Friendship and Sympathy
Communities of Southern Women Writers

Friendship and Sympathy

Communities of Southern Women Writers

Edited by

ROSEMARY M. MAGEE

University Press of Mississippi
Jackson and London

95 94 93 92   4 3 2 1

The paper in this book meets the guidelines for permanence and
durability of the Committee on Production Guidelines for Book
Longevity of the Council on Library Resources.

Library of Congress Cataloging-in-Publication Data

Friendship and sympathy : communities of southern women writers /
    edited by Rosemary M. Magee.
        p. cm.
    Includes bibliographical references.
    ISBN 0-87805-523-1 (cloth : alk. paper).—ISBN 0-87805-545-2
(paper : alk. paper)
    1. American literature—Southern States—History and criticism.
    2. American literature—Women authors—History and criticism.
    3. American literature—20th century—History and criticism.
    4. Women and literature—Southern States—History—20th century.
    5. Southern States—Intellectual life—1865-   I. Magee, Rosemary M.
PS261.F75   1992
810.9'975—dc20   91-25615
                                                                CIP

The editor gratefully acknowledges the following individuals, publishers, and
institutions for permission to reprint the material in this volume:

Lisa Alther, "Introduction" to *A Good Man is Hard to Find* by Flannery
    O'Connor (London: The Women's Press Limited, 1980). Copyright ©
    1980 by Lisa Alther. Reprinted by permission of the author.

Doris Betts, "The Fiction of Anne Tyler," *Southern Quarterly* 21 (1983).
    Copyright © 1983 by the University of Southern Mississippi. Reprinted by
    permission of the University of Southern Mississippi; "More Like an Onion
    than A Map," *Ms.* (March 1975). Copyright © 1975 by Ms. Magazine.
    Reprinted by permission of Ms. Magazine; Review of *Celebration* in *Amer-
    ica* (October 18, 1986). Copyright © 1986 by America Press, Inc. Re-
    printed by permission of America Press, Inc.; "Tyler's Marriage of Op-
    posites," a paper given at a symposium on the fiction of Anne Tyler at Essex
    Community College in Baltimore, April 21–22, 1989. Published in *The
    Fiction of Anne Tyler*, ed. C. Ralph Stephens (Jackson and London: Univer-
    sity Press of Mississippi, 1990). Copyright © 1990 by C. Ralph Stephens.
    Reprinted by permission of C. Ralph Stephens.

Contents

Contents

Acknowledgments

The importance of friendship, sympathy, and community has been reaffirmed for me in the process of creating this collection. I want, first, to thank the writers represented here who have taught me about the many ways of making connections with others through art. I am also grateful for the supportive community that exists for me in the form of friends and colleagues at Emory University. I wish to express my gratitude to Elizabeth Fox-Genovese for many kindnesses but in particular for a conversation over lunch; to David Minter for his friendship and encouragement; to George Jones for his friendship and support; and to Floyd Watkins for his friendship and for more things than can ever be listed. My thanks also extend to Gail Williams, who was as helpful in this endeavor as she has been in every other, to Sharon Armstrong for her meticulous eye, and to Kim Whitehead for her care. I am indebted to Jamie Stanesa for her engagement in this project as well as for her hard work and steady presence. Finally, I wish to thank Seetha Srinivasan who had confidence and patience.

The source of most friendship and sympathy in my life comes from that community that means the most to me: my family. I dedicate this book to my parents for providing me with all the important things, and to Ron, Rebecca, and Sean for always being there to remind me about what is important.

Introduction

"I cannot tell you how much your letter meant to me—and still means," wrote Ellen Glasgow to Marjorie Kinnan Rawlings in the summer of 1941. "It came last night after a trying day, and it brought me a thrilling sense of friendship and sympathy."[1] These words of appreciation, written after an initial meeting between the two writers earlier that year, became part of a brief but meaningful correspondence concluded only by Glasgow's death in November 1945. In their letters they shared information about their personal lives—Rawlings telling Glasgow of her decision to marry—and discussed their views on literature—Glasgow commenting that "as an interpretation of a special aspect of life, *Cross Creek* appears to me to be flawless." She then added quickly, "Not that this, or any other book, can ever take, for me, the place of *The Yearling*."[2] It had been, in fact, in enthusiastic response to the publication of *The Yearling* that Glasgow wrote her first letter in 1939 to Rawlings with an invitation: "If you should go by Richmond on your way North, I hope you will let me know. I should love to talk with you, for I am watching your work with great interest."[3] Although the meeting did not take place for two years, it exceeded their expectations. Afterwards, Rawlings in a letter to Glasgow was to recount a dream she had of the older writer and to state, "I have thought of you oftener than I can tell you."[4] In a final letter, written in 1945, Glasgow in failing health strongly urged Rawlings to go forward with her work. After Ellen Glasgow's death, her literary executor asked Marjorie Kinnan Rawlings to write Glasgow's biography which she worked on (later redefining it as a literary study) until her own death in 1953.

Their brief but intense relationship had a major impact on the lives of both writers and, while unique in some respects, the quality of it characterizes the "friendship and sympathy" shared by many other southern women writers in this century. Vital members and creators of the southern literary world that included William Faulkner, John Crowe Ransom, Allen Tate, and Robert Penn Warren, they often stood on the periphery. But in a way that periphery became defined by a set of intertwining circles—communities not contained by time or space, without the comforts of a shared college campus or the hospitality of the literary establishment—circles that spiral into the present with the continued evolution and emergence of distinctive and distinguished fiction by southern women.

Not that these relationships exist in a vacuum. It would be impossible to overstate, for example, the mutual impact on their lives and works of Allen Tate and Caroline Gordon. Robert Penn Warren wrote elegantly about the fiction of Eudora Welty and Katherine Anne Porter; he served as friend and critic to them and to many others.[5] Sympathetic editors such as Carl Van Doren and Maxwell Perkins were guides and confidants to women writers as well as to men. Perkins at one point encouraged Caroline Gordon gently, "I hope nothing will divert you from going on with the writing. . . . Certainly you have every reason to believe in yourself on the basis of what you have done now." He then added, "I only mention it because it is so much harder for women to write with all the details that they have to think about, than for men." Gordon concurred: "It is certainly much harder for a woman to write than it is for a man."[6]

Mindful of their heritage and appreciative of their tradition, southern women writers have acknowledged an indebtedness to Faulkner and other literary forebears. Many have written essays or reviews about other subjects more often than on one another. In fact, it would be difficult to argue that these were the primary relationships for the writers under consideration. What is significant, however, is their influence and the ways in which they supported one another. It is as if they all acknowledged quietly to themselves and to one another what Caroline Gordon wrote in sympathy to Katherine Anne Porter about John Crowe Ransom: "He can't bear for women to be serious about their art."[7] Despite differences in lifestyle and literary style, they shared a perspective on a world as insiders and outsiders at the same time. Much in need of "friendship and sympathy," they regularly offered support to each other as colleagues.

These ties could even extend beyond the customary racial boundaries, now and then. Rawlings and Zora Neal Hurston became acquainted after Hurston paid Rawlings a visit in St. Augustine. Rawlings described Hurston's work as "superb" and found her visitor to
have "a brilliant mind."[8] She wrote on behalf of Hurston to Maxwell
Perkins impressing upon him that "she has a very great talent. . . . I
am very fond of her."[9] The feeling was apparently returned as Hurston
wrote a mutual friend that she knew Rawlings to be "good and
kind."[10] Similarly, Flannery O'Connor found an admirer in a writer
from a nearby town in Georgia. Alice Walker once described O'Connor
as "the first great modern writer from the South."[11] Although separated geographically by a mere ten miles and chronologically by only
a few years, their cultural experiences in Georgia were vastly different.
But transcending those differences was an appreciation for fiction as a
way to interpret life and meaning and for writing as a means of
understanding the mystery of being and the manners of culture.

Vestiges of relationships among southern women writers are now
interspersed throughout journals, collections of letters, and biographies. Most formally and publicly the influence these writers wielded
over one another is evident in the essays, reviews, and criticism they
wrote about each other and about literature, particularly southern
literature. Here we may observe the enormous impact the fiction of
Flannery O'Connor had on Caroline Gordon and the influence Gordon exercised on O'Connor with her careful criticism; the mutual
respect between Katherine Anne Porter and Eudora Welty; the interre-
lationships between Porter, Gordon, and O'Connor; the significance
of the life and work of Zora Neale Hurston to Alice Walker and the
reconciliation of Walker to Flannery O'Connor; the tutelage of Elizabeth Spencer by Eudora Welty. And the tradition continues with
reviews by Anne Tyler of Doris Betts, Bobbie Ann Mason and Gail
Godwin; reviews by Godwin of Tyler and Mary Lee Settle; articles by
Betts on Tyler's work; and a review by Spencer of fellow Mississippian
Ellen Douglas. Contemporary writers remember their literary precur-
sors as Kaye Gibbons writes about Porter's Miranda stories and Lisa
Alther comments on Flannery O'Connor's short fiction. They struggle
to find their bearings and to articulate the place of their work in
modern American letters.

While most studies of the "literary renaissance" in the South include Porter, Gordon, Glasgow, or O'Connor and McCullers, frequently these writers are not considered to be central to that movement. Attention of critics has traditionally focused on Faulkner and on the Fugitives and their colleagues. Often women have been considered "minor" writers not "major," exemplars of "local color" but not frequently producers of truly great literature. Conventional dating reinforces this view by placing the start of the southern literary renaissance with the publication in 1929 of Thomas Wolfe's *Look Homeward, Angel* and William Faulkner's *The Sound and the Fury*. Some connect this literary phenonemon in the South with broader cultural shifts and the publication of *I'll Take My Stand: The South and the Agrarian Tradition* in 1930. The contributors to this volume were writers and teachers, all men. Perhaps its central thesis is explicated most directly by Allen Tate's question in his essay: "How may the southerner take hold of his Tradition?" Fearing the disintegration of their community, they urged return to a view of the world that upholds agrarian, community values over industrialized, urban ways of life. Cognizant that the trend towards modernization transforms family structures, they were no doubt suspicious of the changing roles of women and the implications for the agrarian way of life.

Though sometimes overlooked in traditional surveys of twentieth-century southern literature, the fiction of Ellen Glasgow flourished in the early decades of this century and provided a foundation for future literary endeavors. Glasgow's role as a central figure in the literary ethos of the time is evident in her efforts to initiate a conference of southern writers in October 1931 in Charlottesville, Virginia, on the topic "The Southern Author and His Public." Glasgow gave the keynote address. Thirty writers attended, including Caroline Gordon, Allen Tate, and William Faulkner. The relationship between Tate and Glasgow, distant before then, improved upon their meeting.[12] Prior to the conference Tate had written to fellow writer Donald Davidson that despite her literary reputation he considered Glasgow "one of the worst novelists in the world" and argued that she demonstrated "an abominable prose style."[13] After the conference he wrote a letter to Stark Young expressing his admiration of Glasgow, and she also informed Young that she was "tremendously drawn" to Tate.[14] With the publication of Glasgow's *The Sheltered Life* Tate expressed his changing assessment of her work in a long letter to Glasgow. The two continued a spirited correspondence, and Tate later read a paper for Glasgow at the Modern Language Association meeting in 1936 on the topic "Empty American Novel"—a discussion of the relationship between imaginative writers and scholars.[15]

Despite close relationships, the times and the customs and the individuals dictated that women were not full-fledged members of literary society. The Fugitives self-consciously referred to one another as "Brother." Caroline Gordon was excluded from literary sessions in Greenwich Village. Malcolm Cowley has commented on her status: "She wasn't 'one of us.' 'We' were mostly poets and intellectuals and men. . . . Caroline was writing unpublished novels that 'we' didn't read. Later she felt—and rightly, in part—that she was a victim of sexual discrimination."[16] Even Tate readily acknowledged that *The House of Fiction,* a collection of short stories with commentaries published in both their names, was largely the work of Gordon.

The literary life for women has not gone without its personal sacrifices. Caroline Gordon struggled with social expectations and her ambitions. Her biographer, Ann Waldron, describes her situation in 1925 shortly after her marriage to Allen Tate: "She, too, wanted to be a writer, a woman of letters, but for now she was a housewife who gardened and cooked and tried to write a novel on the kitchen table."[17] Many of her contemporaries never married; those who did had unusually stormy relationships. Until recently, women writers in the South did not as a rule have children. Some, however, had miscarriages and abortions. One of the few women writers in the early part of the century to have a child, Caroline Gordon, together with her husband Allen Tate, turned over to housekeepers and relatives responsibility for raising their daughter Nancy for long stretches. But such a decision did not come without its costs. Writing from New York to her friend Sally Wood in 1925, when her daughter Nancy was just an infant, she laments, "I'm pretty low just now. Mother took Nancy back to Kentucky with her several weeks ago. I was feeling so feeble I couldn't combat the various forces that were operating against me. It struck everybody as the 'sensible' thing to do, aside from my personal feelings."[18] She shares snapshot glimpses of Nancy with Sally Wood— "She weighs over twelve pounds, laughs out loud, sings and is getting a tooth. (At least Mother says so, though it seems fearfully early.)"[19] Increasingly she believes that Nancy's nurturing is beyond her control; it has been taken over by her mother: "I suppose I try to put the situation as regards Nancy rationally because it seems so hopelessly involved emotionally. I don't know what to do."[20] She could not give Tate the attention he demanded, write as she was compelled to do, and rear a child. That dilemma still not entirely resolved by more contemporary writers, Alice Walker advocated in 1979 "a plan of life that encourages *one* child of one's own, which I consider a meaningful . . . digression within the work(s)."[21] Ann Beattie has commented that though she likes children, "I've never wanted the responsibility of having them."[22]

Perhaps this heart-wrenching experience with her child prepared Gordon for the role she was to assume as compassionate friend and sympathetic mentor to Flannery O'Connor. Through the good graces of Sally and Robert Fitzgerald she came to read and respond in extraordinary depth to O'Connor's works.[23] In a nine-page letter written to O'Connor in 1951, Gordon comments in general on *Wise Blood* and then gives very specific advice on matters of diction, dialogue, and point of view, all the while stating and restating her admiration for the work. She begins the letter enthusiastically: "I think it is terrific!" Later she encourages the younger and now ailing writer—"I admire tremendously the hard core of dramatic action in this book"—while offering detailed commentary and suggestions. But in a postscript she worries that she has not sufficiently indicated her true feelings for the work, and Gordon concludes by offering her "heartiest congratulations on the achievement. It is considerable." O'Connor, in a letter that now exists only in a draft of a fragment, responds appreciatively, "All these comments on writing and my writing have helped along my education considerably and I am certainly obliged to you." In a generous and deliberate manner, Gordon subsequently commented on all of O'Connor's fiction. Writing to her good friend Cecil Dawkins, O'Connor acknowledges her continuing indebtedness: "Whenever I finish a story I send it to Caroline before I consider myself really through with it. She's taught me more than anybody."[24]

Gordon's position in the literary world and her personal dilemmas reflect cultural values which prevented her full participation. Yet it is important to go beyond easy generalizations describing the ethos of southern life and letters in this century as male dominated. Louis D. Rubin, Jr., has established the extent to which "the literature of the southern literary renascence was a college- and university-nurtured literature."[25] The critics and teachers of literature, more often than not, were also part of that tradition. These patterns may have elicited biases with several dimensions in the case of the writers at hand—a bias among feminist writers against southern, rural, and sometimes more traditional fiction and a bias of the prevailing literary establishment against women writers. This is not to say that good fiction has not been published, but sometimes even when published it has not been included in the courses and articles and books that shape the literary canon. As Gordon's experience illustrates, even college-educated women did not have easy and regular access to one another or to an open literary community; they were part of that world yet apart from it.

Issues of gender and literary endeavor persist. In an essay published in 1989, Ursula K. Le Guin asks, "Where does a woman write, what does she look like writing, what is my image, your image, of a woman writing?" She discovers that women may not always have the luxury of a "room of one's own"; they write on the kitchen table or on the subway or waiting for children in carpools. But, finally, she maintains, "Every artist needs some kind of moral support or sense of solidarity, for there *is* a heroic aspect to the practice of art; it is lonely, risky, merciless work. The artist with the least access to social or esthetic solidarity or approbation has been the artist-housewife."[26] Maybe such little attention has been paid to the role of literary communities because societies, clubs, universities, and bars have been so accessible to men that they have been taken for granted. Women, not always in control of where they live and not always able to play a public role in the towns and cities where they reside, have had to create alternate forms of communities. In response to an interviewer's question about the advice she would give young writers, Margaret Walker once replied, "Well, I avoid giving advice because people don't want advice; they want sympathy. They want somebody to bolster and buttress them and say what they're doing is right."[27] It is no wonder that

Glasgow and Rawlings celebrated the closeness they discovered late in their lives and that O'Connor expressed deep gratitude for the thoughtful responses of Gordon to her work.

The importance of a literary community and the impact it can have is evidenced by the recent literary flourishing in North Carolina. Long recognized as a state that nurtures young writers, this value became more formally recognized with the establishment in 1984 of the North Carolina Writers' Network which seeks to help "writers helping writers."[28] Lee Smith admits "almost a duty to help other, younger writers." Kaye Gibbons comments that the state's writing community is both "supportive and self-conscious about its literary tradition." Teachers, critics, editors, and writers alike remark on its importance in their lives, with Kaye Gibbons and Lee Smith and Jill McCorkle acknowledging the support they have received from Louis D. Rubin, Jr. McCorkle expresses her indebtedness to Lee Smith, who encouraged her to believe that "as a 19-year old from a small town I had just as much to say as anybody." Smith articulates her philosophy as a teacher of writers, "Read their works as if they are worth being read and sooner or later they probably will be worth being read." While writers may not require a supportive community in order to work, such relationships can provide much-needed sustenance in a sometimes indifferent or seemingly hostile world.

Many consider the conflict between the old and the new to be the substance and form of the fiction that defined the southern literary renaissance. Allen Tate once asserted that the "backward glance" of the times "gave us the Southern renascence, a literature conscious of the past in the present.[29] More recently, Lewis P. Simpson has wondered if southern literary study can remain vital and vibrant in a time when writers are no longer so closely connected to the past. Even though excellent writers continue to produce in this region, "What one senses is missing is the literary power generated by the encounter between the imagination of a Faulkner, a Warren, a Lytle, a Caroline Gordon, a Richard Wright and the historical society of the South."[30]

In response to such sentiments, Bobbie Ann Mason has restated the issues. An interviewer asked her once if she agreed with William Styron that the qualities that distinguished southern culture in the past (racial tensions, emphasis on family, community, religious life) had become "victims of attrition" so that even though writers continue to write about the South the voice may not be "peculiarly Southern anymore."[31] Mason replies that it is a mistake to view Southern literature in such a static way:

> I'm not so sure those qualities of the Old South were all that terrific. . . . I'm not nostalgic for the past. Times change and I'm interested in writing about what's now. To me, the way the South is changing is very dynamic and full of complexity. There's a certain energy there that I don't notice in other parts of the country. It comes out of an innocent hope of possibility. My characters have more opportunities in their lives than their parents did, and even the parents are more prosperous in their old age than they ever were before. That is what's changing the face of the South—that more and more people are getting in on the good life. But many are still left out . . . so I wouldn't say that tension is gone.[32]

In another interview she admits that she is a southern writer "in a certain way": "I think the culture I write about is very distinctly Southern." But, she further explains, "I don't think the people I write about are obsessed with the past. I don't think they know anything about the Civil War, and I don't think they care."[33] Other contemporary writers have sought to define the persistent qualities of southern literature. Jill McCorkle names the central concern of contemporary southern writers this way: "how you hold onto what you have in the past world but live beyond it and balance the two." Lee Smith maintains that the Southern novel in general is characterized by "leisurely development, care lavished upon developing characters, the importance of place, and the use of history." Concurs McCorkle, "I do think that rootedness, that knowing what has gone on before is very Southern." As a result of such knowledge, argues Kaye Gibbons, "you learn to have a critical eye from the time you can see." A southern writer, she maintains, needs that critical eye but also "a love of the place and a respect for its traditions."[34] There can be little doubt that writers continue to flourish as the region takes on new meanings, new forms, and new territory even as it also seeks to hold on to traditional values and ways of life.

Bridging the world of Katherine Anne Porter, Caroline Gordon, Zora Neale Hurston, and Flannery O'Connor and the world of Lee

Smith, Josephine Humphreys, Alice Walker, and Anne Tyler is Eudora
Welty whose productive life and prolific talent reverberate through the
lives and works of so many others. When asked in a *Paris Review*
interview if she feels part of a community of southern women writers,
Welty responds succinctly: "no." She later acknowledges in another
interview that she feels some connection or kinship with the tradition
of southern writing, "But as far as the act of writing goes, I have never
felt the touch of any other imagination on mine as I write. I think that
must be true of all of us. I can't imagine, for instance, three more
different writers than Katherine Anne Porter, Flannery O'Connor and
myself."[35] Yet she goes on to tell about a time when she and Porter
visited Elizabeth Spencer and about a meeting she had with Flannery
O'Connor. Clearly important to her, these interactions influenced her
life if not directly her writing.

A subject of great interest to readers and critics, influence is impossible to measure. Interviews and panels inevitably get to this question
of the impact of other major literary figures on contemporary writers.
Once when Elizabeth Spencer was asked about the influence of
Faulkner and Welty on her work she answered, "I write my own way, I
don't write according to anybody. But yes, anybody has to acknowledge Faulkner and Welty, because they're the top."[36] Greater testimony is offered by Spencer in dedicating her book *Ship Island* to
Welty.

Writers rarely feel comfortable with the efforts of critics to catego-
rize them according to gender or region. In a review of *Literary Wom-
en* by Ellen Moers, Anne Tyler expresses concern about so much
emphasis on gender: "There is no room in these theories for the
woman as mere individual. . . . In fact the implication here is that
women are unceasingly informed by their femaleness—that it colors
their every thought, vision, and creative effort, at every moment of
their lives." She questions this stance then adds, "It's my personal
feeling that only a portion of my life—and almost none of my writing
life—is much affected by what sex I happen to be. And I can't imagine
that even that portion would be affected in the same way for everyone." Further, women writers cannot simply be defined as victims of
oppression: "The fact is that for every woman writing metaphorically
about her imprisonment, you can surely find at least one man writing

metaphorically about *his* imprisonment—and neither imprisonment is necessarily sex-related."[37] She writes compellingly of the drama of being a writer, a mother, a wife, a walker of dogs and a runner of errands, not as imprisoning but often as competing for her time and attentions. When her children come home from school, she explains, "I have trouble sorting my lives out. The children complain, regularly, that I'm not really paying attention when I let them in, and they're right. I save my afternoons for them, and feel lucky to have such indisputable, ultra-real ties to the everyday world; but still in those first few minutes I'm torn in two directions, and I often wonder what it would be like to live all alone in a shack by the sea and work 23 hours a day."[38] She recognizes that few people, men or women, have this luxury. Anne Tyler's own life and work support Le Guin's argument that the special relationship between mother and children, even as it creates tensions and conflicts, can sometimes nurture the literary impulse.

Writers are becoming increasingly self-conscious about the influence of gender on their work and the importance of community in their lives. During a panel discussion at Furman University in 1988, when asked if she thinks of herself as a "woman writer," Josephine Humphreys responds that initially she had not "considered this question at all," but after publishing, she began to give it some thought. At first she was adverse to the idea which was asked and assumed so often. But she has become increasingly sensitive to the things in her life "related to being a woman, and in particular with children—that affects my writing a lot." Not willing to approach the matter unilaterally, she continues, "In a way, though, writing affects my femininity more than femininity affects my writing. It's sort of an opposite thing for me. Writing has changed my life in so many ways, and that's one of them. It seems to be constantly modifying my perceptions of myself and of what I am doing." One of the hardest parts of writing for her, Humphreys elaborates, is handling the competing demands for her time. At first she concentrated strictly on writing and children, but then she began to feel cut off from everything else—"all my contact with community . . . and I find that the lack of friends and the lack of contact with the human community is killing" (pp. 312–313).

Another writer also talked about the importance of community during the conference at Furman. Through publishing, Louise Shivers discovered friends: "I have had a chance to meet other people who are writing and I didn't have that chance before." What you get from that experience, she believes, is "Knowing that when you are sitting in that room by yourself, and it's just as painful as it has ever been, you are not by yourself." One time when feeling depressed about a book she was working on, she called Josephine Humphreys and they exchanged worries: "It helped just to know she was there." According to Humphreys, "It's also nice to realize that essentially literature is not competitive. . . . I like to know that there are other writers with whom I am not racing and that we like each other's work" (p. 326). The written and spoken words of these writers and many of their contemporaries reveal that they have supported one another, together developed approaches to literature, and with each other pondered what it means to be part of a distinctively southern tradition as women.

To discuss the ways that women writers have flourished in the South is to pay tribute to their talent and determination and the relationships between them. If they could not participate as full-fledged members in the established literary community of their day, they found ways to connect with one another. While letters permitted them to maintain personal contact, critical essays and reviews meshed their need to write—to act as critics and mentors themselves—with their desire to connect with one another and to be part of the literary world. They constructed communities and assumed their place within a tradition. This heritage is one not lost to the writers of today as they write in a world more accepting of what they may have to offer and providing more opportunities for interaction but not always receptive to who they are. Southern women writers of the past and present in offering "friendship and sympathy" to one another transcend the boundaries of time and space, of rigid definitions of literature and life, and they bear witness to a vibrant literary unfolding.

1. Letter from Ellen Glasgow to Marjorie Kinnan Rawlings, July 24, 1941, published in *Atlanta Journal*, April 28, 1946, p. 5. Also included in *Letters of Ellen Glasgow*, ed. Blair Rouse (New York: Harcourt, Brace and Company, 1958), p. 286.

2. Letter from Glasgow to Rawlings, April 20, 1942, in Rouse, *Letters*, p. 293. For an excellent account of this correspondence see Tonette L. Bond, "'A Thrilling Sense of Friendship and Sympathy': The Correspondence of Ellen Glasgow and Marjorie Kinnan Rawlings," *The Ellen Glasgow Newsletter* 16 (March 1982), 3–6.

3. Letter from Glasgow to Rawlings, April 16, 1939 in Rouse, *Letters*, p. 252.

4. Letter from Rawlings to Glasgow, July 19, 1941, *Atlanta Journal*, April 28, 1946. Also included in *Selected Letters of Marjorie Kinnan Rawlings*, ed. Gordon E. Bigelow and Laura V. Monti (Gainesville: University Presses of Florida, 1983), p. 207.

5. In his introduction to a collection of Gordon stories, Warren chooses to connect her with other southern women writers: "Caroline Gordon belongs in that group of Southern women who have been enriching our literature uniquely in this century—all so different in spirit, attitude, and method, but all with the rare gift of the teller of the tale." See "Introduction," *The Collected Stories of Caroline Gordon* (Baton Rouge: Louisiana State University Press, 1990), p. xi.

6. Letter from Maxwell Perkins to Caroline Gordon, July 28, 1931; letter from Gordon to Perkins, August 1, 1931. Quoted in *Close Connections: Caroline Gordon and the Southern Renaissance* (New York: G. P. Putnam's Sons, 1987), p. 94.

7. Caroline Gordon to Katherine Anne Porter, no date, quoted in *Close Connections*, p. 199. Similarly, Rawlings observes in a letter to a friend that Ransom's comment on her work was "disagreeably patronizing—as he meant it to be. To say that he admired them as regional or local color novels, was to deny them all merit on any other counts. If I thought my stuff didn't have something more than local color, I'd stop writing." Letter from Rawlings to Edith Tigert, October 1937, *Selected Letters*, p. 142.

8. Letter from Rawlings to Norman Berg, July 7, 1942, *Selected Letters*, p. 223.

9. Letter from Rawlings to Perkins, April 30, 1947, *Selected Letters*, p. 293.

10. Quoted in a letter from Rawlings to Philip May, March 30, 1948, *Selected Letters*, p. 313.

11. Alice Walker, "Beyond the Peacock: The Reconstruction of Flannery O'Connor," *In Search of Our Mothers' Gardens* (San Diego, New York, London: Harcourt Brace Jovanovich, 1983), p. 52.

12. In the essay "A Week-end at Mr. Jefferson's University," Emily Clark gives a lively summary of the conference. She notes that "Several writers who hated one another's books learned to like one another's personalities so well that they resolved henceforth to tolerate their books." In her synopsis of Ellen Glasgow's address, she comments that "All of what Miss Glasgow said is worth repeating, but the space permitted me can include only a part of it." See *New York Herald Tribune Books*, November 8, 1931, pp. 1–2.

13. Letter from Tate to Davidson, Dec. 12, 1929, in John Tyree Fain and

Thomas Daniel Young, ed., *The Literary Correspondence of Donald Davidson and Allen Tate* (Athens: University of Georgia Press, 1974), p. 243.

14. For more information about their relationship see Ritchie D. Watson, "The Ellen Glasgow-Allen Tate Correspondence: Bridging the Southern Literary Generation Gap," *The Ellen Glasgow Newsletter* 23 (October 1985): 3–24.

15. Glasgow's address was later published in *Saturday Review of Literature*, (January 23, 1937), pp. 3–5, under the title "Elder and Younger Brother."

16. Letter from Malcolm Cowley to Ann Waldron, 1985, quoted in *Close Connections*, p. 39.

17. *Close Connections*, p. 47.

18. Letter from Gordon to Wood, 1925, in *The Southern Mandarins: Letters of Caroline Gordon to Sally Wood, 1924–1937*, ed. Sally Wood (Baton Rouge and London: Louisiana State University Press, 1984), p. 17.

19. Letter from Gordon to Wood, Feb. 5, 1926, in *The Southern Mandarins*, p. 19.

20. Letter from Gordon to Wood, 1926, in *The Southern Mandarins*, p. 29.

21. Alice Walker, "One Child of One's Own: A Meaningful Digression Within the Work(s)," *In Search of Our Mother's Gardens*, p. 362.

22. Quoted in *The Atlanta Journal–The Atlanta Constitution*, February 4, 1990, p. A2.

23. Sally Fitzgerald offers a moving and precise account of this relationship in "A Master Class: From the Correspondence of Caroline Gordon and Flannery O'Connor," *The Georgia Review* 33 (Winter 1979): 827–846. The excerpts in this paragraph are quoted from the correspondence in this essay.

24. Letter from Flannery O'Connor to Cecil Dawkins, December 22, 1957, in *The Habit of Being*, ed. Sally Fitzgerald (New York: Farrar, Straus, Giroux, 1979), p. 260.

25. Louis D. Rubin, Jr., *The Writer in the South: Studies in a Literary Community* (Athens: University of Georgia Press, 1972), p. 105.

26. Ursula K. Le Guin, "The Hand That Rocks the Cradle Writes the Book," *New York Times Book Review*, January 22, 1989, p. 1, 35.

27. Claudia Tate, *Black Women Writers at Work* (New York: Continuum, 1983) p. 204.

28. Barbara Hoffert, "Writer's Renaissance in North Carolina," *Library Journal*, November 1, 1989, pp. 44–48. The quotations in this paragraph are taken from this article.

29. Allen Tate, "The New Provincialism: With an Epilogue on the Southern Novel," *Virginia Quarterly Review* 21 (1945), p. 272.

30. Lewis P. Simpson, "The State of Southern Literary Scholarship," *The Southern Review* 24 (Spring 1988): 242.

31. See Georgann Eubanks, "William Styron: The Confessions of a Southern Writer." *Duke* 71 (Sept.–Oct. 1984), 4.

32. Albert E. Wilhelm, "An Interview with Bobbie Ann Mason." *The Southern Quarterly* 26 (Winter 1988): 37.

33. Wendy Smith, "PW Interviews: Bobbie Ann Mason." *Publisher's Weekly,* August 30, 1985, p. 425.

34. Gibbons, Smith, and McCorkle quoted in "Writers' Renaissance," pp. 45–48.

35. Jan Nordby Gretlund, "An Interview with Eudora Welty," in *Conversations with Eudora Welty,* ed. Peggy Whitman Presnshaw (Jackson: University Press of Mississippi, 1984), p. 218.

36. Charlotte Capers, "An Evening with Eudora Welty and Elizabeth Spencer," *Delta Review* 4 (November 1967): 70.

37. Anne Tyler, "Women Writers: Equal but Separate," *The National Observer,* April 10, 1976, p. 21.

38. Anne Tyler, "Because I Want More Than One Life," *Washington Post,* August 15, 1976, G1; G7.

Friendship and Sympathy
Communities of Southern Women Writers

Traditions

Defining a tradition and finding one's place in it comprises a critical part of the literary enterprise. Unwilling to be passive recipients of an established perspective on the past, Ellen Glasgow, Marjorie Kinnan Rawlings, Carson McCullers, Margaret Walker, and many other southern women writers have sought to understand and configure the tradition which has also defined them. In fact, Ellen Glasgow did much to describe the emerging sense of a literary renaissance in the South. Her central role as a convener of one of the first southern writers conferences gave shape to it and allowed this movement to gather momentum. She also wrote essays on women writers, modern fiction, and many other subjects of importance in her day. Though more a novelist than an essayist or critic, on one occasion Glasgow admitted, "I may confess that spinning theories of fiction is my favourite amusement" and further claimed that she read "with as much interest . . . every treatise on the art of fiction that appeared to me to be promising."[1]

Rawlings, too, sought to engage important literary issues. In a lecture she gave to a group of English teachers the year she was awarded the Pulitzer Prize for *The Yearling*, she complained about certain literary tendencies: "I cannot believe that regionalism, for the sake of regionalism, is valid material for creative fiction. I know it is not literature" (p. 16). Yet there is another way: "It is the approach of the sincere creative writer who has something to say and who uses a specialized locale—a region—as a logical or fitting background for the particular thoughts or emotions that cry out for articulation" (p. 17). Among those who have achieved literary distinction for depicting southern culture yet transcending regionalism she ranks Ellen Glasgow first but also includes Zora Neale Hurston and Elizabeth Madox Roberts as deserving of recognition.

In a similar vein, Carson McCullers sought to probe more deeply into the category of "the Gothic." In so doing, she enlarged her focus beyond south-

3

ern or even American literature by drawing connections between the literature of the South of the twentieth century and Russian literature of the nineteenth. Of particular note, she dates the beginning of modern southern literature with the publication of Glasgow's *Barren Ground* in 1925, four years prior to the publication of *The Sound and the Fury*.

Tracing the roots of southern literature, Margaret Walker starts with John Pendleton Kennedy's *Swallow Barn,* which "marked the beginning of a set of stereotypes from which the literature has yet to free itself. Along with this plantation tradition, both black and white writers have developed a folk tradition that began in the oral tradition of spirituals, work songs, and ballads" (p. 29). She claims that she "cut her teeth" on the works of Zora Neale Hurston as well as Langston Hughes, but also on the fiction of Caroline Gordon and Ellen Glasgow as well as Thomas Wolfe. Walker embroiders into a single fabric two strands of southern literature, thereby demonstrating their connection as well as their tension.

All of these writers have expressed the influence of the dominant tradition, but they also have found a place for one another as they have carved one out for themselves. Thus the ideals of friendship and sympathy which offered texture and richness to their relationships also influenced their interpretation of the tradition of southern literature.

1. "The Sheltered Life," *A Certain Measure: An Interpretation of Prose Fiction* (New York: Harcourt, Brace, and Company, 1943), pp. 190–191.

Ellen Glasgow

Opening Speech
of the Southern Writers Conference

This speech exists only in a manuscript that contains two parts or drafts, marked "Very Rough," and a fragment of a third. Newspaper reports show that passages from both drafts and the fragment were delivered at the Southern Writers Conference, 23–24 October 1931, in Charlottesville, Virginia. Unless otherwise obvious, the brackets in the text indicate passages marked through yet still legible.

The Southern Writers Conference at the University of Virginia was attended by thirty writers. The central committee of the conference consisted of Glasgow (whose idea the conference was), James Branch Cabell, Archibald Henderson, DuBose Heyward, Stark Young, Paul Green, and Thomas Wolfe. (Young and Wolfe, however, did not actually attend the conference.) The central committee was responsible for selecting other writers to be invited to the conference.

This version of Glasgow's speech was edited by Julius Rowan Raper, reprinted here from *Ellen Glasgow's Reasonable Doubts: A Collection of Her Writings* (Louisiana State University Press, 1988).

When I was asked, as the only woman on this committee, to bid you welcome to Virginia, I modestly replied that women come before men only in shipwreck. But Mr. James Branch Cabell, who imposes his duty upon me, is constrained to illustrate his theory that after fifty the only thing worth doing is to decline to do anything. I, on the contrary, believe quite as firmly that the longer one lives in this world of hazard and escapes disaster, the more reckless one should become—at least in the matter of words. Did not Defoe, the father of us all, wait until his adventurous sixties before he dared to write, in *Moll Flanders,* the things that can be said only in print?

Now, as I glance over this *Round Table* I rejoice to find how elastic the term Southern writer may become when it is properly stretched. It isn't necessary to be born in the South in order to become a Southern writer. It isn't necessary even to take the trouble to live here. All that one requires, is the open and eager mind of what I prefer to call the world writer. And because you are not only Southern writers but world writers, you bring to our literature the diversity which is life, not the standardization which is the death of creation. A few years ago every Southern writer fell naturally—or was supposed to fall naturally—into a single class—a kind of Swiss Guard of Defense. But now, thanks to this healthful diversity, we are convincing even those who are not Southerners that the South is more than the South—it is a part of the world. Always, I suppose, the arrogant planter and the classic colonel will return as hardy annuals of journalism. [For I am inclined to believe that when the cockroach or the Japanese beetle finally inherits the earth, he will find that journalistic labels are the solitary survivors of the machine civilization.]

But for the rest of us, the gesture of defense has been so long discarded that we have lost even the art. To defend a civilization would seem to us as impertinent as to defend time. Certainly, the South needs defenders as little as it needs apologists. The Southern scene, as we use it today, is a simply shifting pattern which transmits the colour and movement of life. For the chief concern of the Southern writer, as of every [other?] writer, is life—even though he may have learned long ago that life itself is indefensible. We are, I think, less interested in any social order past or present than we are in that unknown quality which we once called the soul and now call the psychology of mankind. Into this world of psychology we may look as into a wilderness that is forever conquered and yet forever virgin. Here and there, we may see our own small trail which leads on to that vanishing point where all trails disappear. Yet the merest glance into this wilderness much teach us that there is not one truth alone but many truths. Somewhere,—I have forgotten where—I have read a Persian proverb which says, "Many kinds of truth are acceptable to Allah, the Merciful, but the whole truth is not one of them."

There is, for example, what we have agreed to call the truth of life. Then there is that vastly different truth, the truth of art, which includes history and fiction. This, of course, is merely a way of saying that modern psychology or the Theory of Relativity or both together have demolished our conception of truth as an established principle superior to and apart from the thinking subject. We no longer think of truth as a fixed pattern outside of ourselves at which we may nibble for crumbs as mice at a loaf. All of you who write fiction must have felt the shock of finding that when we break off a fragment of the truth of life and place it, without shading and shaping, into the truth of fiction, it sheds a meretricious glare of unreality. And many of us have tried at least once to be so supremely honest that we have taken a single character or incident or even a phrase directly from life—only to be told that this single character or incident or phrase is the one false stroke in an otherwise truthful portrait of experience.

And it is because we have learned this in our work that writers are so very tolerant of other truths than their own. All we ask of any writer is that he shall be honest with himself, that he shall possess artistic integrity. Beyond this, we are perfectly willing, I think, to leave to each individual writer the choice of his own particular subject. For it is the unconscious, not the conscious, will that chooses for us our subject, and over the unconscious we cannot exert prohibitions. But it is this conviction—the conviction that artistic integrity is the only essential—that enables us to enjoy so many varied aspects of truth. We can enjoy, for example, not only the books that are painful, but, in a lesser degree (since we are citizens of a Republic that has been called (and rightly, I think) the masochist among the nations), we are still able—(or, at least some of us are able)—to enjoy the books that are pleasant. Because of this conviction we ask of Mr. Cabell the Cabellian truth, or aspect of truth, and not the truth of Mr. Stark Young or Mr. Allen Tate or Mr. DuBose Heyward or the different truth of Mr. Sherwood Anderson or Mr. Stallings or Mr. Thomas Wolfe. [We see also the subtle truth of Miss Isa Glenn as clearly as we see the [flattering?] truth of Mr. John Peale Bishop—or the quiet truth in that fine new novel *Penhally.* For to the honest novelist, I think, all truth is welcome so long as, like Allah the Merciful, he is not asked to accept the whole truth from any mortal.]

[By this time, you have observed, no doubt, that I have carefully avoided the subject of our general discussion. Candidly, I have little interest in publics. Like presidents, they fail to impress me because I so seldom agree with them. Even when a public appears in Roman dress on the stage, I immediately suspect that it [is] not there for any good, but for purposes of assassination. So I find but one approach to this topic, and that is with the question: How much or how little should a writer participate, as we may say, in his own public?]

When I was asked, as the only woman on this committee, to welcome you to the Round Table, I demurred because I was brought up to believe that women come before men only in shipwreck.[1] And I was perfectly confident that there will [be] no rocking of the boat on this delightful occasion. For never in my experience of committees or parties, have I seen so many persons in one room that I was eager to meet and to know better.

The most charming thing about this gathering is the way it proves once for all, that one can be a Southern writer without being a Southerner. It isn't necessary even to arrange to be born in the South. The only requirement, it appears, is the abiding interest in life everywhere with which every writer worth his salt is provided before he looks about him and reluctantly—for was it ever otherwise?—dips his pen into the ink. When I was a young girl, trying desperately, and with a sinking heart, to get my first book accepted by a publisher, I remember that a very well-known and well-thought-of critic of the late nineties remarked to me with that slightly supercilious air which was then the fashion with intellectuals, "There are writers and there are Southern writers. WE want only writers;" and despairingly, I replied, "But I [don't want Southern nor Northern writers, I want] am a world writer." For this is what pleases me most in this Round Table. It is composed of the elements of the world. We may go into not only romance and realism—faded old terms, but that sounder realism which is romantic and that sounded [sic] romance which is realistic. For in my opinion, no literature in any country, not even in Europe, to which American has for so long played the part of a literary Little

Orphan Annie, can grow and mature except through diversity. In the world of ideas the apollonian [*sic*] and the Dionysian spirits are eternally alive and eternally hostile. Maturity lies not in conquest but in ceaseless struggle and in endless reversals of the situation. And believing this so heartily, I welcome change and conflict and abhor standardization as the earliest sign of death and decay. Always I have felt that it is absurd to say that one prefers the past to the present, the old ways of writing to the new; or the new to the old. Always, I have asked of a book only that it shall be a good book of its kind. Always, I have been willing to leave to a writer the choice of subject to which his temperament has impelled him. For if literature has one virtue it is the virtue of hospitality. There is room for all in the world of letters, and it is safe to assert that the style which occupies the almshouse today will be attired tomorrow in the red and purple—or at least ermine—of authority. And so, having read all your books and liked most of them—though naturally I have liked some of them more than others—I can welcome you with pleasure and pride in your achievement not only as Southern writers but, as my friend of the late nineties would say, as writers. Not only, I feel, are you convincing the South, which sorely needs convincing, that books are more significant [than] smokestacks, you are proving beyond argument [that the] South is in the world and Southerners are people.

As for the immediate discussion, I admit shamelessly that I am more interested in the Southern writer than I am in a public which seems to me to be composed either of words or of a sanguine illusion. [What Southern writers may be, I am perfectly convinced that there is no public.]

I am interested in American literature for what it says and even more I am interested in it for what it does not say—in an age when what we used to call the conspiracy of silence has been broken. If I might have chosen the topic for discussion, I should have avoided the Southern writer and his public, especially since that public is usually situated far away from the South, and have tried to discover why America which suffered so little from the world war in fact should have suffered more deeply in spirit than the defeated countries. It is historically and eternally true that in material defeat there is a spiritual victory. For Germany alone is producing today a literature of pity—and without pity can great books be written? Or is it true, as some psychologists assert, that America, being the most feminine of civilizations, is the masochist among nations? Is this why we enjoy abuse and scorn sympathy in our books? For what does it prove that of all the books written since the war only two are rich in compassion, and that these two, *The Case of Sergeant Grisha* and *The Road Back*, should have come out of Germany? Has the South forgotten defeat? Has it forgotten its heritage of laughter and tragic passion? Who can answer. How does any one know? A year ago, a German professor said to me, "Germany is learning compassion," and I answered, "America is learning brutality." For it is perfectly true that if I were asked by a young writer to point out the quickest road to success in American letters, and especially in Southern letters, I should say, if only half in earnest, "Be brutal. If you have a genius, be brutal. If you have not genius, be more brutal. For the only safe substitute for genius in American literature is brutality."

Why should this be true? Well, the Lord alone could answer, and he will certainly not do so. Perhaps, because we were once too sentimental, we have become like the infant experimented upon by the behaviourists, who was afraid not only of his favorite white rat, but of every other toy he had played with in his innocence, and even of his bottle of milk. Because we cherished our white rat of sentimentality too dearly, have we grown to fear sentiment, which is only another name for pity and understanding. Have we forgotten, in our terror and humiliation, that pity and understanding are the only qualities that justify man's tedious ascent from the troglodyte and perilous descent from the tree-tops. Shall Germany win the intellectual conquest because she is able to see the whole of life in defeat while we can look only as far as the disaster of a physical victory.

And since the most difficult thing on earth is to say what one really means in a little speech, I should like to add that I, who fought sentimentality and prudishness in my youth, who was a convicted heretic in an age when all books were written to win favour with Du Maurier's ubiquitous young person, have never flinched before the barest of truths—not even before that whole truth which was said to be unacceptable to Allah. Only let us learn from Dostoyevsky that if nothing is more terrible than life, nothing is more pitiable. Love may go; sex may go, and not stand upon the order of its going—but, as

Russia knew yesterday and Germany has discovered today, pity survives. Otherwise, the machine age may as well destroy itself while it prepares the world for the insect. For is not the insect the only living creature that is perfect as a machine?[2]

A young girl in the late nineties, I began life as a champion of the oppressed. As a protest against evasive idealism and sentimental complacency, I made the protagonist of my first novel the illegitimate son of an illiterate "poor white." Always, I was in the skin of the fox at every fox hunt and in the skin of the yellow dog under the wagon at every village fair. Only, in the last few years, since there has been a reversal of the situation, and it has become not only fashionable but snobbish to be lowly and despised and rejected, I find my sympathy shifting to that outcast from the machine civilization—the well-bred person. The only distinction is that I think fine breeding springs from the mind and heart, not from arrested tradition. Two at least of the best bred persons I have known were laborers in the soil. The most perfect manner I have ever known was that of an old gentleman who was colored, and this manner was the natural result of simplicity and consideration for others. But in America today, the well-bred persons occupy very much the position of the Kulaks in Russia. They have committed more than a crime; they have committed a blunder. Now and then, when the crowd scatters, we see them scurrying, like terrified pedestrians, to take cover beneath "the mucker pose." For nobody, not even Mr. Sherwood Anderson, of the overflowing heart, has a word to speak in their favor.

I have always liked Goethe's remark that the assassination of Caesar was in very bad taste.

[Before the war would have been an abolitionist.]

[Behaviorist, trained to be President of the U.S.A. We clung to our white rats.][3]

1931

1. What follows seems to be an alternate draft of the speech. It begins much like that above, then moves in a different direction.

2. A final illegible sentence seems intended to guide the meeting back to the subject of general discussion. A separate fragment, which was included in Glasgow's talk according to a newspaper summary, develops a theme she often expounded on elsewhere, sometimes using similar words: her shift in empathy from the "lowly and despised" to "the well-bred."

3. These final notes to herself indicate that Glasgow probably extemporized on themes not fully developed in the written speech.

Marjorie Kinnan Rawlings

Regional Literature of the South

The following paper was written for the Annual Luncheon of the National Council of Teachers of English in New York, 25 November 1939.

I do not know what astute phrase-maker coined the expression "regional literature." The ill-assorted mating must be recent, for *Webster's New Unabridged Dictionary* of 1934 makes no formal acknowledgment of the union. The modern ghost writers for the shade of the great master of words define "regional" as "of or pertaining to a region or territory, especially a geographical region," which does indeed leave the word available to any man's use. "As," says Webster, "regional governments; regional symptoms." I seem to have heard lately of "regional housing," which is an appropriate and decent joining, since the shelters over men's heads must be suitable protection against whatever climatic elements are peculiar to the section. "Regional literature," to the best of my knowledge, is an expression only a few years older than New Deal phraseology. It is as glib as W.P.A., C.C.C., and N.R.A. Time has not yet determined whether these terms are false or true: whether the Works Progress Administration truly progresses, or whether the Civilian Conservation Corps truly conserves. But I believe that the phrase "regional literature" is not only false and unsound but dangerous to a sharp appreciation of values, for the linking of the two words has brought in the connotation that if a piece of writing is regional, it is also literature.

Webster, again, defines literature as "literary productions as a collective body; as: (*a*) The total of preserved writings belonging to a given language or people. (*b*) Specifically, that part of it which is notable for literary form or expression, as distinguished, on the one hand, from works merely technical or erudite, and, on the other, from journalistic or other ephemeral literary writing."

Accepting the specifications of dictionary preciseness, I dare to say, as a writer who often suffers under the epithet of "regional," that there is very little regional literature of the South. I dare go farther and say that the sooner we divorce the two words the sooner shall we discourage the futile outpourings of bad writing whose only excuse is that they are regional, regionalism being at the moment a popular form of literary expression.

Regional stories are obviously stories laid in a circumscribed locale, dealing with characters peculiar to that locale. Somehow or other, regionalism has come to connote ruralism, perhaps because cities are much alike, and offer no localized customs or speech or human types to the field glass and butterfly net of the literary collector. Yet the customs of travel, the mode of life and of thought of natives of New York City are so specialized that a book written about New York City with the passion for detail and the odd patronizing condescension brought to many studies of remote rural sections would be truly a piece of regional writing. It would be tempting to write such a book, for the New Yorker's acceptance of his subways and his taxis and his cliff dwelling seems as outlandish and worthy of note as an Alabama poor white's acceptance of mules, drought, and the boll weevil. The truth is that the congregating of a high percentage of the American population in urban centers and the fluid nature of that population have within a generation made any stationary rural group, maintaining its own customs, a matter for wide-eyed contemplation.

I may be mistaken, but I believe that the words "regional literature" call to the average reader's mind either Middle West farm stories or stories of the South. In a greater number of cases my guess is that the first thought is of the latter. Middle West farm stories have sprung from a common nostalgia, recognized or unrecognized, for the land. They have usually been written either by one who has left the land or by one who has returned to it. Regional stories of the South have sprung from a recent and not quite explicable resurgence of interest in the South and in southern ways.

The Mason and Dixon line is as invisible but as definite as ever. Freer travel back and forth between the two sections has accentuated, rather than minimized, differences in mode of life and thought. Yankee tourists in Florida can be spotted across a hotel dining-room for their fluttery air of knowing themselves to be in a strange land. When grits, looking like Cream of Wheat, are served them for a vegetable, like potatoes, and when their puzzled eyes light on natives buttering or gravying those grits and eating them along with the meat and bread, they are as sheepish and as delighted as any Occidental set down at a Chinese table with a set of chopsticks, or confronted in Hawaii with the first dish of *poi*.

Fortunately, perhaps, though the South still disapproves of the North, the North has come to take—if, indeed, it ever lost it—a literary and faintly maternal interest in the South. It is not too far a step, after all, from the North's preoccupation with Fanny Kemble's *Diary* and Harriet Beecher Stowe's *Uncle Tom's Cabin,* to its horrified and rapturous embracing of *Tobacco Road.* Of recent years the South has been again fresh literary meat. To subtitle a book "A Tale of the South" was to guarantee a closer attention than would be given to a similarly mediocre story laid in Buffalo. The South simply became popular as a divertissement. And, after several generations of mistrust of the "rebels," the southern cause has come to be looked on with a sentimental sympathy.

There is a distinct parallel between recent interest in writings about the South and interest in the Irish revival of letters of a generation or so ago. The Irish cause, lost and losing, was picturesque and remote. Almost any stereotyped tale with the brogue thick enough could be published. And within the last ten years, to make an arbitrary demarcation, almost any articulate story of the South, be it of the past or the present, of a tenant farmer chopping cotton or a julep-drinking aristocrat under the unpainted pseudo-Greek columns of the ancestral mansion, was sure of an audience. The great wave, to the best of my memory, began with *So Red the Rose* and *Tobacco Road,* and reached its crest with *Gone with the Wind.* The success of the last no longer seems phenomenal when, to this peak of interest in the material itself, was added the author's terrific gift for swift narrative and, above all, for characterization. When a milieu that had long fascinated sprang to physical life in the persons of characters so real that one would recognize them in the flesh—giving rise, incidentally, to the passionate furor over a choice of actors and actresses who should not betray that fleshly reality in the cinema version—an entranced reading public took the book to its bosom. That reading public includes the Old World, which has always found the American South glamorous.

The South also reads books about the South. That is because, while not too much concerned with what outsiders say about us, we are all agog to know what we say about one another.

Regional writing may be done either by outsiders or by insiders. It may be done by either outsider or insider from one of two approaches. It may be done deliberately—may I say "perpetrated?"—solely because it is regional. A businessman said to me the other day, "I should think the big market right now would be for war stories. Aren't they the easiest trash in the world to write?" I said, "I wouldn't know. I never wrote trash on purpose." Regionalism written on purpose is perhaps as spurious a form of literary expression as ever reaches print. It is not even a decent bastard, for back of illegitimacy is usually a simple, if ill-timed, honesty. Regional writing done because the author thinks it will be salable is a betrayal of the people of that region. Their speech and customs are turned inside out for the gaze of the curious. They are held up naked, not as human beings, but as literary specimens.

Regional studies are legitimate when the purpose is sociological and scientific. The form in which such studies are presented should be a scientific form. When customs are quaint and speech picturesque, and it is desirable that a record be made, I suggest a Doctor's thesis or the *National Geographic* as proper outlets. I cannot believe that regionalism, for the sake of regionalism, is valid material for creative fiction. I know that it is not literature. I know it from Webster's definition. For literature is, specifically, that part of the preserved writings of a given language or people which is notable for literary form or expression, as distinguished, on the one hand, from works merely technical or erudite, and, on the other, from journalistic or other ephemeral literary writing. Without Webster, I should know it by the sense of shame with which I read it, and the even greater sense of shame with which I sometimes catch myself in a possible danger of writing it.

The second approach to regional writing, whether by an outsider or by an insider, is valid. It may or may not result in literature, but it is honest. It is the approach of the sincere creative writer who has something to say and who uses a specialized locale—a region—as a logical or fitting background for the particular thoughts or emotions that cry out for articulation. This approach results in writing that is only incidentally, sometimes even accidentally, regional. It is only out of this approach that we can look for what may truly be called regional literature. For the producer of literature is not a reporter but a creator. His concern is not with presenting the superficial and external aspects, however engaging, of an actual people. It is with the inner revelation of mankind, thinking and moving against the backdrop of life itself with as much of dramatic or pointed effect as the artistry of the writer can command. The creative writer filters men and women, real and fancied, through his imagination as through a catalytic agent, to resolve the confusion of life into the ordered pattern, the co-ordinated, meaningful design, colored with the creator's own personality, keyed to his own philosophy, that we call art. Occupied with this magic-working, the creative writer finds a fictional character's speech, dress, and daily habits of importance only as they make that character emerge from the printed page with the aura of reality, so that the author has a convincing and effective medium for the tale he means to tell.

The degree of artistry that emerges from regional writing is proportionate to the writer's ability. If he writes badly, the most fascinating material in the world is only a fine horse to carry a crippled rider. If he writes well, he is almost independent of material, for his genius is able to transmute dross into gold and clay into sentience. Yet the best writing is implicit with a profound harmony between the writer and his material, so that many of the greatest books of all time are regional books, in which the author has used, for his own artistic purpose, a background that he loved and deeply understood. Thomas Hardy is a compelling instance.

So it is reasonable, I think, to expect to find this honest and artistic regionalism to a greater degree among native or long-resident writers than among writers-in-search-of-material who may be struck by the novelty and usableness of a particular region.

But while native regionalism is more likely to be honest than what might be called journalistic or itinerant regionalism, it is artistic only as the writer is himself an artist. It is literature only as the author is literary. Without going into the moot question of sectional percentages, and with no intent to imply that the North, or the West, or New England, has a higher quota, I think it is indisputable that the present-day South, which has emitted literally tons of regional writing, has produced very little regional literature.

The matter of personal tastes and prejudices enters, dangerously, any specific evaluation of southern regional writing. The history of literature is crammed with mistakes in contemporary judgments. I have no desire to assume a voluntary and unnecessary martyrdom. I prefer to suggest this demarcation between regional writing and regional literature as a standard of judgment of whose soundness I am certain, and to retreat. Yet martyrdom and folly are more comfortable companions than cowardice, and I am willing to venture my personal opinions on a few southern writers as proof of the courage of my convictions.

To my mind, Ellen Glasgow stands alone in our generation as the creator of the only unmistakable regional literature of the South. Pulitzer prizes for "distinguished" novels are amazing anomalies when they ignore work of her literary distinction. Her literature, like Hardy's, is inherently regional, for while she would have written with great art of whatever people came into the ken of her interest, she is so steeped in the Virginia which she knows that it is an inextricable part of her work, like the colors of a painting or the dye of the wool of a tapestry. But she is first an artist and then a Virginian. If her books—unspectacular, but all the more sound—do not become part of "the total of preserved writings belonging to a given language or people" then I for one am willing to see other bound volumes go unpreserved.

It is, on the other hand, the spectacular quality of *Gone with the Wind,* or, more exactly, the spectacular quality of the book's popular success, that makes me unable to insist with equal certainty that it is literature. At the moment, I am inclined to think that it is. Five years from now, when the tumult and the shouting shall surely have died, and I read it again, I believe I shall know, and others with me. A few critics, like little whirlpools isolated and individual in the sweeping flood of acclaim, have lamented a lack of "style." The charge is serious, if we are to stand firm with Webster on the specific need of literature to be "notable for literary form or expression, as distinguished . . . . from . . . . ephemeral literary writing." Yet we ask of style principally that it be an effective medium of expression for the material itself, and it seems to me that no narrative, no set of characters, could carry the excitement and the living conviction of this book unless the style were at least adequate.

There are three distinctly regional southern writers, some of whose books seem to me very close to literature. Yet, again, permanence, or relative permanence, is too difficult for me to gauge, short of the peculiar certainty that I feel for the work of Ellen Glasgow. These are, especially, Julia Peterkin and after her Elizabeth Madox Roberts and the negress, Zora Neale Hurston. My personal reaction to *Black April* and *Scarlet Sister Mary* is that they are of permanent value. If time deals harshly with them, at least there is no question but that they stand very high indeed in the intermediate zone, between "literature" and "ephemeral literary writings," of contemporary literature.

My reservations as to Elizabeth Madox Roberts are, first, that she evinces such a scholarly preoccupation with dialect speech as to force her work into the class of technical or erudite writings, invalidating its objective artistry; and, second, that the overpoetizing of the prose form invalidates the purity of the literary expression. Yet Mary Webb overpoetized the prose of *Precious Bane,* and the result was still literature. Frankly, I do not know.

It is the newest book by Zora Neale Hurston, *Moses, Man of the Mountain,* that tempts me to admit her to my own private library of literature. The book is reminiscent of Thomas Mann's great *Joseph in Egypt.* A timeless legend, part of man's priceless literary and spiritual heritage, is here revivified through the luminous negro mind. The book is racial, rather than regional, and I had best avoid a positive judgment on the excuse of irrelevancy to my subject matter.

There is a body of workman-like southern writers whose regional writings are completely free from the taint I so deplore, who write out of love and understanding of their sections, but whose ultimate artistry is inadequate for a claim to the creation of literature. The ice here is too thin for me to venture from shore. The list, at best, could only reflect personal prejudice and, no doubt, erroneous judgments. And of the writers guilty of regionalism for its own sake, the less said on a shameful subject the better.

This is patently not the place to discuss other southern writers whose work is not regional. There is perhaps a question as to whether Faulkner is or is not a regional writer, but I should not so classify him. The storm-swept realm of the libido knows no geography.

1940

Carson McCullers

The Russian Realists
and Southern Literature

In the South during the past fifteen years a genre of writing has come about that is sufficiently homogeneous to have led critics to label it "the Gothic School." This tag, however, is unfortunate. The effect of a Gothic tale may be similar to that of a Faulkner story in its evocation of horror, beauty, and emotional ambivalence—but this effect evolves from opposite sources; in the former the means used are romantic or supernatural, in the latter a peculiar and intense realism. Modern Southern writing seems rather to be most indebted to Russian literature, to be the progeny of the Russian realists. And this influence is not accidental. The circumstances under which Southern literature has been produced are strikingly like those under which the Russians functioned. In both old Russia and the South up to the present time a dominant characteristic was the cheapness of human life.

Toward the end of the nineteenth century the Russian novelists, particularly Dostoievsky, were criticized harshly for their so called "cruelty." This same objection is now being raised against the new Southern writers. On first thought the accusation seems puzzling. Art, from the time of the Greek tragedians on, has unhesitatingly portrayed violence, madness, murder, and destruction. No single instance of "cruelty" in Russian or Southern writing could not be matched or outdone by the Greeks, the Elizabethans, or, for that matter, the creators of the Old Testament. Therefore it is not the specific "cruelty" itself that is shocking, but the manner in which it is presented. And it is in this approach to life and suffering that the Southerners are so indebted to the Russians. The technique briefly is this: a bold and outwardly callous juxtaposition of the tragic with the humorous, the immense with the trivial, the sacred with the bawdy, the whole soul of a man with a materialistic detail.

To the reader accustomed to the classical traditions this method has a repellent quality. If, for instance, a child dies and the life and death of this child is presented in a single sentence, and if the author passes over this without comment or apparent pity but goes on with no shift in tone to some trivial detail—this method of presentation seems cynical. The reader is used to having the relative values of an emotional experience categorized by the author. And when the author disclaims this responsibility the reader is confused and offended.

Marmeladov's funeral supper in *Crime and Punishment* and *As I Lay Dying,* by William Faulkner, are good examples of this type of realism. The two works have much in common. Both deal with the subject of death. In both there is a fusion of anguish and farce that acts on the reader with an almost physical force. Marveladov's violent death, Katerina Ivanovna's agitation about the supper, the details of the food served, the clerk "who had not a word to say for himself and smelt abominably"—on the surface the whole situation would seem to be a hopeless emotional rag-bag. In the face of agony and starvation the reader suddenly finds himself laughing at the absurdities between Katerina Ivanovna and the landlady, or smiling at the antics of the little Pole. And unconsciously after the laughter the reader feels guilty; he senses that the author has duped him in some way.

Farce and tragedy have always been used as foils for each other. But it is rare, except in the works of the Russians and the Southerners, that they are superimposed one upon the other so that their effects are experienced simultaneously. It is this emotional composite that has brought about the accusations of "cruelty." D. S. Mirsky, in commenting on a passage from Dostoievksy, says: "Though the element of humor is unmistakably present, it is a kind of humor that requires a rather peculiar constitution to amuse."

In Faulkner's *As I Lay Dying,* this fusion is complete. The story deals with the funeral journey made by Anse Bundren to bury his wife. He is taking the body to his wife's family graveyard some forty miles away; the journey takes him and his children several days and in the course of it the body decomposes in the heat and they meet with a mad plethora of disasters. They lose their mules while fording a stream, one son breaks his leg and it becomes gangrenous, another son goes mad, the daughter is seduced—a more unholy cortege could hardly be imagined. But the immensities of these disasters are given no more accent than the most inconsequential happenings. Anse throughout the story has his mind on the false teeth he is going to buy when he reaches the town. The girl is concerned with some cake she has brought with her to sell. The boy with the gangrenous leg keeps saying of the pain, "It don't bother me none," and his main worry is that his box of carpenter's tools will be lost on the way. The author reports this confusion of values but takes on himself no spiritual responsibility.

To understand this attitude one has to know the South. The South and old Russia have much in common sociologically. The South has always been a section apart from the rest of the United States, having interests and a personality distinctly its own. Economically and in other ways it has been used as a sort of colony to the rest of the nation. The poverty is unlike anything known in other parts of this country. In social structure there is a division of classes similar to that in old Russia. The South is the only part of the nation having a definite peasant class. But in spite of social divisions the people of the South are homogeneous. The Southerner and the Russian are both "types" in that they have certain recognizable and national psychological traits. Hedonistic, imaginative, lazy, and emotional—there is surely a cousinly resemblance.

In both the South and old Russia the cheapness of life is realized at every turn. The thing itself, the material detail, has an exaggerated value. Life is plentiful; children are born and they die, or if they do not die they live and struggle. And in the fight to maintain existence the whole life and suffering of a human being can be bound up in ten acres of washed out land, in a mule, in a bale of cotton. In Chekhov's, "The Peasants," the loss of the samovar in the hut is as sad, if not sadder, than the death of Nikolai or the cruelty of the old grandmother. And in *Tobacco Road*, Jeeter Lester's bargain, the swapping of his daughter for seven dollars and a throw-in, is symbolical. Life, death, the experiences of the spirit, these come and go and we do not know for what reason; but the *thing* is there, it remains to plague or comfort, and its value is immutable.

Gogol is credited to be the first of the realists. In "The Overcoat" the little clerk identifies his whole life with his new winter cloak, and loses heart and dies when it is stolen. From the time of Gogol, or from about 1850 until 1900, imaginative writing in Russia can be regarded as one artistic growth. Chekhov differs certainly from Aksakov and from Turgenev, but taken all in all the approach to their material and the general technique is the same. Morally the attitude is this: human beings are neither good nor evil, they are only unhappy and more or less adjusted to their unhappiness. People are born into a world of confusion, a society in which the system of values is so uncertain that who can say if a man is worth more than a load of hay, or if life itself is precious enough to justify the struggle to obtain the material objects necessary for its maintenance. This attitude was perhaps characteristic of all Russians during those times, and the writers only reported exactly what was true in their time and place. It is the unconscious moral approach, the fundamental spiritual basis of their work. But this by no means precludes a higher conscious level. And it is in the great philosophical novels that the culmination of Russian realism has been reached.

In the space of fourteen years, from 1866 to 1880, Dostoievsky wrote his four masterpieces: *Crime and Punishment, The Idiot, The Possessed,* and *The Brothers Karamazov.* These works are extremely complex. Dostoievsky, in the true Russian tradition, approaches life from a completely unbiased point of view; the evil, the confusion of life, he reports with the sharpest candor, fusing the most diverse emotions into a composite whole. But in addition to this he employs the analytical approach. It is almost as though having long looked on life and having faithfully reflected what he has seen in his art, he is appalled both by life itself and by what he has written. And unable to reject either, or to delude himself, he assumes the supreme responsibility and answers the riddle of life itself. But to do so he would have to be a Messiah. Sociologically these problems could never be altogether solved, and besides Dostoievsky was indifferent to economic theories. And it is in his role as a Messiah that Dostoievsky fails to meet the responsibility he has assumed. The questions he poses are too immense. They are like angry demands to God. Why has man let himself be demeaned and allowed his spirit to be corrupted by matter? Why is there evil? Why poverty and suffering? Dostoievsky demands magnificently, but his solution, the "new Christianity," does not answer; it is almost as though he uses Christ as a contrivance.

The "solution" to *Crime and Punishment* is a personal solution, the problems were metaphysical and universal. Raskolnikov is a symbol of the tragic inability of man to find an inward harmony with this world of disorder. The problem deals with the evils of society, and Raskolnikov is only a result of this discordance. By withdrawal, by personal expiation, by the recognition of a personal God, a Raskolnikov may or may not find a subjective state of grace. But if so only a collateral issue has been resolved; the basic problem remains untouched. It is like trying to reach the Q.E.D. of a geometrical problem by means of primer arithmetic.

As a moral analyst Tolstoi is clearer. He not only demands why, but what and how as well. From the time he was about fifty years of age his *Confessions* give us a beautiful record of a human being in conflict with a world of disharmony. "I felt," he wrote, "that something had broken within me on which my life had always rested, that I had nothing left to hold on to, and that morally my life had stopped." He goes on to admit that from an outward point of view his own personal life was ideal—he was in good health, unworried by finances, content in his family. Yet the whole of life around him seemed grotesquely out of balance. He writes: "The meaningless absurdity of life—it is the only incontestable knowledge accessible to man." Tolstoi's conversion is too well known to need more than mention here. In essence it is the same as Raskolnikov's as it is a purely solitary spiritual experience and fails to solve the problem as a whole.

But the measure of success achieved by these metaphysical and moral explorations is not of the greatest importance in itself. Their value is primarily catalytic. It is the way in which these moral probings affect the work as a whole that counts. And the effect is enormous. For Dostoievsky, Tolstoi, and the minor moralists brought to Russian realism one element that had hitherto been obscure or lacking. That is the element of passion.

Gogol has an imaginative creativeness that is overwhelming. As a satirist he has few equals, and his purely technical equipment is enormous. But of passion he has not a trace. Aksakov, Turgenev, Herzen, Chekhov, diverse as their separate geniuses are, they are alike in lacking this particular level of emotion. In the work of Dostoievsky and Tolstoi it is as though Russian literature suddenly closed its fist, and the whole literary organism was affected; there was a new tenseness, a gathering together of resources, a radically tightened nervous tone. With the moralists Russian realism reached its most fervent and glorious phase.

From the viewpoint of artistic merit it would be absurd to compare the new Southern writers with the Russians. It is only in their approach to their material that analogies can be drawn. The first real novel (this does not include old romances) to be written in the South did not appear until after 1900, when Russian realism was already on the decline. *Barren Ground,* by Ellen Glasgow, marked the beginning of an uncertain period of development, and Southern literature can only be considered to have made its start during the past fifteen years. But with the arrival of Caldwell and Faulkner a new and vital outgrowth began. And the South at the present time boils with literary energy. W. J. Cash in *The Mind of the South* says that if these days you shoot off a gun at random below the Mason-Dixon line you are bound by the law of averages to hit a writer.

An observer should not criticize a work of art on the grounds that it lacks certain qualities that the artist himself never intended to include. The writer has the prerogative of limiting his own scope, of staking the boundaries of his own kingdom. This must be remembered when attempting to appraise the work now being done in the South.

The Southern writers have reacted to their environment in just the same manner as the Russians prior to the time of Dostoievsky and Tolstoi. They have transposed the painful substance of life around them as accurately as possible, without taking the part of emotional panderer between the truth as it is and the feelings of the reader. The "cruelty" of which the Southerners have been accused is at bottom only a sort of naïveté, an acceptance of spiritual inconsistencies without asking the reason why, without attempting to propose an answer.

Undeniably there is an infantile quality about this clarity of vision and rejection of responsibility.

But literature in the South is a young growth, and it cannot be blamed because of its youth. One can only speculate about the possible course of its development or retrogression. Southern writing has reached the limits of a moral realism; something more must be added if it is to continue to flourish. As yet there has been no forerunner of an analytical moralist such as Tolstoi or a mystic like Dostoievsky. But the material with which Southern literature deals seems to demand of itself that certain basic questions be posed. If and when this group of writers is able to assume a philosophical responsibility, the whole tone and structure of their work will be enriched, and Southern writing will enter a more complete and vigorous stage in its evolution.

1941

Margaret Walker

A Brief Introduction
to Southern Literature

A version of this essay was presented at the Mississippi Arts Festival in Jackson, Mississippi, in 1971.

Some of the most distinguished names in literature, in America and in the world at large, are names of southerners of the U.S.A. Because of the nature of more than three hundred years of southern history, the student of American literature tends not to think of the hundreds of writers, Black and white, who were born in the South and claim this region for their native homes, regardless of whether, for one reason or another, they have gone outside the region to develop their writing aptitudes and practice the craft and art of writing.

If we could dispense altogether with regionalism in American literature and see America as a whole, we would have achieved the impossible, for each region has had its place in the sun insofar as American literature is concerned. Scholars speak of the American Renaissance when they mean a resurgence and awakening in New England with the transcendentalists; Hamlin Garland is a name to conjure with in the Midwest, as are Carl Sandburg and Sherwood Anderson. The West claims John Steinbeck and Walter van Tilburg Clark, author of *The Ox-Bow Incident*. I wish I could do justice to the hundreds of names in southern fiction, from John Pendleton Kennedy's *Swallow Barn* (1832) to Margaret Mitchell's *Gone with the Wind* (1936) or from John William DeForest's *Miss Ravenel's Conversion* (1867) to

28

my own *Jubilee* (1966), but that is an impossible task. The history and the literature of the South are a reflection of the life of the people, and the people have had too varied and too myriad an experience for me to deal with boldly and comprehensively. Therefore, I can at best attempt only a brief introduction to this literature.

As early as Kennedy's *Swallow Barn,* a southern tradition existed in American literature. That tradition became known as the plantation tradition, from which came both Paul Laurence Dunbar and Margaret Mitchell, with many others in between. The realm of Black and white minstrels belongs to this tradition. Dialect in its various manifestations was the language most familiar and typical. This marked the beginning of a set of stereotypes from which the literature has yet to free itself. Along with this plantation tradition, both Black and white writers have developed a folk tradition that began in the oral tradition of spirituals, work songs, and ballads. All this was essentially southern. America as a whole became enthralled with southern manners, language, and scenery when Mark Twain, with his Mississippi River stories, opened a classic new chapter in American literature, immortalizing that section of the country from St. Louis to New Orleans. The riverboat, life on the Mississippi, the water commerce, these have contributed to the color not only of the region but of all American literature. New Orleans, Memphis, Charleston, and Atlanta have been at one time or another the queen cities of southern literature, but the rural South is equally as popular.

It is impossible to read our most distinguished writers without being conscious at once of the land as well as the people. The love of the southerner for the land—the southern soil—and the strange agrarian beliefs of such groups of southern writers as the Vanderbilt group, all these have given rise to stories with settings ranging from Texas to the Carolinas and the Gulf Coast through the mountains of Tennessee and Kentucky. There is not a southern state that has not figured prominently in literature. Perhaps in its most striking sense the South has agonized through the Civil War battlegrounds and scenes more than any other region, for this war has seemed most particularly the southern war—the "only war"—and is often considered the southern *Iliad.*

But, what the world knows of this literature, it knows in two widely differing segments. Some of southern literature is known, even at home, scarcely at all because of the nature of the institutions of slavery and segregation. Comparisons between Black writers and white writers can be made in terms of period, subject matter, and form. When this is done, one begins to see more than one side, or facet, of an interesting American theme. During the summer of 1963, a violent year of the sixties in America, I had the rare privilege of taking a course in southern literature under Professor Arlin Turner of Duke University who was teaching that summer in Iowa, and I found myself rereading the fiction of my adolescence, and discovering I had cut my teeth on much of southern fiction, both Black and white. Black writers like Langston Hughes and Arna Bontemps and Zora Neale Hurston were born in the South; white writers like Thomas Wolfe and DuBose Heyward and Julia Peterkin, Caroline Gordon, Ellen Glasgow and Mary Rinehart Roberts had provided me with many a summer's reading. Books like *Black Is My True-Love's Hair* (Elizabeth Maddox Roberts), *Lamb in His Bosom* (Carolin Pafford Miller), *None Shall Look Back* (Caroline Gordon), and *So Red the Rose* (Stark Young), were just as familiar as Hughes's *Not without Laughter,* Bontemps's *Black Thunder,* and Hurston's *Jonah's Gourd Vine.*[1] The southern writer, like all American writers, but perhaps with more intensity, deals largely with race. He or she cannot escape the ever present factor of race and the problems of race as they have grown out of the southern society and affected all of America. The treatment first of the Black man, or the Negro, in southern fiction has been not only the problem of character delineation but also the moral problem of race. The subject of race has been romanticized, and realistically portrayed, and the characters have ranged from wooden stereotypes—flat, mindless, and caricatured as buffoons—to deft and skillful portrayal of both realistic and humanistic proportions. The subject of race has become theme and conflict and character development in southern literature.

Perhaps the single most glaring fault Black Americans find with southern literature by white writers is in the psychology and philosophy, which of necessity in most instances is racist. This has to be understood in terms of the society, the values emphasized in American education, the nature of slavery and segregation, which not only have kept the races apart, separated and polarized in two segregated societies but have ostracized the artistic accomplishments of Black people and ignored their literature. The earliest writers, Black and white, were fighting a racial battle, the white writers were writing apologies for slavery and the Black writers were protesting against the inhumanity of the slave system. With the substitution of segregation, the white child was educated to regard race as more important than humanity and the Black child was educated to imitate a white world as superior to his and thus taught to hate himself. The battle and the conflict can be seen in the literature.

John Esten Cooke, William Gilmore Simms, and Thomas Nelson Page obviously present an altogether different picture from Frederick Douglass, Martin DeLany, and Frances Watkins Harper. Cooke, Simms, and Page served as agents for antebellum southern planter ideals. Their dialect stories, written in the local color tradition, were uncritical in their acceptance of the southern aristocracy that maintained an oppressive slave system. Douglass, DeLany, and Harper, on the other hand, strongly advocated abolishing slavery and found nothing in the slave system to sentimentalize.

Mark Twain's Huck Finn and Jim provide another profile of the treatment of race in southern and American literature. While Twain moved away from the conventions of the sentimental novel, his adaptations of southern humor created Jim and Huck Finn as outsider figures, thus giving way to a new stereotype.

James Russell, Joel Chandler Harris, and Augustus Baldwin Longstreet should be compared with Paul Laurence Dunbar, James Weldon Johnson, and Charles Chestnutt. Harris, Russell, and Longstreet strived to be true to the manners, language and attitudes of their characters. For them, Black nature was not something to be scoffed at or derided, but was a distinctive, if not peculiar, feature of the South. They were among the earliest white writers to recognize the immense creative possibilities of the Black folk expression that Dunbar, Chestnutt, and Johnson used in their works. George Washington Cable and Albion Tourgee are fit writers to compare with W. E. B. Du Bois and the Joseph Seaman Cotters, junior and senior. Cable and Tourgee were the most politically conscious among postbellum white writers. One notes a tinge of social reformism in their work that echoes the concerns of Du Bois and other Black political leaders.

Reading Mark Twain's stories as a child I came across the word *nigger* and put the book down. Years later hearing the ironic incident told as a joke I could not laugh: "Heard about a terrible accident," and one asked, "Did anybody get hurt?" "Nome, just killed a nigger." The full implication was that a Black man was not a human being and this was the racist problem of early southern literature. But it is also important to relate here by the same token much of American literature outside the South did not move me at all. If the South seemed obsessed by race, at least it was a subject. Hemingway's fiction was certainly not as immediate and meaningful, for that same reason, as Faulkner's was to me.

When one thinks of southern literature, the sentimental tradition of moonlight and roses, magnolias and mockingbirds, comes to mind as a definite part of our southern heritage in American literature. But the violent South is a theme that is also evident in southern and American literature from the days of the frontier through the Civil War to the days of the Civil Rights Movement. The violent South gives rise to certain aspects as part of the history of American literature: the Gothic novel, which includes the grotesque, the macabre, the supernatural (such as ghosts); the violence so characteristic in southern fiction is easily accommodated within the Gothic tradition. Edgar Allan Poe is perhaps the single most important figure who influenced a whole school of poetry, the Symbolists, in France including Mallarmé, Rimbaud, Valéry, and Baudelaire. With the southern writer, we automatically think of Poe's tales of ratiocination and mystery when we also think of the Gothic novels of Carson McCullers, Flannery O'Connor, and Alice Walker and the prose of today.

When one reads McCullers, the world becomes inhabited by the isolated; by the lonely vainly groping for escape, as shown in *The Heart Is a Lonely Hunter* (1940). Her world is also one of thwarted homosexuality (*Reflections in a Golden Eye,* 1941); of the physically and emotionally misshapen (*The Ballad of the Sad Cafe,* 1951); or of the ache of the dailiness of life (autobiographical *The Member of the Wedding,* 1946). All are bound by the chord of disjunction, of virulent loneliness. Little sunshine penetrates her dark and Gothic universe. Hope appears to have fled.

With the writers Flannery O'Connor and Alice Walker the landscape is not as sere. But although O'Connor and Walker "lived within minutes of each other on the same Eatonton to Milledgeville road,"[2] they differ in race, in religion, and in thematic treatment. There are, however, areas of likeness. Both offer a somewhat more hopeful picture of life, and both appear to infuse their characters with elements of realism. Black writer Walker has observed that when O'Connor wrote "not a whiff of magnolia hovered in the air."[3] Walker found in O'Connor a truth that surpasses race, thereby achieving a widened vision of the universe: "But essential O'Connor is not about race at all . . . it is 'about' the impact of supernatural grace on human beings."[4]

While O'Connor's characters are mutilated by their quests for salvation (i.e., a seeking for divine mercy from an unyielding God) as shown in the character Motes in *Wise Blood* (1952) and Tarwater in *The Violent Bear It Away* (1960), Walker's protagonists are oppressed from within and from without. Theirs is a universe tyrannized by the rejection of white society (without), and more crucially, Black self-dehumanization (within). *The Third Life of Grange Copeland* (1970) illustrates this two-pronged oppression through three generations. At the core of the oppression is the Black woman—rejected by white society, while being abused by Black men. Such a bitter vision thwarts and twists hopes and dreams. In her award-winning *The Color Purple,* Walker's protagonist, Celie, frees herself from oppression based on race, on sex, and on physical appearance. Unlike O'Connor's God, Walker's God, in *The Color Purple,* can rejoice with woman,[5] thereby freeing her to love and to seek that which liberates and fulfills. Walker thus breaks from O'Connor and McCullers by rejecting the Gothic view and permitting the terror and evil in the world to be overcome by her characters.

It is in William Faulkner, Eudora Welty, and Richard Wright that we see the southern writer rising above time and place, struggling beyond the racist limitations of his or her society into the truly rarified world of the artist, a world in which human values and universal truths take precedence over provincial and philistine notions and bigoted minds. In his acceptance speech for the Nobel prize, William Faulkner expressed his belief in the need of the writer to lift up the human heart in order for the human spirit to struggle to prevail, to triumph over all. Like all great writers they move from the local to the universal, from the immediate to the timeless, and from the simple into the sublime. William Faulkner, Richard Wright, and Eudora Welty are among the most modern of American writers whose native home is the South, and particularly Mississippi. They differ widely in their writings, but they have certain verities in common. They deal with the southern scene; they deal with a violent South, too, but they also work within the framework of a humanistic tradition.

William Faulkner's writing shows a multiracial and multiclass consciousness. Faulkner considers three races in his native Mississippi. His approach is the traditional, such as in all the hackneyed themes of miscegenation and the tragic mulatto, and yet he is innovative and experimental as well. He deals with the southern landscape in a meaningful fashion, and as a symbolist he creates a fictitious world that thoroughly absorbs the American myth about race. Yoknapatawpha is more than the creation of Faulkner's imagination, it is a re-creation of a real southern county in which he lived, as well as a microcosm of much of America on the subject of race.

Eudora Welty skillfully expresses the folk life of her place and time, but she moves beyond these into eternal and universal truths of the human spirit. Like many other people, my favorite short stories are "Why I Live at the P.O." and "A Worn Path." Here she expresses the fundamental philosophies of simple people in an unerring and unforgettable fashion, using humor and pathos without undue sentimentality. I am sure she would not like to be labeled as a member of the Faulkner school when she is also so unlike him, and would doubtless prefer to be associated with the name of Katherine Anne Porter, who has won recognition throughout the world for her craftsmanship as a short story writer. She may have been Miss Welty's teacher, but then often the pupil equals if not surpasses the teacher. Welty's recent novels suggest that indeed she has. I am also sure if you asked Miss Welty about her treatment of race she would say she does no such thing, she writes about people. And therein lies the secret of greatness. The writer is concerned with the human condition. He or she writes about people as people, not as things. Welty sees race superseded by humanity, and as such, she values the human spirit above everything else.

Richard Wright spent his last years far from Mississippi but all that he wrote of significance and strength, and he was a powerful writer, make no mistake about that—power and passion he had—all that he wrote grows out of those nineteen years of his life he spent in the South. The violent South left an indelible impression upon him, and all the rest of his life he was struggling to express the need for men to understand the highest human values as superior to the bigoted notions of race, class, creed and any other prejudices that hinder the human spirit and cloud the human intelligence.

The South has produced a great body of literature, despite all the social hindrances of what James W. Silver calls a "closed society."[6] The South is not alone guilty in terms of racism. All America today suffers from the sickness of racism. All America today also suffers from paranoia. White America seems to have the strange sickness of delusions of grandeur while Black Americans seem to suffer from delusions of persecution. None of us is willing to believe any of it is only a delusion. But our literature reflects our society, and when we are a polarized or segregated society, our literature is also. We would hope for a healing of our sick society, sick of war and division, sick of material values and a quality of life gone sour with pollution, with militarism, racism, and materialism. Our hope for the future must be with the proverbial madmen of the world—the priests and the poets, and the lovers. All of them are mad, drunk with love and religion and the smoke of inspiration. But the artists have always been, too, the avant garde. They have the ideas that the philosophers generate, and they implement the new concepts of the universe in order that man may build a better society. It is therefore in the literature of today that we have cultural hope for change tomorrow. Literature is a cultural instrument, and as such, we build toward a new twenty-first century that will have learned all the sad lessons of the twentieth century. Perhaps we will produce together all that is needed for one race on the face of the earth, the human race.

Two poems express for me the strong sense of the South as I have known and experienced it. I wrote them when I was quite young and a long way from home. "Southern Song" and "Sorrow Home" are from my first book of poems, *For My People:*

Southern Song

I want my body bathed again by southern suns, my soul
   reclaimed again from southern land. I want to rest
   again in southern fields, in grass and hay and clover

bloom; to lay my hand again upon the clay baked by
a southern sun, to touch the rain-soaked earth and
smell the smell of soil.

I want my rest unbroken in the fields of southern earth;
freedom to watch the corn wave silver in the sun and
mark the splashing of a brook, a pond with ducks
and frogs and count the clouds.

I want no mobs to wrench me from my southern rest; no
forms to take me in the night and burn my shack and
make for me a nightmare full of oil and flame.

I want my careless song to strike no minor key; no fiend to
stand between my body's southern song—the fusion of the
South, my body's song and me.

Sorrow Home

My roots are deep in southern life; deeper than John Brown
or Nat Turner or Robert Lee. I was sired and weaned
in a tropic world. The palm tree and banana leaf,
mango and coconut, breadfruit and rubber trees
know me.

Warm skies and gulf blue streams are in my blood. I belong
with the smell of fresh pine, with the trail of coon,
and the spring growth of wild onion.

I am no hot-house bulb to be reared in steam-heated flats
with the music of "L" and subway in my ears, walled
in by steel and wood and brick far from the sky.

I want the cotton fields, tobacco and the cane. I want to walk
along with sacks of seed to drop in fallow ground.
Restless music is in my heart and I am eager to be
gone. O Southland, sorrow home, melody beating in my bone and
blood! How long will the Klan of hate, the hounds
and the chain gangs keep me from my own?[7]

1. All of these books were published during the 1930s. I wish to acknowledge the white southern chronology from Turner's *Southern Stories* (New York: Holt, Rinehart, 1960), and the companion piece on events in the Negro world from *The Negro Caravan*, edited by Sterling Brown, Ulysses Lee, and Arthur P. Davis (New York: Arno Press, 1969).

2. Alice Walker, *In Search of Our Mother's Garden* (New York: Harcourt, Brace, 1983), p. 42.

3. Ibid., p. 52.

4. Ibid., p. 53.

5. Alice Walker, *The Color Purple* (New York: Washington Square Press, 1982), pp. 178, 179, 249.

6. *Mississippi: The Closed Society* (1964) (New enl. ed., New York: Harcourt, Brace & World, 1966) is a remarkable and revealing account of the desegregation of the South, written when Silver was then professor of history at the University of Mississippi.

7. *For My People* (New Haven: Yale University Press, 1942).

1990

Connections

When Katherine Anne Porter, Flannery O'Connor, and Caroline Gordon joined others for a panel discussion in 1960 at Wesleyan College in Macon, Georgia, their gathering reflected relationships that had a major impact on the lives of these three writers. Gordon and Porter frequently traveled in the same social and literary circles; they had many mutual friends—and enemies. Their relationship, while not always characterized by warmth and equanimity, rested on an abiding respect they had for one another. In 1931 when Porter traveled by ship to Germany, a journey that served as the material for her novel *Ship of Fools*, she corresponded regularly with Gordon.[1] She often expressed a deep appreciation of Gordon's craft. In her review of *None Shall Look Back,* Porter describes Gordon as "an ancient chronicler" who "moves about, a disembodied spectator timing her presence expertly" (p. 61). Gordon likewise appreciated Porter's artistry. In *The House of Fiction,* an anthology of thirty short stories edited with Allen Tate, she includes Porter's story "Old Mortality" along with the works of such writers as Nathaniel Hawthorne, Leo Tolstoy, James Joyce, Eudora Welty, and William Faulkner—thus exhibiting her faith in the importance of Porter's work.

Each had a different sort of relationship with Flannery O'Connor. Gordon served as her mentor, Porter as an important source of inspiration. Both Gordon's short story "Old Red" and Porter's "Noon Wine" were models of short fiction for O'Connor. They, in turn, greatly admired the younger writer, as evidenced by their reviews of her work and tributes to her life. All three, while exhibiting disparate lifestyles and approaches to literature, offer testimony to the importance of friendship in enriching their world and in shaping their work.

1. Joan Givner, *Katherine Anne Porter: A Life* (London: Jonathan Cape, 1983), p. 246.

39

Wesleyan College

Recent Southern Fiction:
A Panel Discussion

Wesleyan College, 28 October 1960. Panelists: Katherine Anne Porter, Flannery O'Connor, Caroline Gordon, and Madison Jones. Louis D. Rubin, Jr., Moderator.

Rubin: I suppose you know what a panel discussion is—for the first thirty minutes the moderator tries his best to get the panel members to say something and for the last thirty minutes he does his best to shut them up. I hope we can do that tonight. My own position here with these four distinguished Southern writers on my left is something like the junior member of that famous and often narrated legal firm—Levy, Ginsberg, Cohen, and Kelly. Kelly presses the suits. I thought the first thing we might talk about, if we may, would be writing habits. That is something everyone has one way or another. Mr. Jones, suppose I ask you, how do you write?

    Jones: Well, you mean just physically speaking?

    Rubin: Yes. What time of the day?

    Jones: Well, I usually write from about 8:30 to 12 or 12:30 in the morning.

    Gordon: Every day?

    Jones: Well, every day except Sunday.

    Gordon: You're a genius.

    Rubin: How about you, Miss Porter?

    Porter: Well, I have no hours at all, just such as I can snatch from all the other things I do. Once upon a time I tagged a husband around Europe in the Foreign Service for so many years and never lived for more than two years in one place and never knew where I was going to be and I just wrote when I could and I still do. Once in a while I take the time and run away to an inn and tell them to leave me alone. When I get hungry, I'll come out. And in those times I really get some work done. I wrote two short novels in fourteen days once [*Noon Wine* and *Old Mortality*] but that was twenty-five years ago.

Rubin: How about you, Miss Gordon?

Gordon: I made a horrible discovery this summer. I had a great deal of company and they all wanted to help me with the housework and I discovered I would have to stop writing if I let them do it because my writing and my housework all go together and if they washed the dishes then I didn't get any writing done. That's just my system that I have developed over the years—it works for me except it maddens my friends, because they like to help me wash the dishes.

Rubin: You mean your whole day is part of a very closely worked in regimen?

Gordon: I didn't discover it until this friend came and insisted she wanted to help me.

Rubin: How about you, Miss O'Connor? Do you do your writing along with the dishwashing?

O'Connor: Oh, no. I sit there before the typewriter for three hours every day and if anything comes I am there waiting to receive it. I think there should be a complete separation between literature and dishwashing.

Porter: I was once washing dishes in an old fashioned dishpan at 11 o'clock at night after a party and all of a sudden I just took my hands up like that and went to the typewriter and wrote the short story "Rope" between that time and two o'clock in the morning. I don't know what started me. I know I had it in mind for several years but the moment came suddenly.

Rubin: If that's what dishwashing does, then I'm going to buy a box of Duz in the morning. What I think you all seem to show is that there is no right way or wrong way, I suppose.

Porter: I think Grandma Moses is the most charming old soul. When they asked her how she painted—and they meant, I am sure, how she used the brush—she said, "Well, first I saw a masonite board to the size I want the picture to be." And I think that is what we do.

Rubin: It all sounds like alchemy to me.

Gordon: That is one question that people always ask a writer. How many hours he or she puts in a day. I've often wondered why that is and I just discovered fairly recently. I think they expect you to say you are writing all of the time. If you are mowing the grass you are still thinking about what you are going to write. It is all the time.

Rubin: I always remember reading something the late Bernard De-Voto remarked—that one of his hardest jobs was keeping his wife from thinking that if he looked up out of the window, then that meant he wasn't doing any work at the moment, so that she could ask him about some spending money or something of the sort.

Gordon: I used to have a dentist—an awfully good one—but I quit him because when he was going to hurt me he would say, "Now just relax and think about your novel." I couldn't take that.

Jones: I have always found that when something is going well, I can't think about it at all unless I am right over the paper. Unless I am at work, I can't even get my mind on it away from my environment.

Rubin: Let me change the subject. I'll let Miss Porter answer this one. Miss Porter, do you consider yourself a Southern writer?

Porter: I am a Southerner. I have been told that I wasn't a Southerner, that anyone born in Texas is a South-westerner. But I can't help it. Some of my people came from Virginia, some from Pennsylvania, but we are all from Tennessee, Georgia, the Carolinas, Kentucky, Louisiana. What does it take to be a Southerner? And being a Southerner, I happen to write so I suppose you combine the two and you have a Southern writer, haven't you? What do you think? I do feel an intense sense of location and of background and my tradition and my country exist to me, but I have never really stuck to it in my writing because I have lived too nomadic a life. You know my people started from Virginia and Pennsylvania toward the West in 1776 or 1777 and none of us really ever stopped since and that includes me. So why should I stick to one place or write about one place since I have never lived just in one place?

Rubin: Miss O'Connor, how about you?

O'Connor: Well I admit to being one. My own sense of place is quite unadjustable. I have a friend from Michigan who went to Germany and Japan and who wrote stories about Germans who sounded like Germans and about Japanese who sounded like Japanese. I know if I tried to write stories about credible Japanese they would all sound like Herman Talmadge.

Rubin: Does the State Department know about *this*? How about you, Mr. Jones?

Jones: I feel more or less like Miss O'Connor. No matter where I was or how long I might live there—although my attitude might change—I still have the feeling that everything I would write would be laid in the country that I feel the most communion with, that is the central Tennessee area, or at least a part of it. My imagination just feels at home there. Other places I have been have never tempted me to write about them so I think I am a Southern writer.

Rubin: Miss Gordon, how about you?

Gordon: I agree with him. I wouldn't think about writing anything about anybody from Princeton. They just don't seem to be important. That's dreadful but that's the way I feel. Your own country—that's the first thing you knew—that's important. I did write one story once that was laid in France but it was fifteen years after I lived there. But I think the thing about the Southern writer—I believe there is such a thing—and I think he is very interesting because he knows something that not all other writers in America today know. I feel that very strongly.

Porter: He usually knows who he is and where he is and what he is doing. Some people never know that in a long lifetime. But you see, I write out of my own background about what I know but I can't stay in one place. I write about a country maybe ten years after I have been in it. But that is a part of my experience too, and in a way it is an egotistic thing to do because it is what happened to me. I am writing about my own experience, really, out of my own background and tradition.

Rubin: What do you mean by a sense of place? Do you mean simply your geographical knowledge?

O'Connor: Not so much the geography. I think it is the idiom. Like Mrs. Tate said, people in Princeton don't talk like we do. And these sounds build up a life of their own in your senses.

Gordon: And place is very important too I think.

Jones: And I think it is a check in a way, too, of the honesty in your writing. Somehow in writing you have a way to check yourself by the kind of intimacy you have with your community and home.

Rubin: I don't think myself there is any doubt that there is such a thing as a Southern Writer—capital S, capital W—and that when you pick up a book, a novel, a short story, it doesn't take you very long before you have the feeling that this is by a Southerner. I suppose there are Southern writers that fool you. I mean that you don't think are Southerners. I think that you could pick up some Erskine Caldwell for instance, particularly his later work, and you would never think that this man is from 50 miles from where Flannery O'Connor lives but at the same time—

Gordon: But he says things which are not so. For instance, I forget in what story he has the best hound dogs in the neighborhood down in the well and all of the men are just sitting around talking. None of the men are getting the dogs out of the well. That just couldn't happen. Simply couldn't happen. You can't trust him on detail.

Rubin: I like some of the things in the early Caldwell work.

Gordon: Oh, at times he's very amusing.

Rubin: I was thinking about this the other day. Let's take writers such as Caldwell and Faulkner or Eudora Welty. You think of them as being poles apart. But when you compare either of these writers, with, let's say, Dos Passos, you notice that the Caldwell people and the Welty people are more or less responsible for their own actions. In the stuff Caldwell wrote about 1930 or so he was trying to show, for example, that what was wrong with Jeeter Lester was society and the share cropping system and things like that, but when he wrote about Jeeter Lester you couldn't help feeling that the main reason Jeeter Lester was what he was was because he was Jeeter Lester. Whereas in a book like *USA* I don't think you had this feeling—I think you do accept the author's version of experience that society is what causes it. I think that the individual character somehow being responsible for his own actions is very typical of the Southern writers, and I think this is why we have produced very few naturalists as such. Do you think there is something to that?

Gordon: Why I think we have produced wonderful naturalists.

Rubin: Well, I was using the word in the literary sense.

Gordon: I just don't think you can use it that way. Every good story has naturalistic elements. Look at the sheep, cows and pigs in Miss Porter's story, "Holiday."[1]

Rubin: Well, I was using the word in the philosophical sense of the environment-trapped hero and such as that.

Porter: Don't you think that came out a great deal in the communist doctrine of the locomotive of history—you know, rounding the sharp bend and everybody who doesn't go with it falls off of it—that history makes men instead of men making history, and it takes away the moral responsibility. The same thing can be said of that cry during the war that nobody could be blamed because we are all guilty until we stopped realizing that one has been guiltier perhaps than the other. This whole effort for the past one hundred years has been to remove the moral responsibility from the individual and make him blame his own human wickedness on his society, but he helps to make his society, you see, and he will not take his responsibility for his part in it.

Rubin: Well that's very interesting. I think right there is the difference between Caldwell and Dos Passos. Caldwell was consciously writing out of just that propagandistic position. He wanted to show that these people were victims. Yet because he was a Southerner, because he was writing about these people, they wouldn't behave. They became people instead of symbols.

Gordon: I would like to say one other thing about the Southern writer. I think we have some awfully good Southern writers and I believe one reason they are so good is that we are a conquered people and we know some things that a person who is not a Southern writer cannot envisage as happening. For him they never have happened. We know something he does not know.

Rubin: You know that this isn't necessarily the greatest nation that ever was or ever will be.

Gordon: Well, we know that a nation can go down in defeat. A great many men committed suicide after the Civil War and anyone I have ever heard of left the same note. He said, "This is a great deal worse than I thought it was going to be." Some of them eighty years old. Edmund Ruffin, for example.

Rubin: Tell me this now. Do you think that this is as true of the young Southerner growing up today as it was for the generations of Southerners who wrote the books in the 1920's and 30's?

Gordon: I think the most terrible thing I have ever read about the South was written by my young friend here [Miss O'Connor]—worse than anything Faulkner ever wrote. That scene where that lady, I forgot her name, but her husband is dead and now she gets in a tight place and she goes into the back hall behind some portieres. I can just see them, too. Some of my aunts had portieres. And she sits down at a roll-top desk which is very dusty and has yellow pieces of paper and things, and communes with his spirit. And his spirit says to her, "One man's meat is another man's poison" or something like "The devil you know is better than the devil you don't know." I think that's the most terrible thing that's ever been written about the South. It haunts me.

Rubin: Do you really think that this is changing?

Gordon: Well, I would say here is a young writer who has this terrible vision and such a vision could only come out of great concern.

Rubin: I wondered though. Nowadays I go to my own home town of Charleston, South Carolina, and it still looks the same downtown but you go outside of the city and everything about it looks just like, well I won't say Newark, New Jersey—it's not that bad—but let's say Philadelphia, and I just wondered if the same environment that operated even on Miss O'Connor will still have the emotional impact that it has had on Southern writing, whether the sense of defeat that we were just mentioning is still going to prevail. I think the notion that the South alone of the American sections knew that it is possible to lose a war, that it is possible to do your very best and still lose, is something that has been very true of Southern life, but I wonder whether in the post-Depression prosperity this is still going to be so? I have a feeling that it isn't.

Gordon: I do too.

Porter: It is happening already. There are some extremely interesting young writers. Walter Clemons—I don't want to speak of Texas writers altogether—there is one named George Garrett and there are several others—William Humphrey, Peter Taylor, among them, and I think they are probably the last ones who are going to feel the way they do. And I think these young people are probably the last because I don't see anyone coming after them at all and even they have changed a great deal because they don't have the tragic feeling about the South that we had, you know.

Gordon: One of Peter's best stories and he says it is his best story is "Bad Time." Do you know that story? It's a beaut.

Porter: Yes. But I don't see anybody else coming after and these are greatly changed. You think of young Clemons and then think of ones just before and they are changed. More of them are city people; they are writing about town life. And a kind of life that didn't really interest us, even though we were brought up partly in town. It was the country life that formed us.

Gordon: Peter is kind of a missing link. But he writes about country people going to town.

Jones: I noticed that in the collection of new Southern writings more than half were set in urban areas.

Rubin: You mention William Humphery and to me he is symptomatic of this change. That book [*Home From The Hill*] to me started off extremely well and then suddenly nose-dived, and it nose-dived precisely at the point where the protagonist could no longer do the Faulknerian sort of thing, the hunt and things like that, and was just an adolescent in the city, and it seemed to me we just couldn't take the person seriously enough. Humphrey was still trying to write like Faulkner in a sense—the wrong kind of milieu in the wrong kind of place—and to me the book failed, and this is symptomatic.

Porter: He is an extremely good short story writer. He preceded that book with a number of very good short stories, I think, but he did want to write a successful book if he possibly could, you know, and he got the idea of what is success mixed up with what would be good sales and so he spoiled his book by trying to make it popular.

Rubin: He succeeded in that.

Porter: He did and good luck to him. He was my student for years and I thought he was going to turn out better than that, I must say.

Rubin: I have a feeling about the Southern writing in the last ten years, and that includes Miss O'Connor by the way—and I certainly don't mean it as an insult, Miss O'Connor. There is a kind of distance to the life you describe, a kind of esthetic distance, as if the people are far away from the writer, and this sometimes produces an extremely fine emotional effect. Take for example the difference in Styron's *Lie Down in Darkness* and Faulkner's *The Sound and The Fury*, where in both cases you have someone walking around in a northern city holding a time piece getting ready to take his or her life. Somehow or other the protagonist in the Faulkner novel is still a Yoknapatawpha County citizen. Somehow the protagonist in the Styron novel is away from that, she has left it, she couldn't go back to it if she wanted to or anywhere like that, and to me this feeling runs through so much of the most recent Southern writing. The Southern community is moving farther and farther away. You write about it and do it beautifully, but the distance is farther. You can't take it as seriously.

Jones: But don't you think in *Lie Down in Darkness* that as long as he is at home, Styron makes you feel closer to the character? I mean, that last business about the girl seems to be pretty bad.

Rubin: What I think about that book is that the book takes place in a Southern city, Port Warwick—something like Newport News, but I don't feel that the family in the book are essentially what they are because of the community at all. I think that is what Mr. Styron wanted them to be. He wanted Payton Loftis to suffer because of several generations, etc., but I don't think she does. I think it is purely because of these particular people involved. Their little private things are apart from the community, and I don't get the same sense of community even when they are writing about things in Port Warwick that you would have in a Faulkner novel.

Porter: I have a feeling about Styron, you know the way he develops piles of agonies and horrors and that sort of thing, and I think it masks a lack of feeling. I think he has all the vocabulary of feeling and rhythm of feeling and knows he ought to feel but he does not. I can't read him with any patience at all. I want to say, "Take off those whiskers, come out of the bushes and fight fair."

Rubin: I find him a very provocative writer myself.

Porter: Well, you remember the story about the man and the two people who come to play cards, I think this was in Rome. They are terrible card cheats and everybody gets frightfully drunk and he winds up perfectly senselessly without any clothes on, robbed and beaten, in a horribly filthy hotel and his wife has to come and get him and you say—now let me see, what was it about? What did it mean? It means absolutely nothing. One feels, well, the police just should have put this one in jail until he sobered up. And such a thing is not interesting for the simple reason that the man to whom it happened is of no interest. That is my quarrel with him, and it is a quarrel, too.

Rubin: If there is anything to this feeling of distance, I have the feeling that the Southern writer now isn't taking the things that go on in the community with the same kind of importance. He takes it with equal importance, but with a different kind of importance than, let's say, Faulkner did. Take someone like Sutpen in Faulkner, or Colonel Sartoris. What they did seemed to Faulkner to be very logical and important, even though it may be mad, but at the same time he wasn't writing about it in the sense that he thought he was handling a sort of primitive, or something like that.

Jones: Well, in that kind of community I guess that when someone jumps in the water you feel the ripple, but now it is hard to feel it.

Porter: I think Styron's trouble may be he really is alienated, you know, from that place and he can't get back home himself. Thomas Wolfe said, "You can't go home again," and I said "Nonsense, that it is the only place you can go. You go there all the time."

Rubin: He certainly can't write about Southerners in the sense that they are importantly in the South acting on Southern concerns. His last one takes place in Italy.

Porter: It's curious. He may be able to do it. He has been living there for years. But I don't know what is happening to him.

Rubin: Miss O'Connor, I know this is a question that writers don't think of and only literary critics like myself think of and ask, but do you think that the Southern community you see, that your relationship to it, is different from the way that Eudora Welty or Faulkner looks at the Southern community?

O'Connor: Well, I don't know how either Eudora Welty or Faulkner looks at it. I only know how I look at it and I don't feel that I am writing about the community at all. I feel that I am taking things in the community that I can show the whole western world, the whole edition of the present generation of people, of what I can use of the Southern situation.

Rubin: I surely agree with that.

Porter: You made that pretty clear yesterday. You know that was one of the things you talked about. It was most interesting.[2]

O'Connor: You know, people say that Southern life is not the way you picture it. Well, Lord help us, let's hope not.

Rubin: Well, I think that this is one of the tremendous appeals that Southern writing has had—the universality of its creative materials—

but to me there has been some relation between this universality and the particularity with which it is done. You couldn't have one without the other. But I think the fact that you are all writing about the South in the sense that this is the way the people talk, etc., somehow does make possible a meaningful, broader reading that people give it.

Jones: It does give you something to check yourself against.

Rubin: I think that is a very good notion. It is the thorough grounding in actuality.

O'Connor: Well, the South is not the Bible Belt for nothing.

Porter: Someone said that the resemblance of the real Southerner to the Frenchman was that we have no organized, impersonal abstract murder. That is, a good Southerner doesn't kill anybody he doesn't know.

Rubin: I wonder if even that isn't changing. Speaking of the Bible belt, I think that it has more than one relevance to what we are dealing with. I think it also involves this question of language. I think that Southerners do and did read the Bible a great deal and somehow, more in the King James Bible, this rolling feeling for language comes through.

Gordon: They read a lot of Cicero, too.

O'Connor: More than the language it seems to me it is simply the concrete, the business of being a story teller. I have Boston cousins and when they come South they discuss problems, they don't tell stories. We tell stories.

Rubin: Well look now, how about our audience? I am sure that our panel will be glad to parry any questions you would like to throw at them. Doesn't someone have a question or two to ask?

Question: Would someone care to comment on the great number of old people and children in Southern writing?

Porter: Well, they are very much there.

Gordon: How many children in that family you were reading about last night?

Porter: Well, there were eight under the age of ten—counting one not yet born—belonging to two women. That isn't bad, is it? And I have known them to do better than that. And with the old people who always seem to live forever and everybody always lived in the same house, all the generations. It was one way of getting acquainted with the generations. We simply would have old people and we would have children in the house together, and they were important, both ends of the line. It was really the ones in mid-life who took the gaff, didn't they? Because they had the young on one side and the old on the other.

Rubin: They were too young to be tolerated and not old enough to be characters.

Porter: A friend of mine said the other day, "Now there are only three degrees of age—young, mature, and remarkable."

Question: Miss O'Connor, you said yesterday that the South was Christ-haunted instead of Christ-centered. I don't quite understand this and how it effects our Southern literature. Would you please explain this?

O'Connor: I shouldn't have said that, should I? Well, as I said, the South didn't seem to me as a writer to be Christ-centered. I don't think anyone would object to that at all. I think all you would have to do is to read the newspapers to agree with me, but I said that we seemed to me to be Christ-haunted and that ghosts cast strange shadows, very fierce shadows, particularly in our literature. It is hard to explain a flat statement like that. I would hate to talk off the top of my head on a subject like that. I think it is a subject that a book could be written about but it would take me ten or twelve years to do it.

Gordon: When I was young, old gentlemen sat under the trees reading. That was all they did all of the time, and shall we call it the movement which is sometimes called The Death of God, that controversy that Hegel the Philosopher had with Heine the Poet. There was quite a lot of talk about the death of God, but God crossed the border, and I think that is what you are talking about. It's cast its shadow.

O'Connor: It's gone underneath and come out in distorted forms.

Question: I would like particularly Miss Porter to comment on religious symbolism in her work—if you think there is any and how you go about it in your work.

Porter: Symbolism happens of its own self and it comes out of something so deep in your own consciousness and your own experience that I don't think that most writers are at all conscious of their use of symbols. I never am until I see them. They come of themselves because they belong to me and have meaning to me, but they come of themselves. I have no way of explaining them but I have a great deal of religious symbolism in my stories because I have a very deep sense of religion and also I have a religious training. And I suppose you don't invent symbolism. You don't say, "I am going to have the flowering Judas tree stand for betrayal," but, of course, it does.

O'Connor: I would second everything Miss Porter says. I really didn't know what a symbol was until I started reading about them. It seemed I was going to have to know about them if I was going to be a respectable literary person. Now I have the notion that a symbol is sort of like the engine in a story and I usually discover as I write something in the story that is taking on more and more meaning so that as I go along, before long, that something is turning or working the story.

Rubin: Do you ever have to try to stop yourselves from thinking about your work in terms of symbols as you are working?

O'Connor: I wouldn't say so.

Porter: No, May I tell this very famous little story about Mary McCarthy and symbols. Well, she was in a college and she had a writers' class and there was a young person who wrote her a story and she said, "You have done a very nice piece of work. You are on the right road, now go on to something else." And the young person said, "But my teacher read this and said, 'Well all right, but now we have to go back and put in the symbols.'"

Rubin: How about you, Mr. Jones?

Jones: Am I a symbol man? Well, I don't think so. The story is the thing after all and I don't see how a writer can think about anything but the story. The story has got to carry him. I think it is bound to occur to you finally that something you have come across—maybe in the middle of coming across it it might occur to you—that this has certain symbolic value and maybe you would to a certain extent elaborate it in terms of this realization, but I don't think it is a plan of any kind where you say I am heading for a symbol and when I get there I am going to do so and so to it. It just comes out of the context. Of course, writing is full of symbols. Nearly everything is a symbol of some kind but some of them expand for you accidentally.

O'Connor: So many students approach a story as if it were a problem in algebra: find X and when they find X they can dismiss the rest of it.

Porter: Well and then another thing, everything can be used as a symbol. Take two of the most innocent and charming sounding, for example, just in western Christianity, let us say the dove and the rose. Well, the dove begins by being a symbol of sensuality, it is the bird of Venus, you know, and then it goes on through the whole range of every kind of thing until it becomes the Holy Ghost. It's the same way with the rose which begins as a female sexual symbol and ends as the rose of fire in Highest Heaven. So you see the symbol would have the meaning of its context. I hope that makes sense.

Question: Is tradition an important part of contemporary Southern writing?

Rubin: What about you, Miss Gordon, do you have a tradition you go back to when you are writing? You told me today that you are writing an historical novel.

Gordon: All novels are historical. I don't think I told you I was writing an historical novel. I said it went back to 1532.

Rubin: Well, that sounds pretty historical.

Gordon: The word has become so debased. I wrote two novels, one in Civil War times and one in pioneer times, but people didn't know how to read them. I wouldn't like to be accused of writing what is known as an historical novel.

Rubin: Well, instead of saying tradition, do you think Southerners do things in certain ways because that is the way they have always been done rather than thinking about it at all, and if so, is this the way you see the Southerner in what you write?

Gordon: Well, I don't see it that way. I sit there or I walk around or I wash dishes until I see these people doing something and hear them and then I record it as best I can.

Rubin: It is very hard to get people to talk in terms of these abstractions because I don't think anyone uses tradition with a capital T. And yet there is a lot of tradition in what they do.

Question: I meant white columns, magnolias, worship of family— tradition in this sense.

Gordon: Well, after the Civil War there was a school of literature foisted on us by Northern publishers. They demanded moonlight and magnolias and a lot of people furnished it to them and that idea stuck in peoples' heads ever since. If a Southerner writes a novel now, whoever is reviewing for the *New York Times* will make a point of saying it isn't moonlight and magnolias. It's all nonsense. We are a conquered nation and abominably treated and we paid the greatest tribute perhaps ever paid by any conquered nation. Our history was miswritten and our children were taught lies and therefore the Northerners could not bear the image of us as we were and therefore the Northern publishers would publish only novels full of white columns and magnolias.

Porter: But this very place right this minute is absolutely filled to the chin with moonlight and magnolias. All you have to do is look outside.

Rubin: I think the position of that particular role of moonlight and magnolias tradition in Southern literature is very true. In the case of someone like George Washington Cable, for example. He tried to write one book without it and it was a flop. Nobody paid any attention to it so he went back and wrote the flowery sort of war romances. This was the only thing he could write. I must say that this ain't so no more, and I think it has been people like Miss Porter who ended all that. Many people read their books for what the books *say,* instead of what the people *thought* they should say. I think that the tremendous importance of Southern literature in our own time represents a breaking away from the stereotype. Writers who have done this, having published their first books in the 20's and 30's, have performed a great service for future generations of Southern writers. Not that that was what you were trying to do at the time, but I think the young ones are going to be eternally grateful for it.

O'Connor: Walker Percy wrote somewhere that his generation of Southerners had no more interest in the Civil War than in the Boer War. I think that is probably quite true.

Rubin: I think there is something to that and yet I heard many an argument in the Army during the last war. You get one or two Southerners in a barracks with a bunch of Northerners and maybe the Southerners were just kidding but let anyone say anything too outrageous and the fight was on.

Jones: That's true. They'll still fight but they don't know what they are talking about. They have no real information and so it is more a matter of just being a personal insult.

Question: Do you think that the South is being exploited now for its immediate fictional gains, let's say commercial gain, etc., is it too popular? Is it too much *Southern* writing?

O'Connor: I don't know any Southern writers who are making a big killing except Faulkner, you know. We are all just limping along.

Rubin: I think when you have a group of very fine writers who approach a group of people and subjects in a certain way it is then easier to imitate that than to do something on your own. And therefore a lot of second rate writers will come along and imitate it, and I know I see the publisher announcement sheets every fall. On one page of almost all announcement sheets from every publishing house there is announced a new Southern writer and most of them are never announced more than once. But I do feel very definitely there is a great deal of writing about the South, because these people here have shown how it can be done, and therefore someone is not going to do something on his or her own when this is the best lead to follow.

Question: I would like to know if your writing is strictly for a Southern reading audience or if you have in mind any reading audience.

O'Connor: The *London Times Literary Supplement* had an issue on Southern writing once and they said that Southerners only wrote books, they didn't read them.

Porter: Well, that's just the opposite from the old South because they only read them, they never wrote them. At least before The War Between the States writing was not really a gentleman's occupation except as privately. He wrote letters, memoirs, and maybe essays. But they all had libraries and collections of books.

Rubin: The South has long had the reputation for being the worst market for books in the U.S., per capita, among the publishers. I think any Southern writer who wrote primarily for Southerners would have to write a syndicated column for a newspaper or he would starve to death. I don't really think that these people think in terms of who is going to read what they are going to write, unless I am mistaken.

Jones: I was just going to say that I don't know who I write for but it seems to me that I have a person or two who is my audience rather than any group. But I think about one person and perhaps the standards that I absorbed from that person tends to be my audience rather than any group. I hope that a group will buy a book but I don't think I direct a book at any large group of people.

Rubin: John Bishop wrote that he wrote his books to be read by Edmund Wilson and Allen Tate.

Gordon: But you see he never wrote but one novel. Well, I know I have one reader, a Frenchman. He is the only person I know of who understands my work and I think that is why I think about him but I don't think I would under other circumstances. He knows a great deal about techniques of fiction and, perhaps this is a little off the subject, but people very much dislike any revolution in technique. If an author uses a technique that has never been used before, everybody will dislike it. And there is no record of any literary critic ever recognizing an innovation in technique. It has never happened. It is always recognized by another artist. So I have gotten to the point that I write for the person who will know what I am doing.

Question: Mr. Jones, you mentioned this afternoon that Southern writers have a stronger than usual sense of guilt and natural depravity. If this is so, what means of redemption do you see as possible?

Jones: You asked me a very complex question. I don't know whether I can answer the whole thing or not. You said that Southern writers have a sense of natural depravity. Do I think they do? Well, I do have the feeling that if it is not still, it certainly was the case with the first important Southern writers in that there was very little question about the sense of man's guilt. There was a consciousness of that and a perfect willingness to accept it and I think that is very notable in all the best Southern writers of the last generation. I don't know why that should particularly be the case with Southern writers except partly because, as I said, of Southern Fundamentalism which has kept that fact before them. And perhaps the Civil War had something to do with it. Not that I feel that the Southerners felt guilty about the Civil War but perhaps even though we felt we were right before the war, nevertheless we were defeated and didn't achieve all we thought we could even though we thought we were right and something must be wrong. I am sure there would be a great many other reasons that someone else could elaborate on. Man is of a less than perfect nature.

Porter: I am sure that we are all naturally depraved but we are all naturally redeemable, too. The idea, Calvin really put it into action, that God somehow rewarded spiritual virtue with material things, which is to say that if you were living right God would reward you with health and money, a good reputation, or the goods of this world is to me an appalling doctrine. I happen to have a faith that says the opposite, you see, that goods of this world have nothing to do with your spiritual good and your standing with God and I think that this attitude of the South, when you say they felt that if they had been right God would not have permitted them to lose that war is dreadful, you know. I think it is a terrible fallacy and a terrible mistaken way to feel because some very good people have had the worst times in this world and have lost all their wars, don't you know, have lost everything altogether. Defeat in this world is no disgrace and that is what they cannot understand. If you really fought well and fought for the right thing.

Rubin: That is a very good point. You know, I think it is about time we finished. I would like to question you a bit on that Calvin business if it weren't. I think we had better say one thing. We have been talking about a number of characteristics and we say, now *this* is Southern, and *this* Southern, and then somebody comes along and says, well don't you think that New England writers, or Western writers, have a notion about the natural depravity of man? Is this something that was invented in the South? I think the answer would be is that there are a number of qualities that people assign to Southern writing and say, "This is true of Southern writing." It isn't the uniqueness of the qualities, but I would say the combination of a certain number of qualities at one time, which has made this achievement possible and I think that whatever the achievement is, it has been a considerable thing; and I, myself, am not particularly pessimistic about it continuing, what with the people seated at the table with me tonight. We have hashed over the problems of writers and writing in the South for about an hour now and tried to answer some questions, and I think we'll quit. I would like to say on behalf of the panel what a wonderful time we have had and how grateful we are to Wesleyan College and to everybody for coming.

1. "Holiday," read by Miss Porter on the preceding evening, appears in the December, 1960 issue of *The Atlantic*.

2. Miss O'Connor's talk was entitled "Some Thoughts on the Grotesque in Southern Fiction."

1960

Katherine Anne Porter

Dulce et Decorum Est

Review of *None Shall Look Back* by Caroline Gordon

Fontaine Allard, tobacco planter, slave holder full of cares and responsibilities, an old man walking in a part of his Kentucky woods, "had a strange feeling, as if a voice said to him, 'these are your father's and your fathers' before him' . . . he had actually for a moment been overcome by his attachment for that earth, those trees." This is in the beginning of "None Shall Look Back." Toward the end, his son Ned returns from the lost war, a skeleton, a dying man. "The land's still there, I reckon," he says, and goes back to it, hoping to live, but certain at least that he shall die there, where he belongs, unchanged in his belief in the way of life he had fought for.

His brother Jim, unfit for war, had stayed at home and profited by the changing times, taking advantage of his chances with the rising merchants and industrialists. Alienated, hostile, secretly hoping that Ned may die, he watches him go, a breathing reproach, supported by two women of his family. Miss Gordon makes it quite clear, in this short bitter scene, that Jim is the truly defeated man, the lost soul who thinks nothing is worth fighting for, who sets himself to survive and profit meanly by whatever occasion offers him.

This form of opportunism is sometimes at present called "interpreting history correctly"—that is, having the foresight to get on the bandwagon and make the most of the parade. With such shabbiness Miss Gordon has nothing to do. Her story is a legend in praise of heroes, of those who fought well and lost their battle, and their lives. It seems fresh and timely at this moment when we have before our eyes the spectacle of a death-dedicated people holding out in a struggle against overwhelming odds. Of all human impulses, that of heroism changes least in its character and shape, from one epoch to another. He is forever the same, then and forever unanswerable, the man who throws his life away as if he hated living, in defense of the one thing, whatever it may be, that he cares to live for. Causes change perpetually, die, go out of fashion, are superseded according to shifting political schemes, economics, religions, but the men ready to die for them are reborn again and again, always the same men.

Miss Gordon's heart is fixed on the memory of those men who died in a single, superbly fought lost cause, in nothing diminished for being lost, and this devotion has focused her feelings and imagination to a point of fire. She states clearly in every line of her story her mystical faith that what a man lives by, he must if the time comes, die for; to live beyond or to acknowledge defeat is to die twice, and shamefully. The motive of this faith is the pride of Lucifer, and Miss Gordon makes no pretense, either for herself or for her characters, to the maudlin virtue of humility in questions of principle.

All seeing as an ancient chronicler, she has created a panorama of a society engaged in battle for its life. The author moves about, a disembodied spectator timing her presence expertly, over her familiar territory, Kentucky, Georgia, Tennessee, Mississippi. Time, 1860 to 1864, dates which are, after 1776, the most portentous in the history of this country. Having chosen to observe from all points of view, rather than to stand on a knoll above the battle and watch a set procession of events through a field glass, she makes her scenes move rapidly from Federal lines to Confederate, from hospitals to prisons, to the plantations; the effect could easily have become diffuse without firm handling, and the central inalterable sympathies of the chronicler herself. She might have done the neat conventional thing, and told her story through the adventures of her unlucky young pair of lovers, Lucy Churchill and her cousin, Rives Allard. But they take their proper places in the midst of a tragedy of which their own tragedy is only a part. I know of nothing more humanly touching and immediate than the story of the brief, broken marriage of Rives and Lucy; but the book is not theirs, nor was it meant to be. Rives goes to die as a scout for Nathan Bedford Forrest, that unaccountable genius of war, who remained a mystery and a figure of legend even to his own soldiers, those who knew him best. There is no accounting for Forrest and Miss Gordon does not attempt the impossible. He remains what he was, a hero and a genius.

The Allard family is a center, or rather, a point of departure and return: in the beginning they are clearly seen, alive, each one a human being with his individual destiny, which gradually is merged with the destiny of his time and place. Their ends are symbolically exact: the old man lapses into the escape of imbecility, the old mother into perpetual blind grief, Rives into death in battle, Jim into moral dry rot, Lucy into numbness. In the meantime, we have seen them as they were born to be, busy with the full rich occupations of family life, the work of the plantation, the unpretentious gayety. Life for the Kentucky planters was never so grand as it was in Virginia and Louisiana, or even in Mississippi, with its slightly parvenu manners, if one takes Mr. Stark Young's account at face value. The Kentucky planters were down-to-earth men, and the most tenderly bred women were not above taking a hand in the cookery. They much more resembled Madame Washington than they did Mr. Young's jewelry-conscious belles. This tone is here, properly; it pervades the book like a fresh aroma of green woods and plowed fields.

This seems to me in a great many ways a better book than "Penhally" or "Aleck Maury, Sportsman," Miss Gordon's other two novels. The good firm style, at once homely, rhythmical and distinguished, is in all three of them, but at its best, so far, in "None Shall Look Back." It is true I know her story by heart, but I have never heard it told better. The effect is of brilliant, instant life; there is a clear daylight over a landscape I need not close my eyes to see, peopled with figures I know well. I have always known the end, as I know the end of so many tales of love, and heroism, and death. In this retelling, it all happened only yesterday. Those men on the field are not buried yet, those women have just put on their mourning.

1937

Caroline Gordon

With a Glitter of Evil

Review of *A Good Man Is Hard to Find*

by Flannery O'Connor

This first collection of short stories by Flannery O'Connor exhibits what Henry James, in "a partial portrait" of Guy de Maupassant, called "the artful brevity of a master." James added that Maupassant was "a 'case,' an embarrassment, a lion in the path." The contemporary reviewer, called upon to evaluate the achievement of the young American writer, may well feel that a lioness has strayed across *his* path. Miss O'Connor's works, like Maupassant's, are characterized by precision, density and an almost alarming circumscription. There are few landscapes in her stories. Her characters seem to move in the hard, white glare of a searchlight—or perhaps it is more as if the author viewed her subjects through the knothole in a fence or wall.

James complained that Maupassant's work lacked a dimension, because he "took no account of the moral nature of man. . . . The very compact mansion in which he dwells presents on that side a perfectly dead wall." This charge cannot be laid at Miss O'Connor's door. The difference lies in the eye that is applied to the crack in the wall of her "very compact mansion." Miss O'Connor, for all her apparent preoccupation with the visible scene, is also fiercely concerned with moral, even theological, problems. In these stories the rural South is, for the first time, viewed by a writer whose orthodoxy matches her talent. The results are revolutionary.

Miss O'Connor has an unerring eye in the selection of detail and the most exquisite ear I know of for the cadences of everyday speech. The longer, statelier sentence which has come down to us from the great masters of English prose and which, in the hands of a writer like Joyce, throws into such dramatic relief his mastery of the vernacular, is not as yet in her repertory. She is, like Maupassant, very much of her time; and her stories, like his, have a certain glitter, as it were, of evil, which pervades them and astonishingly contributes to their lifelikeness.

In "A Good Man Is Hard to Find" an American family, father, mother, three children and grandmother, set off on a vacation motor trip, their aim being to cover as much ground as possible in the time allotted for the vacation. "Let's go through Georgia fast, so we won't have to look at it much" is the way 8-year-old John Wesley puts it. Before they are through they have all six confronted eternity—through the agency of a gunman escaped from a penitentiary who employs the interval, during which his two henchmen are off in the wood murdering the father and mother and three children, in discussing the problem of death and resurrection with the grandmother.

In "The Displaced Person" Mrs. Shortley, the wife of a dairyman, reads the Apocalypse and communes with her soul so long and earnestly that she has visions. Mrs. McIntyre, the owner of the dairy farm, being more sophisticated than Mrs. Shortley, does not have as easy access to spiritual comforts and, when hard pressed, turns to the memory of her late husband, "the Judge." She sometimes sits and meditates in his study, which she has kept unchanged since his death as a sort of memorial to him.

Mrs. McIntyre married the Judge because she thought he was rich—and wise. His estate proved to consist of "fifty acres and the house." His wisdom is still embodied in pithy vulgarization of proverbs: "One fellow's misery is the other fellow's gain." "The devil you know is better than the devil you don't."

Miss O'Connor is as realistic and down to earth a writer as one can find. Yet many people profess to find her work hard to understand. This may be because she uses symbolism in a way in which it has not been used by any of her young contemporaries. Mrs. Hopewell in "Good Country People" is thrifty, kind-hearted and optimistic, abounding in aphorisms such as "A smile never hurt anyone," "It takes all kinds to make a world." She cannot understand why her daughter Joy is not happy. Joy, who had her leg blown off when she

conversion is elaborately prepared for and underwritten by the force of Jungian psychology will be overlooked by those who are not willing to accept the reality of supernatural grace. Making grace believable to the contemporary reader is the almost insurmountable problem of the novelist who writes from the standpoint of Christian orthodoxy. *The Malefactors* is undoubtedly the most serious and successful fictional treatment of a conversion by an American writer to date.

1956

Flannery O'Connor

Review of *How to Read a Novel*
by Caroline Gordon

By now all are familiar with the famous ad found in a diocesan paper: "Let a Catholic do your termite work." In connection with literature, which is almost as dangerous as termites, this fraternal attitude abounds. Miss Gordon's book can therefore be recommended on the grounds that it is a Catholic who is writing. It would be painful to leave it at this.

As Miss Gordon points out, it requires a certain humility to read a novel; and perhaps also it requires a certain humility to read a book called *How to Read a Novel,* for everyone thinks novel-reading well within his competence. This book should satisfy any reader that it is not; and it can be particularly recommended for Catholics because Catholic groups are often vocal on the subject of "bad" literature, without knowing "good" literature when they see it. To pronounce judgment on a novel, one must first be able to read it. The suspicion with which the average Catholic approaches this particular art form is lessened only if the label Catholic can be applied to it in some way. Those moral principles which save us from counting ourselves among the admirers of such works as *Peyton Place* seldom operate in more subtle cases of corruption. We are liable to praise prose as poor, structure as weak, and psychology as dishonest if only the characters involved live, or at least die, according to the precepts of the Church. This is a cultural deficiency but it implies and it fosters a lack of moral insight.

No one will go through Miss Gordon's book and begin forthwith to read adequately, but he will begin to read more slowly and some of the fiction which satisfied him before will no longer do so. This book, along with Maritain's *Art and Scholasticism,* should be studied by any Catholic group making public pronouncements about literature.

1957

Caroline Gordon

Flannery O'Connor's *Wise Blood*

The talent of Flannery O'Connor, one of the most original among younger American writers, was recognized soon after the publication of her first short stories. Her originality has been to some extent obscured by the resemblance of her work to the work of other American writers who belong, roughly, to the same literary generation.

This resemblance has been noted so often and so widely that it has come to be taken for granted; a critic recently asserted that if the name of the author were deleted it would be hard to tell a story by Miss O'Connor from a story by Truman Capote, Carson McCullers or Tennessee Williams.

Miss O'Connor's work does, indeed, resemble the work of some of her gifted contemporaries and the resemblance is not superficial. Their characters have what we might almost call a "family likeness." They often behave in the same way, talk the same way. (One may observe in passing that these writers are gifted with an exquisite ear for the common speech.)

Miss O'Connor's work, however, has a characteristic which does not occur in the work of any of her contemporaries. Its presence in everything she writes, coupled with her extraordinary talent, makes her, I suspect, one of the most important writers of our age.

We may be in a better position to define the nature of this characteristic if we first consider the resemblances between Miss O'Connor's work and the works to which it is most frequently compared. What, for instance, do *Wise Blood* and Truman Capote's *Other Voices, Other Rooms* have in common?

Marguerite Young says of Truman Capote: "His chief preoccupation is the everyday monstrous—modern Gothic; people who haunt or are haunted." Mr. Capote's hero, Joel Knox, an adolescent boy, sets out in search of his father and ends trapped in the same half-world in which his father lies paralyzed and all but mindless. Mr. Capote's world is one of horror but it has its strange beauty: miasmic swamps where tiger lilies "the size of a man's head" glow above luminous sunken logs, a ruined hotel whose "swan stairs soft with mildewed carpet curve upward from the hotel's [long-deserted] lobby," a parlor with gold-colored curtains, tied with satin tassels, a love seat of lilac velvet, a cabinet gleaming with ivory figurines. And Joel himself is an attractive boy with large brown eyes and gold-brown hair.

Haze Motes, the Tennessee hill-billy who is the hero of *Wise Blood*, has eyes "the color of pecan shells," wears a suit of "glass blue" and moves always in the harsh light of every day. But he, like Joel, bears one of the marks of a hero; he has set forth alone on a quest that may cost him his life. We see him first in a train, sitting "at a forward angle on the green plush seat, looking one minute at the window as if he might want to jump out of it." Haze was brought up strictly in the Tennessee hills by a mother who, whenever she punished him, which was often, did not fail to remind him that "Jesus died to redeem you." "I never ast him," Haze invariably mutters. While serving in World War Two he has lost whatever religious faith has survived his mother's whippings and is on his way to the town of Taulkinham on what he considers his life mission: the spreading of the gospel of "the Church of Christ Without Christ."

Like most fanatics, he eschews the pleasures of the senses, but he feels impelled to do anything which his "jesus" would disapprove of and, on the train, he copies down from the wall of a toilet the address of a prostitute:

> Mrs. Leora Watts!
> 60 Buckley Road
> The Friendliest Bed in Town!
> Brother.

He lives with Mrs. Watts until he meets another woman who poses as a child and is the daughter of a supposedly blind itinerant street preacher.

Joel Knox has a girl friend, Idabel Tompkins, "[a] skinny girl with fiery, chopped-off red hair," who, when she is not swaggering about, accompanied by a flea-bitten hound, Henry, stands "dead still, her hands cocked on her hips." "Her face was flat, and rather impertinent; a network of big ugly freckles spanned her nose. Her eyes, squinty and bright green, moved swiftly from face to face, but showed none a sign of recognition; they paused a cool instant on Joel, then traveled elsewhere."

Haze's girl, Sabbath Lily Hawks, wears "a black knitted cap, pulled down low on her forehead," with "a fringe of brown hair sticking out." She has "a long face and a short sharp nose" and her eyes, too, are remarkable, glittering like "two chips of green bottle glass."

On the surface the two young women much resemble each other. One is tempted to call them both freaks. And indeed, a good many critics have asserted that the worlds of both these writers are peopled almost exclusively by freaks. Joel Knox's cousin, Randolph, his cousin, Amy, the Negro woman, Missouri, her grandfather, Jesus Fever, are all twisted by life into shapes which show themselves as monstrous through the veilings of Mr. Capote's lush prose. Miss O'Connor writes lean, stripped, at times almost too flat-footed a prose, and her characters, as I have said, move always in the harsh glare of every day. But they, too, are warped and misshapen by life—in short, freaks. The difference between her work and that of her gifted contemporaries lies in the nature and the causes of their freakishness.

Idabel Tompkins is an appealing figure, in spite of her appearance and swaggering ways. Joel feels her attraction and tries to make love to her but the affair comes to nothing—she repulses him and in so doing gives him the final push towards the twilit world in which he will eventually take refuge.

The affair between Haze Motes and Sabbath Lily Hawks proceeds to a logical and more terrifying conclusion. Sabbath Lily is actually less prepossessing than Idabel. She differs from her in being fiercely womanly. She will go to almost any lengths to get her man and to even greater length to fulfil another womanly function, maternity. Haze yields to her blandishments partly as a way of proving his faith in the

Church of Christ Without Christ. They set up housekeeping in a rented room. Haze's friend—or enemy—Enoch Emery, obeying a compulsive impulse, or, as he would put it, his "wise blood," steals a mummy from a city museum. He hears Haze preaching his gospel: "The Church Without Christ don't have a Jesus but it needs one! It needs a new jesus"—and he rushes home, wraps the mummy up and deposits it at Haze's door. Haze is lying on the bed, a bandage over his eyes. Sabbath receives the bundle, unwraps it and after a few moments, during which her face has "an empty look, as if she didn't know what she thought about him or didn't think anything," cradles him in her arms and begins to croon to him. The unholy family is now complete.

Miss O'Connor does not stop there but piles horror on horror. The idea of "a new jesus" catches on. A consumptive named Solace Layfield impersonates Haze, wearing the same white hat and "glare-blue suit. Haze is struck by the resemblance to himself and stops his preaching long enough to listen to the new "prophet." He comes to the conclusion that Layfield actually believes in Jesus and is so enraged by what seems to him heresy that he runs the automobile which is his own pulpit over the prophet. The prophet forces Haze to listen to his dying confession. From that time forward Haze subjects his body to fierce mortifications, wears barbed wire twisted about his waist and fills his shoes with gravel and bits of broken glass. He finally loses his "pulpit." Two patrolmen decide that his rattle-trap old car is a menace to public safety and push it off the highway and down an embankment. In despair and, like Oedipus, unable to look at what is before his eyes, Haze blinds himself.

In comparison with *Wise Blood, Other Voices, Other Rooms* reads like a case history. The reader may feel distress when Joel Knox, abandoned by the maternal, middle-aged woman who is his only remaining link with reality, descends into the twilit world of Scully's Landing, but Mr. Capote merely tells us what happened. No moral judgment is implied and there is throughout the action of the story no frame of reference such as one finds in Hawthorne or Balzac, for instance.

This lack of a frame of reference larger than that of the individual action is characteristic of most contemporary fiction. Nowadays a story by any fiction writer who came on the scene later than, say, Scott

Fitzgerald is likely to read like a case history. Moll Flanders used occasionally to refer—if hypocritically—to the life she ought to have led. Such reflections rarely occur to the characters in modern fiction. "This," they seem to be saying breathlessly, "is the way it was or is with me." Never the way it should have been or might be.

Miss O'Connor's talent, occurring in such a milieu, is as startling, as disconcerting as a blast from a furnace which one had thought stone-cold but which is still red-hot.

Haze Motes, Miss O'Connor's hero, is illiterate and of lowly origins, but he is spiritually kin to more highly placed Americans. His whole life is given over to a speculation on the nature of Christ, the union of the divine with the human which theologians term "the hypostatic union." The philosopher and amateur theologian, Henry James the elder, whom the critic, Austin Warren, numbers among his "New England saints," spent his life in a similar preoccupation. Haze, being illiterate, states his disbelief in words of one syllable: "My Church is the Church Without Christ." The elder James, better educated, speaks of "the venomous tradition of a disproportion between Man and his Maker." Haze has a broken-down flivver as his pulpit. The elder Henry James also had a high regard for locomotion as a means of arriving at the truth. "The horse car," he once remarked, "is the true Shechinah of our day." Like Haze, he was bent on founding a church, his "New Church," of which, as somebody wittily remarked, he was the only member. But he was a philosopher rather than a man of action and spent the greater part of his life at his desk, writing the same book over and over, as his son, William James, observed in the preface he wrote for his father's works. Haze, a man of action and, it seems to me, a tragic hero, dies in a ditch, self-blinded as the penalty of his disbelief.

Malcolm Cowley and other critics have remarked the prevalence of the Christ figure in contemporary fiction and in the fiction of the past twenty years. Faulkner's corporal in *A Fable,* Robert Jordan in *For Whom the Bell Tolls,* Dick Diver in *Tender Is the Night,* Gatsby—all seem bent on laying down their lives in the hope of finding a fuller life. Even Thomas Wolfe's hero in *You Can't Go Home Again* hopes to "leave this world for fuller living."

But the works of all these writers, with the exception of Fitzgerald,

whose Catholic bias and apprehension of theological truths was perhaps deeper than he himself realized, reveal a lack of acquaintance
with fundamental Christian doctrine. Ours is the first age in which a
man could call himself educated and know no theology. This indif-
ference to and ignorance of the "Science of Sciences" is by no means
confined to American writers. Albert Camus' brilliant, uneven novel,
The Fall, is a case in point. The subject matter of the novel is the
depravity, which, according to Christian doctrine, is inherent in all of
us since the Fall of Man, and the action is an exercise in theological
dialectic on the part of the hero and the partner he has chosen for this
exercise. But the author's lack of acquaintance with his subject matter
renders his technique infirm. At the moment when the reader should
be intent on the *dénouement*—on *what is happening*—his attention is
likely to stray. He may even find himself indulging in speculation, his
credulity perhaps over-taxed by the hero's modernistic and highly
individual interpretation of the Crucifixion. M. Camus' hero holds
that Christ forced the Jews and Romans to crucify him in order to rid
himself of the "guilt complex" he had incurred as the result of Herod's
Slaughter of the Innocents.

The fiction writer, as Chekhov once pointed out to an over-sensitive
lady reader, has the right, indeed the duty, to deal with any manifestations of human life which come within the province of his art. He has
another responsibility fully as grave. No matter what kind of people
he portrays, no matter what they are doing, he must make his portrayal so life-like that (while we are reading his book) we must be
convinced that this is what really happened. A novelist who has a
plumber, or a pimp, or a nuclear physicist, say, for his hero would
presumably go to some pains to acquaint himself with the kinds of
lives led by the majority of plumbers or pimps or nuclear physicists.
But M. Camus seems curiously ignorant of the "vital statistics" of the
times of which he is writing. Ancient hagiographers put the number of
"Holy Innocents" slain at 144,000 as an "accommodation" to a passage in the Apocalypse. The Syrian menologies estimated it at 64,000,
but modern hagiographers, from Alban Butler down, point out that a
town the size of Bethlehem could not have produced more than twenty-five boy babies eligible for Herod's slaughter. The guilt complex
which M. Camus ascribes to the Savior of the World is so dispropor-

tionate to its cause that the structure of the novel is disjointed. The action does not resolve itself satisfactorily. As a result, the edifice which the author has been at such pains to erect, is flawed at its base, and totters.

But Miss O'Connor is, after all, an American. It is perhaps more profitable to compare her work with that of another distinguished American writer who is, like her, a Southerner.

The corporal in William Faulkner's *A Fable* has twelve disciples who inevitably remind the reader of the Twelve Disciples and he lays down his life for others, but the analogy to the Christ figure stops there. The reader who has come to expect from this author a higher degree of verisimilitude than most fiction writers achieve is considerably taken aback when a Roman Catholic priest begins voicing beliefs which his training and his profession would seem to preclude his uttering, in short, begins talking like a Haze Motes:

> "It wasn't He with his humility and pity and sacrifice that converted the world; it was pagan and bloody Rome which did it with His martyrdom; furious and intractable dreamers had been bringing that same dream out of Asia Minor for three hundred years until at last one found a caesar foolish enough to crucify Him. . . . Because only Rome could have done it, accomplished it, and even He knew . . . knew it, felt and sensed this, furious and intractable dreamer though He was. Because He even said it Himself: *On this rock I found My church,* even while He didn't—and never would—realise the true significance of what He was saying. . . ."

Mr. Faulkner's theology—what there is of it—would appear to have come down to him from his grandfather's time, derived, perhaps, from a reading of Renan. His priest's statement, slightly clouded by rhetoric, is the kind of heresy to which Renan subscribed. Miss O'Connor's "prophet" is fully as heretical but his logical processes are more exact. And he speaks—terrifyingly—for our own time. Is that because he is, in his way, an Existentialist?

> I preach there are all kinds of truth, your truth and somebody else's, but behind all of them, there's only one truth and that is that there's no truth. . . . No truth behind all truths is what I and this church preach! Where you come from is gone, where you thought you were going to never was there, and where you are is no good unless you can get away from it. Where is there a place for you to be? No place.

In Miss O'Connor's vision of modern man—a vision not limited to Southern rural humanity—all her characters are "displaced persons," not merely the people in the story of that name. They are "off center," out of place, because they are victims of a rejection of the Scheme of Redemption. They are lost in that abyss which opens for man when he sets up as God. This theological framework is never explicit in Miss O'Connor's fiction. It is so much a part of her direct gaze at human conduct that she seems herself to be scarcely aware of it. I believe that this accounts to a great extent for her power. It is a Blakean vision, not through symbol as such but through the actuality of human behavior; and it has Blake's explosive honesty, such as we find in

> But most thro' midnight streets I hear
> How the youthful harlot's curse
> Blasts the new-born infant's tear
> And blights with plagues the marriage hearse.

1958

Katherine Anne Porter

Gracious Greatness

I saw our lovely and gifted Flannery O'Connor only three times over a period, I think, of three years or more, but each meeting was spontaneously an occasion and I want to write about her just as she impressed me.

I want to tell what she looked like and how she carried herself and how she sounded standing balanced lightly on her aluminum crutches, whistling to her peacocks who came floating and rustling to her, calling in their rusty voices.

I do not want to speak of her work because we all know what it was and we don't need to say what we think about it but to read and understand what she was trying to tell us.

Now and again there hovers on the margin of the future a presence that one feels as imminent—if I may use stylish vocabulary. She came up among us like a presence, a carrier of a gift not to be disputed but welcomed. She lived among us like a presence and went away early, leaving her harvest perhaps not yet all together gathered, though, like so many geniuses who have small time in this world, I think she had her warning and accepted it and did her work even if we all would like to have had her stay on forever and do more.

It is all very well for those who are left to console themselves. She said what she had to say. I'm pretty certain that her work was finished. We shouldn't mourn for her but for ourselves and our loves.

After all, I saw her just twice—memory has counted it three—for

78

the second time was a day-long affair at a Conference and a party given by Flannery's mother in the evening. And I want to tell you something I think is amusing because Flannery lived in such an old-fashioned southern village very celebrated in southern history on account of what took place during the War. But in the lovely, old, aerie, tall country house and the life of a young girl living with her mother in a country town so that there was almost no way for her knowing the difficulties of human beings and her general knowledge of this was really very impressive because she was so very young and you wondered where—how—she had learned all that. But this is a question that everybody always asks himself about genius. I want to just tell something to illustrate the southern custom.

Ladies in Society there—in that particular society, I mean—were nearly always known, no matter if they were married once or twice, they were known to their dying day by their maiden names. They were called "Miss Mary" or whoever it was. And so, Flannery's mother, too; her maiden name was Regina Cline and so she was still known as "Miss Regina Cline" and one evening at a party when I was there after the Conference, someone mentioned Flannery's name and another—a neighbor, mind you, who had probably been around there all her life—said, "Who is Flannery O'Connor? I keep hearing about her." the other one said, "Oh, you know! Why, that's Regina Cline's daughter: that little girl who writes." And that was the atmosphere in which her genius developed and her life was lived and her work was done. I myself think it was a very healthy, good atmosphere because nobody got in her way, nobody tried to interfere with her or direct her and she lived easily and simply and in her own atmosphere and her own way of thinking. I believe this is the best possible way for a genius to live. I think that they're too often tortured by this world and when people discover that someone has a gift, they all come with their claws out, trying to snatch something of it, trying to share some thing they have no right even to touch. And she was safe from that: she had a mother who really took care of her. And I just think that's something we ought to mention, ought to speak of.

She managed to mix, somehow, two very different kinds of chickens and produced a bird hitherto unseen in this world. I asked her if she were going to send it to the County Fair. "I might, but first I must find

a name for it. You name it!" she said. I thought of it many times but
no fitting name for that creature ever occurred to me. And no fitting
word now occurs to me to describe her stories, her particular style, her
view of life, but I know its greatness and I see it—and see that it was
one of the great gifts of our times.

I want to speak a little of her religious life though it was very sacred
and quiet. She was as reserved about it as any saint. When I first met
her, she and her mother were about to go for a seventeen day trip to
Lourdes. I said, "Oh, I wish I could go with you!" She said, "I wish
you could. But I'll write you a letter." She never wrote that letter. She
just sent a post card and she wrote: "The sight of Faith and affliction
joined in prayer—very impressive." That was all.

In some newspaper notice of her death mention of her self-portrait
with her favorite peacock was made. It spoke of her plain features. She
had unusual features but they were anything but plain. I saw that
portrait in her home and she had not flattered herself. The portrait
does have her features, in a way, but here's something else. She had a
young softness and gentleness of face and expression. The look—
something in the depth of the eyes and the fixed mouth; the whole
pose fiercely intent gives an uncompromising glimpse of her character.
Something you might not see on first or even second glance in that
tenderly fresh-colored, young, smiling face; something she saw in
herself, knew about herself, that she was trying to tell us in a way less
personal, yet more vivid than words.

That portrait, I'm trying to say, looked like the girl who wrote those
blood-curdling stories about human evil—NOT the living Flannery,
whistling to her peacocks, showing off her delightfully freakish breed
of chickens.

I want to thank you for giving me the opportunity to tell you about
the Flannery O'Connor I know. I loved and valued her dearly, her
work and her strange unworldly radiance of spirit in a human being
so intelligent and so undeceived by the appearance of things. I would
feel too badly if I did not honor myself by saying a word in her honor:
it is a great loss.

1964

Caroline Gordon

An American Girl

Some years ago Witter Bynner sent Henry James a copy of one of Willa Cather's novels. James thanked him for the gift and deplored his inability to read "promiscuous novels"—"particularly when written by young ladies." I think we may assume that when James used the adjective "promiscuous" in his letter to the poet-editor that he was using it in a technical sense. In other words, that it is charged with meaning in the way so many words in his notebooks are charged with meaning. James was certainly what Percy Lubbock dubbed him: "the scholar of the novel." But the novelist has little or no technical vocabulary at his command. James so felt the need of one that he invented his own terminology and used it boldly both in his self-communings in his notebooks and in his public discussions of the mysteries of his art. He has told us that a novel "should consist of 'a single impression.'" I take it that when he refers to a "promiscuous novel" that he means a novel which may be original and highly readable but which is, nevertheless, not constructed so that every incident in it contributes to this "single impression." Confronted with such a novel, James is likely to react the way a veteran architect might react at the sight of a building erected on shifting sands and already exhibiting—to his practiced eye, at least—a slight list. One can almost hear him suavely declining the invitation: "No, thank you, I never enter buildings designed by young ladies!"

The student of James's novels, his criticism and his notebooks, expe-

81

riences a recurring pleasure in observing the analogies between his life and his work. Everything which he, himself, wrote, it seems to me, if viewed in large enough perspective, contributes toward that "single impression" which he found the chief requisite for the novel. I believe, indeed, that statements which, on the surface, appear contradictory, will reconcile themselves if contemplated long enough. For instance, his refusal to read "promiscuous novels by young ladies" may, at first glance, appear to negate what he has to say about the American girl in *The American Scene,* the book he wrote as the result of a visit to his native land after many years' absence. James was impressed by the social dominance of women both in Washington and other cities. He came to the conclusion that largely as the result of this dominance, the cultural future of this country was in the hands of the American girl, American men being too busy trying to make money to concern themselves with culture.

He expresses his fear that the American girl will not be equal to the task and even dramatizes her own fear that she will not be able to live up to her awesome responsibilities in a fictional apostrophe which is half baby talk and half the gibberish of a mind on the verge of dissolution.

I gather that James never read any of Miss Cather's novels and so never discovered that although she was still then a comparatively young lady, she was, nevertheless, a master of the architectonics of illusion. It is a matter of regret for Miss Cather's many admirers that he never knew her work. I find myself regretting, too, that he never had an opportunity to read Flannery O'Connor's short stories and novels. I think that he would have felt a kinship with her that might have transcended his innate conviction that the writing of novels—a difficult and dangerous task, to begin with—is a task for which men are by nature better fitted than women.

If he had lived to read Miss O'Connor's stories, I suspect that he would also have derived from them the pleasure which any of us feels when he finds his own words coming true. For this young woman, who died recently at the age of thirty-nine, comes nearer than anyone I can think of to enacting the role of "the American girl" whom James foresaw as charged with such great responsibilities.

If Miss O'Connor was James's "American girl" she wasted little time in baby talk or in bewailing her fate! She seems to have early envisioned the task that lay before her and during her short life all her energies were concentrated on its performance.

Her task, I think, resembled James's own task in many particulars. I believe, however, that the chief resemblance between the two writers consists in the fact that each was faced with an obstacle which, for a fiction writer, is almost always insuperable in his own lifetime. In order to create the world of illusion—which for him embodied fictional truth—both writers had to use a technique which was revolutionary.

The world contrived by the novelist or short story writer is, of course, an illusory world. Nevertheless, the analogy between fiction and real life holds—and must of necessity hold—if the novelist is to attain the verisimilitude which is his goal. The analogy holds, chiefly, I believe, because of the attitude which the reader shares with the natural man. The readers of novels are as firmly opposed to the use of any revolutionary technique in any novel as any one of us is naturally opposed to any invention which may change our way of life. We accept the inventions in the end, usually, but, as a rule, a great deal of energy has to be expended by somebody or many somebodies before we do accept it. The descendants of these people who used to shout "get a horse!" when the first automobile rolled past are doubtless crying out as shrilly as their grandfathers did at this moment, and in the same spirit. It is only the words of the slogan that have changed.

The history of literature provides a succession of examples of the reader's natural antipathy to revolutionary techniques; the reading public is consistent in its abhorrence of any innovation which enables a fiction writer to attain artistic effects which have not been attained before. Many a young novelist, however, has been astonished, dismayed, and profoundly depressed when he found that this attitude has been shared by the literary critics. As far as I can gather, there is no instance of a revolutionary talent—or technique—being recognized by any literary critic, who was not himself an artist. The first instance that comes to mind is Baudelaire's review of *Madame Bovary,* which, according to Flaubert, was the only review of the book which made sense to him. It was written by a fellow artist who happened to have a fine critical intelligence. James, himself, acknowledged the existence of this particular form of incomprehension in a review he wrote of one of Emil Faguet's books on Flaubert. He recognized M. Faguet's biography as definitive but he pointed out that the scholar's grasp is too "lax" to apprehend certain fictional effects.

Most literary critics, however, do not err through a kind of laxity of grasp but through misplaced belligerence. Ordinarily, the literary critic, when confronted with a revolutionary technique, not only refuses to accept it but hastens to fill the void of his incomprehension with brickbats, as it were. Witness the criticism which the contemporary literary critics accorded the early works of T. S. Eliot and James Joyce. Henry James, himself, contended with this lack of comprehension for a great part—the most important part—of his working life. So much so that he once wrote in his journal immediately after speaking of "the reader"—"Oh, if there only *were* a reader!"

Flaubert, whose works are still on the Index, chiefly, I have been told, because nobody has attempted to have them taken off, wrote Mme. Maurice Schlesinger that "*Madame Bovary* is a page out of the liturgy" but, he added, "the good folk who have the liturgy in their keeping cannot read very well." If Flaubert were alive today, I think that he might be inclined to revise his statement. I can even conceive his pointing out that some of "the good folk" are not only reading very well but writing very well! Certainly, anyone who surveys the contemporary literary scene cannot fail to be impressed by the fact that so many of our most talented young fiction writers not only write from a Catholic background (as Flaubert did, for all his personal scepticism), but are themselves practicing Catholics.

Of these young fiction writers Flannery O'Connor seems to me the most talented—and the most professional. My admiration for her work was first evoked when, in the line of duty, I contemplated the structure of "A Good Man Is Hard to Find" and found it written "in the one way that is mathematically right"—to borrow a phrase from James's notebooks.

Any expert performance is always more or less interesting to an audience. The spectacle of a young fiction writer achieving popular triumphs by the use of a technique which is not only revolutionary but universally derided is, for a fellow novelist, as exciting an experience as—a bullfight, say, can be for one who is *aficionado*. Indeed, I think we can profitably reflect upon one of those metaphors from the bull-ring in which Ernest Hemingway embodied his most profound conclusions about the art of fiction. He tells us in *The Sun Also Rises* that in a bullfight "there is the *terrain* of the man and the *terrain* of the bull." In a bullfight the unforgettable moments are those in which the matador sustains the invasion by the bull of his territory or, himself, invades the territory of the bull. During her short life, Miss O'Connor worked always "within the terrain of the bull." Perhaps that is one reason why she did not live longer.

Evelyn Waugh, when he first read one of her books, expressed a doubt that it had been written "by a young lady." Certainly, James's adjective "promiscuous" does not apply to her work. She, herself, felt that she was primarily a short story writer although she wrote two novels, *Wise Blood* and *The Violent Bear It Away*. Her best work, however, whether in the novel or the short story, has an outstanding characteristic. It is never "promiscuous." Her story is never "jerry-built"—if I understand James's use of that term. Indeed, it seems to me that she has a firmer grasp of the architectonics of fiction than any of her contemporaries. She has written four short stories, "A Good Man Is Hard to Find," "Good Country People," "The Displaced Person," and "The River" which seem to me to nearly approach perfection. "The Enduring Chill," "A Circle in the Fire" and "A Temple of the Holy Ghost" do not seem to me as successful.

But when Miss O'Connor falls short of her best work, the flaw is always in the *execution* of the story, not in its *structure*. In her architectural creations a turret may loom indistinctly or a roof line will slant so steeply that the eye follows it with difficulty but turret and roof and even battlements indistinctly limned are nevertheless recognized as integral parts of the structure. All her work is based upon the same architectural principle. This principle, fundamental but in our own times so fallen into disrepute that it has actually come to be thought of as an innovation, is, I think, the fact that any good story, no matter when it was written or in what language, or what its ostensible subject matter, shows both natural and supernatural grace operating in the lives of human beings. Her firm grasp of this great architectural principle is, I believe, in large part, responsible for Miss O'Connor's successes. A variety of causes may account for her failures or near-failures. Chief of them, of course, is the immense difficulty inherent in her subject matter. The chasm between natural and supernatural grace is sometimes an abyss, so deep that only the heroes—in fiction as in real life—can bear to contemplate it. "Look at the abyss long enough and it will look back at you," said Nietzsche, who was to experience at firsthand what he was talking about. In all her stories Miss O'Connor sets out to bridge this chasm, or, to speak more precisely, to do away with it. It is a task to appall the hardiest. No wonder her hand sometimes falters when the moment comes for the joining of the two terrains, as in "A Circle in the Fire" when "the Child" who figures frequently in Miss O'Connor's stories, sees in her mother's face "the new misery" she, herself, has just felt and sees also "[an old misery that] looked as if it might have belonged to anybody, a Negro or a European or to Powell himself" (232). Powell, the adolescent boy, finding that he can no longer even in memory possess the farm on which he spent the happiest days of his life, has just set the woods on fire.

> The child turned her head quickly, and past the Negroes' ambling fig-
> ures she could see the column of smoke rising and widening unchecked
> inside the granite line of trees. She stood taut, listening, and could just
> catch in the distance a few wild high shrieks of joy as if the prophets
> were dancing in the fiery furnace, in the circle the angel had cleared for
> them (232).

The transition from the natural world to the supernatural seems to me too abrupt. Powell's response to the natural world is sensitive and passionate—"It was a horse named Gene . . . and a horse named George"—but so far he has excited only our compassion. We are not agile enough to visualize him as either Meshach, Shadrach or Abednego or even as enjoying the protection of an angel.

Sister Mariella Gable, O.S.B., speaks of Miss O'Connor as "the first great writer of ecumenical fiction anywhere in the world."[1] Catholic literary critics are not noted for their moderation or their interest in professional techniques. Time will doubtless tell us whether Miss O'Connor is one of our great fiction writers or whether she belongs in the ranks of the fine minor writers (where, after all, she would have quite distinguished company). But anyone who has followed the news of the world even casually may find himself agreeing with a part of Sister Mariella's encomium. It is an easily verifiable fact that Miss O'Connor was writing fiction in which men and women were involved in some of the same predicaments which were the subjects of discussion at the first ecumenical council—a good many years before John XXIII became Pope. She may not have considered her writing "ecumenical" but she was aware of its profound implications and their significance. This is evidenced by a letter she wrote Sister Mariella in 1963:

> Ideal Christianity doesn't exist, because anything the human being touches, even Christian truth, he deforms slightly to his own image. . . . To a lot of Protestants I know monks and nuns are fanatics, none greater. And to a lot of monks and nuns I know my Protestant prophets are fanatics. For my part, I think that the only difference between them is that if you are a Catholic and have this intensity of belief you join a convent and are heard of no more; whereas if you are Protestant and have it, there is no convent for you to join and you go about the world getting into all sorts of trouble and drawing the wrath of people who don't believe much of anything at all down on your heard. . . .[2]

Philip Scharper has pointed out that "Flannery O'Connor was one of those artists—rare in any age—who saw life *sub specie aeternitatis.*"[3] It is certainly true that in her stories every incident is seen in the light of eternity, one of the marks of a creative imagination of the first rank. But she has another distinction, one which is unique in our day. She was a pioneer in a field which is not only considered dangerous for the fiction writer but is commonly regarded as forbidden ground. She was the first fiction writer to view her own region—it happened to be the rural South—through the eyes of Roman Catholic orthodoxy. In doing this she ran counter to the belief held by most novel readers and nearly all reviewers that religious conversion or, indeed, any of the operations of supernatural grace are not subjects for fictional rendition.

James, who in his notebooks referred to the writing of fiction as "the sacred calling," would not have hesitated, I suspect, to brand this conviction as a "heresy." It may be a sign of the degeneracy of letters in our times—where would Dante or Shakespeare have been if confronted with such a taboo? But no one can deny that it is firmly rooted in the contemporary mind. The literary magazines publish endless discussions of the "handicaps" which the novelist who is a practicing Catholic supposedly works under. The reviewers, if confronted, as one is inevitably confronted in any fictional masterpiece, with the workings of supernatural grace, are as prudish (theologically) as the Victorian lady is supposed to have been when apprised of some of the grosser manifestations of sex.

This taboo has had a constrictive effect on some of the best fictional talents of our times. The novelist who is a Catholic (and in some cases is a novelist because he is a Catholic) cannot fail to take the workings of supernatural grace into account in his novels but his rendition of its workings is frequently *sub rosa* and so oblique that the reader is not quite sure what has happened. In many cases the creative imagination suffers another kind of constriction. The novelist is so bewildered by the clamor from the marketplace that he cannot allow his imagination free play; the incident in which supernatural grace figures is not allowed to attain the proportions which are necessary if it is to have its desired effect. The result is a fictional structure which is "jerry-built." At any rate, such a novel does not create "the single impression" which James found requisite.

Miss O'Connor, almost alone among her contemporaries, adheres strictly to the great architectural principle (upon which James's three great later novels are based) that in the life of certain human beings supernatural grace operates as freely as natural grace—if only when being resisted.

Her work owed its first popularity to the fact that her stage is peopled by so many freaks. We like—everybody has always liked—to contemplate monsters—from a distance. One of Miss O'Connor's early critics wrote that one could not tell the difference between the characters in one of her stories and the characters in one of Truman Capote's stories.[4] There is all the difference in the world—both in the natural and the supernatural world! When we finish reading one of Mr. Capote's stories we are not in any doubt as to the fate of the chief character but weeks or months later we may find ourselves speculating as to how he "got that way." Such speculations do not arise in connection with Miss O'Connor's characters. If they are freaks, they are freaks for one reason only: they have been deprived of the sacraments. Of the Blood of Christ, as Enoch Emery and Haze Motes are deprived in *Wise Blood,* as the boy, Harry, is deprived in "The River," as the one-legged female doctor of philosophy and her seducer, the false Bible salesman, are deprived in "Good Country People."

The serious student of Miss O'Connor's stories will find it profitable, I think, to compare her life's work with that of Henry James. The novels of his "later" period deal with the imposition of supernatural grace upon natural grace. Lambert Strether's last meeting with Mme. de Vionnet is in a room in which the candles flicker as if upon "an altar." The "voice of Paris," which spoke to him so compellingly on the day of his first arrival in the city, comes in through the open windows but the vague, murmurous voices speak to him now of the tumult which accompanied the fall of the Bastille. They cry out for "Blood!" Mme. de Vionnet is dressed this evening in a way which reminds him of the way Mme. Roland must have looked as she rode in the tumbril to the guillotine. Mme. de Vionnet, who is clearly cast in the role of sacrificial victim, shows us that she understands her role when, in her conversation with Strether, she paraphrases one of the Beatitudes: "The thing is to give . . . never to take. That is the only thing that never plays you false." *The Wings of the Dove* rests similarly on a Christian foundation. Kate Croy and her fiance, Merton Densher, are happy enough in their love for each other but Kate feels that they would be happier if they were not so poor. She persuades Densher to pay court to the ailing heiress, Milly Theale, in the hope that if he marries her she will leave them her money at her death. The woman tempted him and he fell. Milly Theale does leave her money to Densher when she dies, sooner than she would have died in the ordinary course of events. Densher is so overcome by the realization of his guilt that the Angel of the Flaming Sword speaks through his lips when he says to Kate: "We shall never again be as we were!"

Through his genius James apprehended the archetypal Christian patterns. He tells us, however, in *Notes of a Son and Brother* that neither he nor any of his brothers or his sister were "allowed to divine an item of devotional practice" in their childhood. Instead, they were sent to churches of first one denomination then another in order that they might choose the religion that suited them best. He records that he wondered, even as a small child, why "we were so religious" and

yet practiced no religion. One of those great metaphors which illuminate his writings may have arisen first in his infant imagination. He
visualized his household as a temple dedicated to what his mother
called "Father's ideas." His mother, he tells us, seemed to enact the
role of priestess. At least, she was nearly always to be found on the
steps of the temple where "beakers of the divine fluid" were also
always to be found, "though," he says, "I cannot remember that any
of us ever quaffed from them."

That percipient critic, Austin Warren, has included the elder Henry
James in his roster of *New England Saints*. The novelist's father was
certainly a saintly figure. Henry James, Jr. paints a moving picture of
his father seated every morning at his desk, pausing sometimes to sigh
and pass his hand eerily over his forehead, then returning to his task:
"the one book he was all his life writing."

The elder James, like many thoughtful men of his day, was influenced by the writings of Emanuel Swedenborg, but he was not wholly
in agreement with him. Indeed, he was not wholly in agreement with
anybody. His "New Church," whose tenets he spent his life setting
forth, contained only one member, himself, or so one of his friends
wittily averred.

His son, William James, said that editing his father's literary remains was the hardest task he ever faced. But both he and his brother,
Henry James, Jr., felt that he did his father's memory full justice. A
paragraph from a book called *Society the Redeemed Form of Man:
An Earnest of God's Providence* shows us that William's task was,
indeed, no easy one:

> It is in fact the venomous tradition of a natural as well as a personal
> disproportion between man and his maker—speciously cloaked as it is
> under the ascription of a supernatural being and existence to God,—
> that alone gives its intolerable odium and poignancy to men's otherwise
> healthful and restorative conscience of sin. That man's personality
> should utterly alienate him from God,—that is to say make him infi-
> nitely other and opposite to God,—this I grant you with all my heart;
> since if God were the least like me personally, all my hope in him would
> perish. . . . But that God should be also an infinitely *foreign* substance
> to me,—an infinitely other or foreign *nature*,—this wounds my spon-

taneous faith in him to its core, or leaves it a mere mercenary and servile homage. . . .

I do not know that Miss O'Connor was consciously influenced by the novelist, Henry James's work. I am inclined to think that the affinity between the two writers is instinctive and unconscious. One of Miss O'Connor's "prophets," Hazel Motes, who preaches "The Church of Jesus Christ Without Christ" strongly resembles the elder Henry James. Both men have one lifelong preoccupation: theology. In the case of both men it is coupled with an inability to believe in the divinity of Christ. Both men are indifferent to worldly goods. The elder James never envisaged for any of his children a career which took into account the making of money. Hazel lives on the pension he receives for a disability incurred in the war. When his landlady calls his attention to four one dollar bills she has found in his wastebasket, he tells her that he threw them there because "they were left over." In addition to his practice of an almost Franciscan poverty, he practices mortifications of the flesh, putting pebbles and bits of broken glass in the bottoms of his shoes while he wears a strand of barbed wire coiled about his waist. In the end, he blinds himself with quicklime in his frenzied effort to see more clearly—that which is invisible to mortal eyes.

James left us, along with the prodigious body of his work, a complete, detailed record of his life as an artist. Those of us who still cannot read his novels, cannot plead in self-defense that he has not given us any clue how to go about reading them, for he has given us explicit directions.

Miss O'Connor is almost as well documented as to her artistic intentions. Dialogues, panels, discussions of the nature of the creative process are much in vogue these days. Almost every novelist has had to take part in such discussions on some occasion. Miss O'Connor has been subjected to as many questionnaires as any writer I can think of. She has submitted with an unusually good grace. Over and over she has explained, as best she could, what she has been trying to do. I find her intentions admirably summed up in a colloquy which took place between her and Gerard Sherry, editor of the *Georgia Bulletin:*

MR. SHERRY: What do you think is stifling the Catholic writer of today . . .?

MISS O'CONNOR: I think it's the lack of a large intelligent reading audience which believes Christ is God.[5]

I believe that a personal reminiscence may not be out of place here. I had the privilege of visiting Flannery O'Connor in a hospital a few weeks before her death. She told me that the doctor had forbidden her to do any work. He said that it was all right to write a little fiction, though, she added with a grin and drew a notebook out from under her pillow. She kept it there, she told me, and was trying to finish a story which she hoped to include in the volume which we both knew would be published posthumously. The story, "Parker's Back,"[6] does not have the perfection of phrasing which characterizes "Good Country People" or "A Good Man Is Hard to Find" but it is as sound architecturally as either of them. Parker, a Georgia hillbilly, becomes a collector of tattoos during his service in the Navy. Only his back is unornamented. Finally, in an effort to impress his wife, a religious fanatic, who tells him that the tiger and panther which adorn his shoulders, the cobra coiled about a torch on his chest, the hawks on his thighs are all "Vanity of vanities," he approaches an unusually high-priced "artist" and tells him that he wants a picture of God tattooed on his back. The artist asks:

"Father, Son or Spirit?"
"Just God," Parker said impatiently. "Christ. I don't care. Just so it's God" (*Everything*, 234).

He selects from the catalogue which the artist places before him a representation of a "stern Christ with all-demanding eyes," which the reader recognizes as Byzantine. After he has made his choice he "sat there trembling; his heart began slowly to beat again as if it were being brought to life by a subtle power" (*Everything*, 235).

Parker tells the artist that his new tattoo is to be a surprise for his wife. "You think she'll like it and lay off you for a while?" the artist asks shrewdly. "She can't hep herself," Parker said. "She can't say she don't like the looks of God" (*Everything*, 238).

Parker's wife wastes no words, however, when she sees the image of Christ tattooed on his back. She seizes a broom and belabors him until he is nearly senseless and the face of the Christ is covered with bleeding welts. The American girl has succeeded where the great

Flaubert failed! In this story in which there are no theological references other than those which might be found on the lips of "good country people," the author has embodied that particular heresy which denies Our Lord corporeal substance. During his lifetime, Henry James never found the reader he so ardently desired but I think that in Flannery O'Connor there was a disciple of whom he could have been proud.

1. "The Ecumenic Core in the Fiction of Flannery O'Connor," *American Benedictine Review,* XV (June, 1964), 127–43.

2. *Ibid.*

3. "Flannery O'Connor—a tribute," *Esprit,* VIII (Winter, 1964), 45.

4. William Esty, "In America, Intellectual Bomb Shelters," *Commonweal,* LXVII (March 7, 1958), 586–88.

5. "An Interview with Flannery O'Connor," *Critic,* XXI (June–July, 1963), 29.

6. *Everything That Rises Must Converge,* pp. 219–44.

1966

The Wide Net

Eudora Welty's presence in the tradition of southern literature is solid and enduring. She has influenced many writers who have identified with her vision and looked to her work for guidance and inspiration. But the image that emerges from her exchanges with Katherine Anne Porter and Elizabeth Spencer is not so much one of mentoring as one of friendship. These writers are linked by their belonging to the South: the site of their life experiences and the setting of much of their fiction. Porter praises Welty as "a child of her time and place" (p. 98), a position Welty herself claims openly, later telling Alice Walker that Jackson, Mississippi, is "my piece of the world" (p. 157). Spencer identifies with Welty as a sister Mississippian, revering her as a writer who "leaves things the same but different . . . because touched by her special alchemy" (p. 138). In turn, Welty admires Porter's ability to see "down to the bones" and recognizes a certain childhood affinity in her bond with Spencer.

Contemporary writers continue to look to Eudora Welty for inspiration. Alice Walker attempts to confront her own southern past in both Welty and Flannery O'Connor, an endeavor that culminates in a difficult trip back to Georgia where she finds O'Connor's childhood home intact but her own long since destroyed. And through Zora Neale Hurston, Walker locates her own particular southern literary heritage. By establishing a dialogue with the past through the works of O'Connor and Hurston, and through her interview with Welty, Walker identifies with them as southerners and as women while implicitly probing the place of the African-American writer in the southern literary tradition.

Still other writers have looked to Welty, Porter, and O'Connor for sustenance and identity, and for a southern sense of place important to their own work. Lisa Alther admires the keen detail and particularity in O'Connor's stories and considers her role as a woman writer in southern tradition. Lee

Smith, like Welty and Spencer before her, explores the issues of objectivity and point of view in her own work with respect to that of her predecessors; she finds in Welty and O'Connor a recognition of what it means to "write what you know." Through their writings these women and others confirm their kinship with women from their literary past, writers they have discovered in footnotes, in margins, or in the asides of college lectures on American, African-American, and southern literature. Welty's presence in particular, both in her early friendships and in her continuing influence on many contemporary writers, attests to the sense of community these women share among themselves—their sense of place as women and as southerners which joins them in respect and admiration, friendship and sympathy.

Katherine Anne Porter

Eudora Welty and *A Curtain of Green*

Friends of us both first brought Eudora Welty to visit me two and a half years ago in Louisiana. It was hot midsummer, they had driven over from Mississippi, her home state, and we spent a pleasant evening together talking in the cool old house with all the windows open. Miss Welty sat listening, as she must have done a great deal of listening on many such occasions. She was and is a quiet, tranquil-looking, modest girl, and unlike the young Englishman of the story, she has something to be modest about, as *A Curtain of Green* proves.

She considers her personal history as hardly worth mentioning, a fact in itself surprising enough, since a vivid personal career of fabulous ups and downs, hardships and strokes of luck, travels in far countries, spiritual and intellectual exile, defensive flight, homesick return with a determined groping for native roots, and a confusion of contradictory jobs have long been the mere conventions of an American author's life. Miss Welty was born and brought up in Jackson, Mississippi, where her father, now dead, was president of a Southern insurance company. Family life was cheerful and thriving; she seems to have got on excellently with both her parents and her two brothers. Education, in the Southern manner with daughters, was continuous, indulgent, and precisely as serious as she chose to make it. She went from school in Mississippi to the University of Wisconsin, thence to Columbia, New York, and so home again where she lives with her mother, among her lifelong friends and acquaintances, quite simply and amiably. She tried a job or two because that seemed the next thing, and did some publicity and newspaper work; but as she had no real need of a job, she gave up the notion and settled down to writing.

She loves music, listens to a great deal of it, all kinds; grows flowers very successfully, and remarks that she is "underfoot locally," meaning that she has a normal amount of social life. Normal social life in a medium-sized Southern town can become a pretty absorbing occupation, and the only comment her friends make when a new story appears is, "Why, Eudora, when did you write that?" Not how, or even why, just when. They see her about so much, what time has she for writing? Yet she spends an immense amount of time at it. "I haven't a literary life at all," she wrote once, "not much of a confession, maybe. But I do feel that the people and things I love are of a true and human world, and there is no clutter about them. . . . I would not understand a literary life."

We can do no less than dismiss that topic as casually as she does. Being the child of her place and time, profiting perhaps without being aware of it by the cluttered experiences, foreign travels, and disorders of the generation immediately preceding her, she will never have to go away and live among the Eskimos, or Mexican Indians; she need not follow a war and smell death to feel herself alive: she knows about death already. She shall not need even to live in New York in order to feel that she is having the kind of experience, the sense of "life" proper to a serious author. She gets her right nourishment from the source natural to her—her experience so far has been quite enough for her and of precisely the right kind. She began writing spontaneously when she was a child, being a born writer; she continued without any plan for a profession, without any particular encouragement, and, as it proved, not needing any. For a good number of years she believed she was going to be a painter, and painted quite earnestly while she wrote without much effort.

Nearly all the Southern writers I know were early, omnivorous, insatiable readers, and Miss Welty runs reassuringly true to this pattern. She had at arm's reach the typical collection of books which existed as a matter of course in a certain kind of Southern family, so that she had read the ancient Greek and Roman poetry, history and fable, Shakespeare, Milton, Dante, the eighteenth-century English and the nineteenth-century French novelists, with a dash of Tolstoy and Dostoievsky, before she realized what she was reading. When she first discovered contemporary literature, she was just the right age to find first W. B. Yeats and Virginia Woolf in the air around her; but always, from the beginning until now, she loved folk tales, fairy tales, old legends, and she likes to listen to the songs and stories of people who live in old communities whose culture is recollected and bequeathed orally.

She has never studied the writing craft in any college. She has never belonged to a literary group, and until after her first collection was ready to be published she had never discussed with any colleague or older artist any problem of her craft. Nothing else that I know about her could be more satisfactory to me than this; it seems to be immensely right, the very way a young artist should grow, with pride and independence and the courage really to face out the individual struggle; to make and correct mistakes and take the consequences of them, to stand firmly on his own feet in the end. I believe in the rightness of Miss Welty's instinctive knowledge that writing cannot be taught, but only learned, and learned by the individual in his own way, at his own pace and in his own time, for the process of mastering the medium is part of a cellular growth in a most complex organism; it is a way of life and a mode of being which cannot be divided from the kind of human creature you were the day you were born, and only in obeying the law of this singular being can the artist know his true directions and the right ends for him.

Miss Welty escaped, by miracle, the whole corrupting and destructive influence of the contemporary, organized tampering with young and promising talents by professional teachers who are rather monotonously divided into two major sorts: those theorists who are incapable of producing one passable specimen of the art they profess to teach; or good, sometimes first-rate, artists who are humanly unable to resist forming disciples and imitators among their students. It is all well enough to say that, of this second class, the able talent will throw off the master's influence and strike out for himself. Such influence has merely added new obstacles to an already difficult road. Miss Welty escaped also a militant social consciousness, in the current radical-intellectual sense, she never professed communism, and she has not expressed, except implicitly, any attitude at all on the state of politics or the condition of society. But there is an ancient system of ethics, an unanswerable, indispensable moral law, on which she is grounded firmly, and this, it would seem to me, is ample domain enough; these laws have never been the peculiar property of any party or creed or nation, they relate to that true and human world of which the artist is a living part; and when he dissociates himself from it in favor of a set of political, which is to say, inhuman, rules, he cuts himself away from his proper society—living men.

There exist documents of political and social theory which belong, if not to poetry, certainly to the department of humane letters. They are reassuring statements of the great hopes and dearest faiths of mankind and they are acts of high imagination. But all working, practical political systems, even those professing to originate in moral grandeur, are based upon and operate by contempt of human life and the individual fate; in accepting any one of them and shaping his mind and work to that mold, the artist dehumanizes himself, unfits himself for the practice of any art.

Not being in a hurry, Miss Welty was past twenty-six years when she offered her first story, "The Death of a Traveling Salesman," to the editor of a little magazine unable to pay, for she could not believe that anyone would buy a story from her; the magazine was *Manuscript*, the editor John Rood, and he accepted it gladly. Rather surprised, Miss Welty next tried the *Southern Review*, where she met with a great welcome and the enduring partisanship of Albert Erskine, who regarded her as his personal discovery. The story was "A Piece of News" and it was followed by others published in the *Southern Review*, the *Atlantic Monthly*, and *Harper's Bazaar*.

She has, then, never been neglected, never unappreciated, and she feels simply lucky about it. She wrote to a friend: "When I think of Ford Madox Ford! You remember how you gave him my name and how he tried his best to find a publisher for my book of stories all that last year of his life; and he wrote me so many charming notes, all of his time going to his little brood of promising writers, the kind of thing that could have gone on forever. Once I read in the *Saturday Review* an article of his on the species and the way they were neglected by publishers, and he used me as the example chosen at random. He ended his cry with 'What is to become of both branches of Anglo-Saxondom if this state of things continues?' Wasn't that wonderful, really, and typical? I may have been more impressed by that than would other readers who knew him. I did not know him, but I knew it was typical. And here I myself have turned out to be not at all the martyred promising writer, but have had all the good luck and all the good things Ford chided the world for withholding from me and my kind."

But there is a trap lying just ahead, and all short-story writers know what it is—The Novel. That novel which every publisher hopes to obtain from every short-story writer of any gifts at all, and who finally does obtain it, nine times out of ten. Already publishers have told her, "Give us first a novel, and then we will publish your short stories." It is a special sort of trap for poets, too, though quite often a good poet can and does write a good novel. Miss Welty has tried her hand at novels, laboriously, dutifully, youthfully thinking herself perhaps in the wrong to refuse, since so many authoritarians have told her that was the next step. It is by no means the next step. She can very well become a master of the short story, there are almost perfect stories in *A Curtain of Green*. The short story is a special and difficult medium, and contrary to a widely spread popular superstition it has no formula that can be taught by correspondence school. There is nothing to hinder her from writing novels if she wishes or believes she can. I only say that her good gift, just as it is now, alive and flourishing, should not be retarded by a perfectly artificial demand upon her to do the conventional thing. It is a fact that the public for short stories is smaller than the public for novels; this seems to me no good reason for depriving that minority. I remember a reader writing to an editor, complaining that he did not like collections of short stories because, just as he had got himself worked into one mood or frame of mind, he was called upon to change to another. If that is an important objection, we might also apply it to music. We might compare the novel to a symphony, and a collection of short stories to a good concert recital. In any case, this complainant is not our reader, yet our reader does exist, and there would be more of him if more and better short stories were offered.

The stories in *A Curtain of Green* offer an extraordinary range of mood, pace, tone, and variety of material. The scene is limited to a town the author knows well; the farthest reaches of that scene never go beyond the boundaries of her own state, and many of the characters are of the sort that caused a Bostonian to remark that he would not care to meet them socially. Lily Daw is a half-witted girl in the grip of social forces represented by a group of earnest ladies bent on doing the best thing for her, no matter what the consequences. Keela, the Outcast Indian Maid, is a crippled little Negro who represents a type of man considered most unfortunate by W. B. Yeats: one whose experience was more important than he, and completely beyond his powers of absorption. But the really unfortunate man in this story is the ignorant young white boy, who had innocently assisted at a wrong done the little Negro, and for a most complex reason, finds that no reparation is possible, or even desirable to the victim. . . . The heroine of "Why I live at the P.O." is a terrifying family poltergeist, when one reconsiders it. While reading, it is gorgeously funny. In this first group—for the stories may be loosely classified on three separate levels—the spirit is satire and the key grim comedy. Of these, "The Petrified Man" offers a fine clinical study of vulgarity—vulgarity absolute, chemically pure, exposed mercilessly to its final subhuman depths. Dullness, bitterness, rancor, self-pity, baseness of all kinds, can be most interesting material for a story provided these are not also the main elements in the mind of the author. There is nothing in the least vulgar or frustrated in Miss Welty's mind. She has simply an eye and an ear sharp, shrewd, and true as a tuning fork. She has given to this little story all her wit and observation, her blistering humor and her just cruelty; for she has none of that slack tolerance or sentimental tenderness toward symptomatic evils that amounts to criminal collusion between author and character. Her use of this material raises the quite awfully sordid little tale to a level above its natural habitat, and its realism seems almost to have the quality of caricature, as complete realism so often does. Yet, as painters of the grotesque make only detailed reports of actual living types observed more keenly than the average eye is capable of observing, so Miss Welty's little human monsters are not really caricatures at all, but individuals exactly and clearly presented: which is perhaps a case against realism, if we cared to go into it.

She does better on another level—for the important reason that the themes are richer—in such beautiful stories as "Death of a Traveling Salesman," "A Memory," "A Worn Path." Let me admit a deeply personal preference for this particular kind of story, where external act and the internal voiceless life of the human imagination almost meet and mingle on the mysterious threshold between dream and waking, one reality refusing to admit or confirm the existence of the other, yet both conspiring toward the same end. This is not easy to accomplish, but it is always worth trying, and Miss Welty is so successful at it, it would seem her most familiar territory. There is no blurring at the edges, but evidences of an active and disciplined imagination working firmly in a strong line of continuity, the waking faculty of daylight reason recollecting and recording the crazy logic of the dream. There is in none of these stories any trace of autobiography in the prime sense, except as the author is omnipresent, and knows each character she writes about as only the artist knows the thing he has made, by first experiencing it in imagination. But perhaps in "A Memory," one of the best stories, there might be something of early personal history in the story of the child on the beach, estranged from the world of adult knowledge by her state of childhood, who hoped to learn the secrets of life by looking at everything, squaring her hands before her eyes to bring the observed thing into a frame—the gesture of one born to select, to arrange, to bring apparently disparate elements into harmony within deliberately fixed boundaries. But the author is freed already in her youth from self-love, self-pity, self-preoccupation, that triple damnation of too many of the young and gifted, and has reached an admirable objectivity. In such stories as "Old Mr. Marblehall," "Powerhouse," "The Hitch-Hikers," she combines an objective reporting with great perception of mental or emotional states, and in "Clytie" the very shape of madness takes place before your eyes in a straight account of actions and speech, the personal appearance and habits of dress of the main character and her family.

In all of these stories, varying as they do in excellence, I find nothing false or labored, no diffusion of interest, no wavering of mood—the approach is direct and simple in method, though the themes and moods are anything but simple, and there is even in the smallest story a sense of power in reserve which makes me believe firmly that, splendid beginning that this is, it is only the beginning.

1961

Eudora Welty

Katherine Anne Porter:
The Eye of the Story

In "Old Mortality" how stirring the horse race is! At the finish the crowd breaks into its long roar "like the falling walls of Jericho." This we hear, and it is almost like seeing, and we know Miss Lucy has won. But beyond a fleeting glimpse—the "mahogany streak" of Miss Lucy on the track—we never get much sight of the race with our eyes. What we see comes afterward. Then we have it up close: Miss Lucy bleeding at the nose. For Miranda has got to say "That's winning too." The race would never have got into the story except that Miranda's heart is being prepared to reject victory, to reject the glamour of the race and the cheering grandstand; to distrust from now on all evidence except what she, out of her own experience, can testify to. By the time we *see* Miss Lucy, she is a sight for Miranda's eyes alone: as much symbol as horse.

Most good stories are about the interior of our lives, but Katherine Anne Porter's stories take place there; they show surface only at her choosing. Her use of the physical world is enough to meet her needs and no more; she is not wasteful with anything. This artist, writing her stories with a power that stamps them to their last detail on the memory, does so to an extraordinary degree without sensory imagery.

I have the most common type of mind, the visual, and when first I began to read her stories it stood in the way of my trust in my own certainty of what was there that, for all my being bowled over by them, I couldn't see them happening. This was a very good thing for me. As her work has done in many other respects, it has shown me a thing or two about the eye of fiction, about fiction's visibility and invisibility, about its clarity, its radiance.

Heaven knows she can see. Katherine Anne Porter has seen all her life, sees today, most intimately, most specifically, and down to the bones, and she could date the bones. There is, above all, "Noon Wine" to establish it forever that when she wants a story to be visible, it is. "Noon Wine" is visible all the way through, full of scenes charged with dramatic energy; everything is brought forth into movement, dialogue; the title itself is Mr. Helton's tune on the harmonica. "Noon Wine" is the most beautifully objective work she has done. And nothing has been sacrificed to its being so (or she wouldn't have done it); to the contrary. I find Mr. Hatch the scariest character she ever made, and he's just set down there in Texas like a chair. There he stands, part of the everyday furniture of living. He's opaque, and he's the devil. Walking in at Mr. Thompson's gate—the same gate by which his tracked-down victim walked in first—he is that much more horrifying, almost too solid to the eyes to be countenanced. (So much for the visual mind.)

Katherine Anne Porter has not in general chosen to cast her stories in scenes. Her sense of human encounter is profound, is fundamental to her work, I believe, but she has not often allowed it the dramatic character it takes in "Noon Wine." We may not see the significant moment happen within the story's present; we may not watch it occur between the two characters it joins. Instead, a silent blow falls while one character is alone—the most alone in his life, perhaps. (And this is the case in "Noon Wine" too.) Often the revelation that pierces a character's mind and heart and shows him his life or his death comes in a dream, in retrospect, in illness or in utter defeat, the moment of vanishing hope, the moment of dying. What Miss Porter makes us see are those subjective worlds of hallucination, obsession, fever, guilt. The presence of death hovering about Granny Weatherall she makes as real and brings as near as Granny's own familiar room that stands about her bed—realer, nearer, for we recognize not only death's presence but the character death has come in for Granny Weatherall.

The flash of revelation is revelation but is unshared. But how unsuspecting we are to imagine so for a moment—it *is* shared, and by ourselves, her readers, who must share it feeling the doubled anguish of knowing this fact, doubled still again when it is borne in upon us how close to life this is, to *our* lives.

It is to be remembered that the world of fiction is not of itself visible. A story may or may not be born in sensory images in a given writer's mind. Experience itself is stored in no telling how many ways in a writer's memory. (It was "the sound of the sea, and Beryl fanning her hair at the window" that years later and thousands of miles away brought Katherine Mansfield to writing "At the Bay.") But if the physical world *is* visible or audible in the story, it has to be made so. Its materialization is as much a created thing as are the story's characters and what they think or do or say.

Katherine Anne Porter shows us that we do not have to see a story happen to know what is taking place. For all we are to know, she is not looking at it happen herself when she writes it; for her eyes are always looking through the gauze of the passing scene, not distracted by the immediate and transitory; her vision is reflective.

Her imagery is as likely as not to belong to a time other than the story's present, and beyond that it always differs from it in nature; it is *memory* imagery, coming into the story from memory's remove. It is a distilled, a re-formed imagery, for it is part of a language made to speak directly of premonition, warning, surmise, anger, despair.

It was soon borne in upon me that Katherine Anne Porter's moral convictions have given her readers another way to see. Surely these convictions represent the fixed points about which her work has turned, and not only that, but they govern her stories down to the smallest detail. Her work has formed a constellation, with its own North Star.

Is the writer who does not give us the pictures and bring us the sounds of a story as it unfolds shutting out part of life? In Katherine Anne Porter's stories the effect has surely been never to diminish life but always to intensify life in the part significant to her story. It is a darkening of the house as the curtain goes up on this stage of her own.

Her stories of Mexico, Germany, Texas all happen there: where love and hate, trust and betrayal happen. And so their author's gaze is turned not outward but inward, and has confronted the mysterious dark from her work's beginning.

Since her subject is what lies beneath the surface, her way—quite direct—is to penetrate, brush the stuff away. It is the writer like Chekhov whose way of working is indirect. He moved indeed toward the same heart and core but by building up some corresponding illusion of life. Writers of Chekhov's side of the family are themselves illusionists and have necessarily a certain fondness for, lenience toward, the whole shimmering fabric as such. Here we have the professional scientist, the good doctor, working with illusion and the born romantic artist—is she not?—working without it. Perhaps it is always the lyrical spirit that takes on instantaneous color, shape, pattern of motion in work, while the meditative spirit must fly as quickly as possible out of the shell.

All the stories she has written are moral stories about love and the hate that is love's twin, love's imposter and enemy and death. Rejection, betrayal, desertion, theft roam the pages of her stories as they roam the world. The madam kicking the girl in "Magic" and the rest of the brutality in the characters' treatment of one another; the thieving that in one form or another infects their relationships; the protests they make, from the weakness of false dreams or of lying down with a cold cloth over the eyes, on up to towering rages—all this is a way of showing to the inward eye: Look at what you are doing to human love.

We hear in how many more stories than the one the litany of the little boy at the end of "The Downward Path to Wisdom," his "comfortable, sleeping song": "I hate Papa, I hate Mama, I hate Grandma, I hate Uncle David, I hate Old Janet, I hate Marjory, I hate Papa, I hate Mama . . ." It is like the long list of remembered losses in the story "Theft" made vocal, and we remember how that loser's decision to go on and let herself be robbed coincides with the rising "in her blood" of a "deep almost murderous anger."

"If one is afraid of looking into a face, one hits the face," remarked W. B. Yeats, and I think we must conclude that to Katherine Anne Porter's characters this face is the challenging face of love itself. And I think it is the faces—the inner, secret faces—of her characters, in their self-delusion, their venom and pain, that their author herself is contemplating. More than either looking at the face or hitting it, she has made a story out of her anger.

If outrage is the emotion she has most strongly expressed, she is using outrage as her cool instrument. She uses it with precision to show what monstrosities of feeling come about not from the lack of the existence of love but from love's repudiation, betrayal. From which there is no safety anywhere. Granny Weatherall, eighty, wise, affectionate and good, and now after a full life dying in her bed with the priest beside her, "knew hell when she saw it."

The anger that speaks everywhere in the stories would trouble the heart for their author whom we love except that her anger is pure, the reason for it evident and clear, and the effect exhilarating. She has made it the tool of her work; what we do is rejoice in it. We are aware of the compassion that guides it, as well. Only compassion could have looked where she looks, could have seen and probed what she sees. Real compassion is perhaps always in the end unsparing; it must make itself a part of knowing. Self-pity does not exist here; these stories come out trenchant, bold, defying; they are tough as sanity, unrelinquished sanity, is tough.

Despair is here, as well described as if it were Mexico. It is a despair, however, that is robust and sane, open to negotiation by the light of day. Life seen as a savage ordeal has been investigated by a straightforward courage, unshaken nerve, a rescuing wit, and above all, with the searching intelligence that is quite plainly not to be daunted. In the end the stories move us not to despair ourselves but to an emotion quite opposite because they are so seriously and clear-sightedly pointing out what they have been formed to show: that which is true under the skin, that which will remain a fact of the spirit.

Miranda, by the end of "Old Mortality" rebelling against the ties of the blood, resenting their very existence, planning to run away now from these and as soon as she can from her own escape into marriage, Miranda saying "I hate loving and being loved," is hating what destroys loving and what prevents being loved. She is, in her own particular and her own right, fighting back at the cheat she has discovered in all that's been handed down to her as gospel truth.

Seeing what is not there, putting trust in a false picture of life, has been one of the worst nightmares that assail her characters. "My dreams never renege on me, Mr. Richards. They're all I have to go by," says Rosaleen. (The Irish are no better than the Southerners in this respect.) Not only in the comic and touching Rosaleen, the lovely and sentient and tragic Miranda, but in many other characters throughout the stories we watch the romantic and the anti-romantic pulling each other to pieces. Is the romantic ever scotched? I believe not. Even if there rises a new refrain, even if the most ecstatic words ever spoken turn out to be "I hate you," the battle is not over for good. That battle is in itself a romance.

Nothing is so naturally subject to false interpretation as the romantic, and in furnishing that interpretation the Old South can beat all the rest. Yet some romantic things happen also to be true. Miss Porter's stories are not so much a stand against the romantic as such, as a repudiation of the false. What alone can instruct the heart is the experience of living, experience which can be vile; but what can never do it any good, what harms it more than vileness, are those tales, those legends of more than any South, those universal false dreams, the hopes sentimental and ubiquitous, which are not on any account to be gone by.

For there comes a confrontation. It is then that Miss Porter's characters, behaving so entirely like ourselves, make the fatally wrong choice. Enter betrayal. Again and again, enter betrayal. We meet the betrayal that lies in rejection, in saying No to other or No to the self, or that lies with still more cunning in saying Yes when this time it should have been No.

And though we are all but sure what will happen, we are possessed by suspense.

It appears to me irrelevant whether or not the story is conceived and put down in sensory images, whether or not it is dramatic in construction, so long as its hold is a death-grip. In my own belief, the suspense—so acute and so real—in Katherine Anne Porter's work never did depend for its life on disclosure of the happenings of the narrative (nothing is going to turn out very well) but in the writing of the story, which becomes one single long sustained moment for the reader. Its suspense is one with its meaning. It must arise, then, from the mind, heart, spirit by which it moves and breathes.

It is a current like a strand of quicksilver through the serenity of her prose. In fiction of any substance, serenity can only be an achievement of the work itself, for any sentence that is alive with meaning is speaking out of passion. Serenity never belonged to the *now* of writing; it belongs to the later *now* offered its readers. In Katherine Anne Porter's work the forces of passion and self-possession seem equal, holding each other in balance from one moment to the next. The suspense born of the writing abides there in its own character, using the story for its realm, a quiet and well-commanded suspense, but a genie.

There was an instinct I had, trustworthy or not, that the matter of visibility in her stories had something to do with time. Time permeates them. It is a grave and formidable force.

Ask what time it is in her stories and you are certain to get the answer: the hour is fateful. It is not necessary to see the hands of the clock in her work. It is a time of racing urgency, and it is already too late. And then recall how many of her characters are surviving today only for the sake of tomorrow, are living on tomorrow's coming; think how we see them clearest in reference to tomorrow. Granny Weatherall, up to the last—when God gives her no sign acceptable to her and jilts her Himself—is thinking: "There was always so much to be done, let me see: tomorrow." Laura in "Flowering Judas" is "waiting for tomorrow with a bitter anxiety as if tomorrow may not come." Ordinary, self-respecting and—up to a certain August day—fairly well blessed Mr. Thompson, because he has been the one to kill the abominable Mr. Hatch, is self-tried, self-pleaded for, and self-condemned to no tomorrow; neither does he leave his sons much of a tomorrow, and certainly he leaves still less of one to poor, red-eyed Mrs. Thompson, who had "so wanted to believe that tomorrow, or at least the day after, life, such a battle at best, was going to be better." In "Old Mortality" time takes Miranda by the hand and leads her into promising herself "in her hopefulness, her ignorance": "At least I can know the truth about what happens to me." In "Pale Horse, Pale Rider" the older Miranda asks Adam, out of her suffering, "Why can we not save each other?" and the straight answer is that there is no time. The story ends with the unforgettable words "Now there would be time for everything" because tomorrow has turned into oblivion, the ultimate betrayer is death itself.

But time, one of the main actors in her stories—teacher, fake healer, conspirator in betrayal, ally of death—is also, within the complete control of Miss Porter, with his inimical powers made use of, one of the movers of her writing, a friend to her work. It occurred to me that what is *seeing* the story is the dispassionate eye of time. Her passionate mind has asked itself, schooled itself, to use time's eye. Perhaps Time is the genie's name.

Laura is stuck in time, we are told in "Flowering Judas"—and told in the timeless present tense of dreaming, a brilliant working upon our very nerves to let us know precisely Laura's dilemma. There is in all Katherine Anne Porter's work the strongest sense of unity in all the parts; and if it is in any degree a sound guess that an important dramatic element in the story has another role, a working role, in the writing of the story, might this not be one source of a unity so deeply felt? Such a thing in the practice of an art is unsurprising. Who can separate a story from the story's writing?

And there is too, in all the stories, a sense of long, learning life, the life that is the story's own, beginning from very far back, extending somewhere into the future. As we read, the initial spark is not being struck before our eyes; the fire we see has already purified its nature and burns steadied by purpose, unwavering in meaning. It is no longer impulse, it is a signal, a beacon.

To me, it is the image of the eye of time that remains the longest in the mind at her story's end. There is a judgment to be passed. A moral judgment has to be, in all reason, what she has been getting at. But in a still further act of judiciousness, I feel, she lets Time pass that judgment.

Above all, I feel that what we are responding to in Katherine Anne Porter's work is the intensity of its life, which is more powerful and more profound than even its cry for justice.

They are excoriating stories. Does she have any hope for us at all? Well, do we not feel its implication everywhere—a desperate hope for the understanding that may come, if we use great effort, out of tomorrow, or if not then, maybe the day after? Clearly it has to become at some point an act of faith. It is toward this that her stories all point: here, it seems to me, is the North Star.

And how calm is the surface, the invisible surface of it all! In a style as invisible as the rhythm of a voice, and as much her own as her own voice, she tells her stories of horror and humiliation and in the doing fills her readers with a rising joy. The exemplary prose that is without waste or extravagance or self-indulgence or display, without any claim for its triumph, is full of pride. And her reader shares in that pride, as well he might: it is pride in the language, pride in using the language to search out human meanings, pride in the making of a good piece of work. A personal spell is about the stories, the something of her own that we refer to most often, perhaps, when we mention its beauty, and I think this comes from the *making* of the stories.

Readers have long been in the habit of praising (or could it be at times reproaching?) Katherine Anne Porter by calling her a perfectionist. I do not agree that this is the highest praise, and I would think the word misleading, suggesting as it does in the author a personal vanity in technique and a rigidity, even a deadness, in her prose. To me she is something more serious than a perfectionist. I celebrate her for being a blessed achiever. First she is an artist, of course, and as an artist she is an achiever.

That she hasn't wasted precious time repeating herself in her stories is sign enough, if it were needed, that she was never interested in doing the thing she knew already that she was able to bring off, that she hasn't been showing off for the sake of high marks (from whom?), but has patiently done what was to her her born necessity, quietly and in her own time, and each time the way she saw fit.

We are left with a sense of statement. Virginia Woolf set down in her diary, on the day when she felt she had seen that great brave difficult novel *The Waves* past a certain point in the writing: "But I think it possible that I have got my statues against the sky." It is the achieving of this crucial, this monumental moment in the work itself that we feel has mattered to Katherine Anne Porter. The reader who looks for the flawless result can find it, but looking for that alone he misses the true excitement, exhilaration, of reading, of rereading. It is the achieving—in a constant present tense—of the work that shines in the mind when we think of her name; and in that achieving lies, it seems to me, the radiance of the work and our recognition of it as unmistakably her own.

And unmistakable is its source. Katherine Anne Porter's deep sense of fairness and justice, her ardent conviction that we need to give and to receive in loving kindness all the human warmth we can make—

here is where her stories come from. If they are made by the mind and address the mind, they draw their eloquence from a passionate heart. And for all their pain, they draw their wit, do they not, from a reserve of natural gaiety? I have wondered before now if it isn't those who were born gay who can devote themselves most wholeheartedly in their work to seriousness, who have seriousness to burn. The gay are the rich in feeling, and don't need to save any of it back.

Unmistakable, too, is what this artist has made. Order and form no more spring out of order and form than they come riding in to us upon seashells through the spray. In fiction they have to be made out of their very antithesis, life. The art of making is the thing that has meaning, and I think beauty is likely to be something that has for a time lain under good, patient hands. Whether the finished work of art was easy or hard to make, whether it demanded a few hours or many years, concerns nobody but the maker, but the making itself has shaped that work for good and all. In Katherine Anne Porter's stories we feel their making as a bestowal of grace.

It is out of the response to her particular order and form that I believe I may have learned the simplest and surest reason for why I cannot see her stories in their every passing minute, and why it was never necessary or intended that a reader should. Katherine Anne Porter is writing stories of the spirit, and the time that fills those moments is eternity.

1965

Eudora Welty

Post Mortem

Review of *The Never-Ending Wrong*

by Katherine Anne Porter

As this is being written, the Governor of Massachusetts has issued a proclamation calling for a memorial day on Aug. 23, the anniversary of the electrocution of Sacco and Vanzetti in the Charlestown Prison for a holdup and murder, and his legal counsel has cited "the very real possibility that a grievous miscarriage of justice occurred with their deaths." It has taken the law exactly 50 years to acknowledge publicly that it might have made a mistake. But after that same 50 years, the renowned short-story writer and novelist Katherine Anne Porter has written a book, "The Never-Ending Wrong," also to be published on Aug. 23; and it seems to her that she still believes and feels today the same as she believed and felt at that time on that scene.

This book of 63 pages, a "plain, full record of a crime that belongs to history" as she states in a foreword, was not intended to establish the guilt or innocence of Nicola Sacco and Bartolomeo Vanzetti, but rather to examine the guilt or innocence of those on the outside, all those gathered there, like herself, to see the final scene played out.

"I did not know then and I still do not know whether they were guilty . . . but I had my reasons for being there to protest the terrible penalty they were being condemned to suffer; these reasons were of the heart, which I believe appears in these pages with emphasis."

Her own participation was outwardly of little substance—a matter of typing letters Sacco and Vanzetti wrote to their friends on the outside, of showing up in the picket line and going through the motions of being arrested, jailed and bailed out. She knew herself to be largely in the dark about what was really going on. Questions rose out of personal feeling—deeply serious questions. She made some notes. This book, their eventual result, is a searching of a personal experience, whose troubling of the heart has never abated and whose meaning has kept on asking to be understood. The notes of that time have been added to, she says, "in the hope of a clearer statement," but the account is "unchanged in feeling and point of view."

The picket line in which she marched included the poets and novelists Edna St. Vincent Millay, John Dos Passos, Michael Gold, Grace Lumpkin, Lola Ridge. "I wouldn't have expected to see them on the same street, much less the same picket line and in the same jail."

By today's standards, the conduct of these exercises was almost demure. "I never saw a lady—or a gentleman—being rude to a policeman in that picket line, nor any act of rudeness from a single policeman. That sort of thing was to come later, from officers on different duty. The first time I was arrested, my policeman and I walked along stealing perplexed, questioning glances at each other; . . . neither of us wished to deny that the other was a human being, there was no natural hostility between us."

She made notes:

"*Second day*:

"He (taking my elbow and drawing me out of the line; I go like a lamb): 'Well, what have you been doing since yesterday?'

"I: 'Mostly copying Sacco and Vanzetti's letters. I wish you could read them. You'd believe in them if you could read the letters.'

"He: 'Well, I don't have much time for reading.'"

On the day they were all aware that the battle was lost, she said to him, "I expect this will be the last time you'll have to arrest me. You've been very kind and patient and I thank you." "Thank you," he replied.

They were bailed out by the same kind soul every time they were put in jail. Edward James, Henry James's nephew, invariably appeared and put up the money for all of them, even those who did not wish to be bailed out, "getting us set free for the next round."

But it appeared, Sacco and Vanzetti did not trust their would-be rescuers. "Many of the anxious friends from another class of society found [it] very hard to deal with, not to be met on their own bright, generous terms in this crisis of life and death; to be saying, in effect, we are all brothers and equal citizens; to receive, in effect, the reserved answer: No, not yet. It is clear now that the condemned men understood and realized their predicament much better than any individual working with any organization devoted to their rescue." They "knew well from the beginning that they had every reason to despair, they did not really trust these strangers from the upper world who furnished the judges and lawyers to the courts, the politicians to the offices, the faculties to the universities, who had all the money and the influence. . . . "

What they may not have known, says Miss Porter, was that "some of the groups apparently working for them, people of their own class in many cases, were using the occasion for Communist propaganda, and hoping only for their deaths as a political argument. I know this because I heard and I saw."

It was a certain Rosa Baron who made this clear through her own words to Katherine Anne Porter, who had expressed the hope that even yet the men might be saved. This "grim little person" headed Miss Porter's particular group during the Boston demonstrations, and what Miss Porter remembers most vividly through the 50 years of time are Rosa Baron's "little pinpoints of eyes glittering through her spectacles at me and her shrill, accusing voice: 'Saved? Who wants them saved? What earthly good would they do us alive?'"

"In the reckless phrase of the confirmed joiner in the fight for whatever relief oppressed humanity was fighting for, I had volunteered 'to be useful wherever and however I could best serve,' and was drafted into a Communist outfit all unknowing."

The account of her experience is clear and has the strength of an essence, not simply by virtue of its long distillation. It is clear through candor, as well. Miss Porter says of herself at this time:

"I was not an inexperienced girl, I was thirty-seven years old; I knew a good deal about the evils and abuses and cruelties—of the world; I had known victims of injustice, of crime, I was not ignorant of history, nor of literature; I had witnessed a revolution in Mexico, had in a way taken part in it, and had seen it follow the classic trail of all revolutions. Besides all the moral force and irreproachable motives of so many, I knew the deviousness and wickedness of both sides, on all sides, and the mixed motives—plain love of making mischief, love of irresponsible power, unscrupulous ambition of many men who never stopped short of murder, if murder would advance their careers an inch. But this was something very different, unfamiliar."

"There were many such groups, for this demonstration had been agitated for and prepared for many years by the Communists. They had not originated the protest, I believe, but had joined in and tried to take over, as their policy was, and is. . . ."

Being used! The outrage she had found unbearable for the men on trial in court she realized was also the outrage being inflicted on those who had tried to help them, and on others more vulnerable than picketers in their line.

Through Miss Porter's eyes we see their wives, Rosa Sacco and Luigia Vanzetti, being marched through the streets at the head of a crowd massing at a rally, on the night before the scheduled execution.

". . . and the two timid women faced the raging crowd, mostly Italians, who rose at them in savage sympathy, shouting, tears pouring down their faces, shaking their fists and calling . . . 'Never you mind. Rosina! You wait, Luigia! They'll pay, they'll pay!' It was the most awesome, the most bitter scene I had ever witnessed."

But the crowd assembled to await the execution itself was in contrast "a silent, intent assembly of citizens—of anxious people come to bear witness and to protest against the terrible wrong about to be committed, not only against the two men about to die, but against all of us, against our common humanity. . . . " The mounted police galloped about, bearing down on anybody who ventured beyond the edge of the crowd and rearing up over their heads.

"One tall, thin figure of a woman stepped out alone, a good distance into the empty square, and when the police came down at her and the horse's hoofs beat over her head, she did not move, but stood with her shoulders slightly bowed, entirely still. The charge was repeated again and again, but she was not to be driven away." Then she was recognized as Lola Ridge, and dragged to safety by one of her own; the strange, poignant, almost archetypical figure Miss Porter describes must remain indelible.

After that night was all over, the picketers themselves were given a trial; that is, "simply our representatives" (Edna St. Vincent Millay was one) "were tried in a group in about five minutes." The judge "portentously, as if pronouncing another death sentence, found us guilty of loitering and obstructing traffic, fined us five dollars each, and the tragic farce took its place in history."

The aftermath was numbness, silence; disbanding and going home. Miss Porter writes: "In all this I should speak only for myself, for never in my life have I felt so isolated as I did in that host of people, all presumably moved in the same impulse, with the same or at least sympathetic motive; when one might think hearts would have opened, minds would respond with kindness, we did not find it so, but precisely the contrary."

Katherine Anne Porter's fine, grave honesty has required of her, and she has given it to this account, a clarity of statement, a respect for proportion, an avoidance of exaggeration, a watchfulness against any self-indulgence, and a regard for uncompromising accuracy.

But the essence of the book's strength lies in its insight into human motivations, and the unique gifts she has brought to her fiction have been of value to her here as well—even in the specific matter of her subject. The theme of betrayal has always run in a strong current through her work. The worst villains of her stories are the liars, and those most evil are the users of others. Elements of guilt, the abandonment of responsibilities in human relationships, the betrayal of good faith and the taking away of trust and love are what her tragic stories are made of. Betrayal of justice is not very different from the betrayal of love.

And a nation is a living human organism. Like a person, a nation sometimes needs years to comprehend the full scope and seriousness of some wound that has happened to it or some act it has brought itself to perform. Though an experience in its history may have hurt it deeply, left a scar and caused it recurring discomfort and bad dreams, yet only slowly may its meaning grow clear to the sufferer.

"The never-ending wrong," says Miss Porter, "is the anguish that human beings inflict on each other," which she pronounces at the end "forever incurable." And she finds that "The evils prophesied by that crisis have all come true."

As no concerned citizen can argue, this book she has written out of her own life is of profound contemporary significance.

1977

Eudora Welty

My Introduction to Katherine Anne Porter

When in 1937 Robert Penn Warren, Cleanth Brooks, and Albert Erskine, editors of *The Southern Review,* had decided to use two of my stories, the significance of that acceptance was not lost on me. They had thought my work good enough to take a chance on, to encourage. Still I had not been prepared for a letter out of the blue from Katherine Anne Porter after the stories appeared. She was not an editor, but a *writer,* a writer of short stories; she was out in the world, at Baton Rouge:

> 961 America Street
> Baton Rouge, Louisiana
> October 25, 1938
>
> Dear Miss Welty:
>
> Ford Madox Ford has been given control of the fiction department of the Dial Press, and asked me to help him look about for candidates for publication. I thought of you first, with your admirable short stories. It seems to me that if you have no other plans, and have a book length collection of stories, it would be an excellent idea to write to Ford, giving him some notion of your manuscript. He will then no doubt ask to see it.
>
> Also, if you like, I would be glad to name you as candidate for a Guggenheim Fellowship for next year—rather, for application in the fall of 1939 and 1940 Fellowship. I have already named a candidate for this year. This is done by request of the Secretary of the Foundation who

looks constantly for likely candidates, and naturally is no sort of engagement or promise. But if you should care to apply, I should at once write a letter about you to Mr. Moe.

I take this liberty because of my admiration for your very fine work.

Katherine Anne Porter

I seized on the belief Miss Porter offered me; she was the writer of short stories I revered. Her letter was an act of faith, and I was able to recognize this. It also foretold something about her lifelong habit of mind: there was no mistaking the seriousness of her meaning; there never must be, with her, as all learned sooner or later about K.A.P. She spoke truth as she saw it about the written word, about the writing of the written word, the act itself.

She was to give encouragement to me from that time on in the ways that always applied to the serious meaning of a young writer's work—and life; as indeed she gave encouragement to many young writers.

Thus I'd sent along my stories to Ford Madox Ford, who turned out to think well enough of them to try to place them in England up until the time of his death not very long afterward. I'd applied for the Guggenheim in 1940 with Katherine Anne's blessing. It wasn't awarded on that first application. But it was the existence of Katherine Anne Porter's hopes for me themselves, successful and unsuccessful alike, that filled me with gratitude.

However I had been able to express this to her, she wrote back:

1050 Government Street
Baton Rouge, Louisiana
March 7, 1940

Dear Eudora:

Please remember that my recommendation of your work costs me nothing; that it gives me pleasure, and is the best proof I can offer of my faith in your talent and hopes for the future. It is no doubt one of the marks of your seriousness of character and intention that you take obligation for any little help offered or received; in this case, let me assure you, a purely imaginary, self-assumed sense of obligation. Try not to remember it; I would much prefer your friendship, in the most unburdensome meaning of that word. And it would really disturb me if you felt in my debt for such a small thing as a word of praise from me.

I am still hoping that your luck will be good this year. Enough for the present, for if this year is good, the others can take care of themselves. . .[1]

Katherine Anne

And even if this year turns out *not* so good, that is no sign at all that the coming ones shall be unlucky!

In September 1940, as I was travelling to Vermont, she invited me to stop off at Yaddo, the artists' colony where she was spending a time working. She wrote to me afterwards:

Yaddo, Saratoga Springs
New York, September 18
1940

Dear Eudora:

It was simply lovely having you here even for such a little while, and I wish you could come back now, for I'm moved upstairs to a much pleasanter place and there are bedrooms all over the house, unoccupied . . .

Diarmuid Russell[2] wrote me, and I wrote him and he wrote me again and I just answered, so you see we are getting on splendidly. He gave me some advice which I followed and it worked; and he is a most secure admirer of you and your work, so it is delightful to know you are going to be looked after. He is really in earnest about it; says he finds himself mentally shaking his finger at editors about you. I feel serenely conscious that it is all going to end well. Yours will be a war of attrition, as mine was, Eudora. You just go the way you're going and the editors will fall in, in time. And you have all the time in the world, and all the gift you can handle; in fact, you've got a handful, perhaps more than you know.

I have out of a clear sky but not without premeditation, finished two short stories—whales, about eight thousand words each. One to S.R., one to Harper's Bazaar, as usual. I think I was working on the first when you were here. Well, there are two now. "Season of Fear" and "The Leaning Tower." That makes enough floating around for a collection, and I'm going to get out another book of short stories, willy-nilly; they can take it or leave it. We have *got* to beat down this conspiracy against collections of short stories . . . It's a long war, but we will win.

Katherine Anne

By 1941, Diarmuid Russell after two years' unremitting work had succeeded in placing all my stories in magazines, which had made them acceptable as a collection to a publisher who would risk a book of short stories. And now, John Woodburn of Doubleday, Doran in New York had by his long and patient work persuaded his house to publish it. The book was given a title, *A Curtain of Green*. To cap this, he had invited and persuaded Katherine Anne Porter to write an Introduction to it. She added to this wonderful news by writing to me:

February 19, 1941—Olivet
[Olivet College, Michigan]

Dearest Eudora:

All the news about you is good news and makes me happy for you, and for myself, because nothing is better than to see you getting off so bravely.

I write with pencil because I am in bed with a crick in the neck which seems to be my way of having a cold, and all my paper, pens, etc., are on the other side of this blizzard-swept campus in my office. A splendid letter from Diarmuid full of rejoicing about you and the new baby.[3] Please tell him in your next I have his letter and will write when I am better able.

Meantime—Send the collection *with* "The Robber Bridegroom"[4] et al to Yaddo. I will do what I can to have it included—Above all, tell me *when, where* the preface should be sent; deadlines are my snare—But I will make it.

I know well already what I think of your work, but reading all the stories will give pointers.

No more for the moment. Albert Erskine will be delighted with this news. Meantime my love and good wishes, may all your good beginnings bring you to a happy end!

Katherine Anne

And soon after:

Yaddo, Saratoga Springs
New York, May 2, 1941

Dear Eudora:

Elizabeth Ames tells me you have been invited here for early June, and I hope you like the place and can stay a long time if you want . . . It will be lovely to see you. Mrs. Ames had said something about inviting you before the regular season, but I heard no more of it.

Your letter was useful and I am keeping it with my notes for the preface, just for the tone. We'll talk all that over when you get here . . .

Nothing more just now, I am at the last gasp of that novel, and must finish now before I do anything else. But after, I shall be free; and meantime I scribble down something else about your work as it comes to me, so the notes are piling up nicely against the day . . .

I got the deed to South Farm, today. So it is really mine, and the work is beginning on it almost at once . . . The end of the summer should see me in it. But believe me, this novel is the foundation of this whole thing, and it must go soon . . . I've written it so often, really, it is high time to let go, now!

Waiting to see you, with my love,

Katherine Anne

I showed your collection to Glenway Wescott, and he was pretty well bowled over. I said, "My money is on her nose for the next race," and he said, "Mine, too. She is marvelous." So your audience grows. He is a good friend to have—never will let his friends hear the last of you . . .

I arrived at Saratoga Springs as one in a dream.

Yaddo was in the old, rural, comfortably settled part of New York State west of Albany, near the town of Saratoga Springs. The estate was private and well guarded, though its gardens were, at that innocent time, open to the public. The Mansion faced you head-on as you approached it through forest trees; it was huge, elaborately constructed: it looked made by impulse for eternity, out of the rock on which it stood. The artists came for their summer at Yaddo solely by invitation. Elizabeth Ames gave her life to being its director—a woman of Quaker-like calm and decisiveness; she was beautiful and to some extent deaf. She stood ready for crises.

The artists—painters, composers, writers, sculptors—lived in the reaches of the Mansion, and beyond their rooms they were given studios to suit their particular needs; these stood hidden away among the old forest trees, at various calculated degrees of remoteness. Artists ate their lunch alone; it arrived in a tin box left silently outside their doors at noon.

Katherine Anne and I were enviably installed in the "farmhouse," a

small frame building a distance away from the Mansion on its hill
across the road. We shared the farmhouse with only two others, congenial both—a Canadian composer and an Armenian-American
etcher, who did work all day in their respective studios.

Upstairs, across the hall from Katherine Anne's combined bedroom
and studio, was my bedroom. My studio was downstairs in the farmhouse kitchen. On the outside of the studio door was a sign tacked up:
"SILENCE. WRITER AT WORK WITHIN." My immediate work consisted
of reading the proofs of my forthcoming book, and that was over
quickly. Already, though, my editor John Woodburn, in New York,
had begun to write me little bulletins, instructing me to remind Katherine Anne about the Introduction: "And kid, you keep after her!
She promised to write it *now!* Remind her we've got a deadline."

And I knew I couldn't do that.

In the early evening of each long summer's day, Katherine Anne—with
her spring-heeled step, catching up her long skirts—and I set out in
single file walking the woodland path up to the great stone Mansion
for dinner. This was the only hour of the twenty-four when all the
guests came out and showed themselves. They had supposedly been
solitary all day behind their studio doors, working.

Within the Mansion, the atmosphere, even the hour, seemed
changed; it was hushed, moody, and somehow public. The great room
we entered spread out like a stage set for a grand opera on which the
curtain might at any moment go up. An overture was in the making:
an interior fountain close to us was murmuring, and offstage somewhere an organ began to growl; it was possible that one of the resident
poets was still at work, thinking something through.

I began to feel apprehensive that we were all expected to *perform*
here, that the assigned soloists and the combined chorus were *us*. The
great hall was appointed with throne chairs, divans, velvet stools (one
also noticed a sleigh), with candelabra, wine glasses, wine.

If I supposed our opera would be one about the arts, or artists,
something like *La Bohème*, I wasn't on the right track. This was 1941.
The company was in great part European. Elizabeth Ames had come
to the aid of many artists who no longer had homes and were seeking
refuge and a place to carry on their work. Our evening was indeed

operatic, but it wasn't about the arts; it was about politics. Katherine Anne rose to the occasion—her clear voice would enter as if on cue with cries of "*Au contraire!*" One end of the great room gave onto the coming night; the window was a great tall frame holding the Yaddo moon, and I watched it climbing. Out there beyond and below the stone balustrade, the garden descended, with its statues of the Graces rising from the beds like another chorus. I could smell, without seeing it, the summer stock, the nicotiana. They made me think of home. That first night, I knew for certain only what the *garden* was doing.

From New York, John Woodburn, who was my champion, who had staked so much in bringing out this first book by an unknown, young, Southern, female, short-story writer, wrote to me nearly every day. "How far along is she? How's the Introduction coming?" "Keep after her, kid! Tell her one more time about the deadline!" "Get it out of her, baby."

Was she writing it indeed? If I heard from across the hall her little Olivetti typewriter start up, or still more, if I heard it stop, I felt like an eavesdropper. I let myself out of the house and walked down the road to Saratoga Springs.

It was lovely to arrive there, too, in the bright Northern summer morning. Lining either side of the main street, the great hotels stood facing each other under the meeting boughs of lofty elms, the United States Hotel and all its sisterhood: their red faces, their black iron columns across the front, twisted like Venetian barge poles, and the figures of black, turbaned, Oriental slaves mounted at the top of the steps with an arm crooked up to hold branching lamps with clusters of globes made for gaslight.

The length of the street was strung overhead with banners and flags bidding Welcome. Along the sidewalks I moved with a wonderful crowd of perambulators here for the waters, the races, the sights and parades: invalids, sporting people, sightseers, families stalled in circles on the sidewalk in a chorus of argument over what to do next. I visited the racetrack where the horses were working out, and the busy public halls where the waters were being dispensed.

By the time I walked home to Yaddo, I might be carrying onions, soup bones, maybe a fresh stalk of celery or bunch of carrots to Katherine Anne, who liked to keep the soup pot going on her little stove, as well as her windup gramophone going, and sometimes now her Olivetti going.

I knew it was to be a wonderfully happy and carefree summer for me—if only I didn't have Katherine Anne's awful deadline hanging over my head: the unmentionable.

Outside our farmhouse sat a brand new Studebaker car—it was Katherine Anne's. She had not quite learned to drive it yet. But I could drive it, and she said she had something to show me: we would take the day off from work!

It was a little distance off, in deep country: the house her letter had told me about securing the deed for. She confided that she was actually now in the very process of restoring it. She had christened it "South Hill." She would finish it, make it all her own, move into it, settle down and *write*. It became a part of nearly every day to jump into the Studebaker and drive out to South Hill.

She could count on a Mr. Somebody who came to see to everything. So a yellow-coned cement mixer churned away among the trees, and at times drowned out the birdsong, and the carpenters who stripped the upstairs walls now down to the laths found little feminine slippers that K.A.P. identified as being a hundred years old, and further came on—roused up—bees in the walls too, which had been at work storing honey there for, she estimated, the same length of time. K.A.P. and I stretched out on the long sweet meadow grass in another part of the shade. At peace, we puffed on our cigarettes, and I listened to her tell the way she had discovered Joyce for herself: somehow a copy of *Ulysses* had been carried into this country and ended up on a secondhand bookstall in Galveston, Texas; Katherine Anne had walked by and just picked it up.

When the spirit moved us, we would jump into the Studebaker and ride all the way to Albany and there find six wonderful French antique dining-room chairs, or cinch a roll of ruby-red carpeting, perfect for the stairs when they were made ready to climb (at present we were crawling up a plank to reach the upstairs). All were now entrusted to storage. It was the clearest thing to K.A.P. that everything we engaged in all day long was South Hill in the making. There was supporting magic attached to finding treasures that would take their rightful place in it. There popped into my head the lovely little French virginal that Katherine Anne had showed to me, the very first thing, on the day when I'd come on her invitation to see her for the first time; it was in her new house in Baton Rouge. Where was the virginal now? I wondered, but did not ask. It must be in storage somewhere.

We sank into the luxury of talking books as easily as we sank into the long, sweet meadow grass; we had all day and a picnic lunch. We listened to the birdsong and the carpenters at work. Katherine Anne would often be laughing out loud.

But if it was hard for me, being there night and day with my very presence putting Katherine Anne on the spot, did I think of how hard it was for Katherine Anne? I am certain beyond a doubt that I could not have written the first line about anybody who was, at the time, staying in the house with me three steps away across the hall. And if that person knew about my purpose, and was waiting on me daily to set down the words on paper? And if at the same time that person had turned out to be a friend? I'm afraid the possibility never occurred to me that I *could* conclude my stay at Yaddo before my invitation was up.

Then the day came when she tapped at my door and came in holding out to me a whole sheaf of typewritten pages. "You may read this," she said, "if you would like." It was what she'd been working on, the first seventy-five pages of *No Safe Harbor*—her novel (which of course was to become, in the end, *Ship of Fools*). In allowing me to read it, and at its beginning, she had made me a gift of her clear confidence in me. As far as I was concerned, the Introduction she was going to write for me had been conveyed to me by way of a blessing. If its significance was to relate to her literary trust in me, I had already received it.

The novel was years later on to appear in the finality of print, but what I had been living across the hall from was the immediacy, the presence, and something of the terror, of its pages coming into being one by one. I'd *heard* the living words coming through her fingers and out of her skin. I don't think I was ever again as stirred, and as captivated, to hold a fresh manuscript in my hands and realize what I held.

The summer was deepening, and with it the pleasures of Yaddo. By then, friendships had ripened among the set of artists, informality had caught up with formality, and picnics sneaked into the lazy noons. Katherine Anne made onion soup for her friends. That could take all day, and as we all agreed, it was worth every minute of it. There was music in the evening at the Mansion, but music was *always* to be heard at our farmhouse. The gramophone would be kept wound up and playing. K.A.P. kept stacks of French records, from Piaf back to Gluck, back to madrigals. In the performance of the opera *Orphée*, when the moment arrived that I listened for—Cerberus barking—a live little dog filled the role.

There was everything going on at once those days. Some way or another, the little Olivetti was seizing its chances, too. From across our hall, I heard it very well—its insistencies, its halts, and again its resuming, the long runs as if this runner could not now stop for breath. And we didn't leave out driving nearly every day to visit South Hill—what else was the Studebaker for?

At South Hill Katherine Anne and I sat in the meadow downhill from what was going on, and watched the building slowly come to pass before our eyes. For the plain, century-old house (looking something like an ark) that she was making her own, the elation, the intensity, the triumph, the impatience of her vision of it took hold of her afresh every day. It made me aware that the planner was profoundly a story writer.

As I look back now, I believe she was putting the house together like a story in her head, restoring to it its history—a story that had as much to do with her past as it had to do with her future. It was a work-in-progress she was highly conscious of, and scrupulously attentive to, a self-assignment she was meeting, an autobiographical deadline.

"How far along *is* the Introduction?" wrote John Woodburn to me. How hard this was on John too, and how well I knew it! He adored Katherine Anne. He had travelled up to Yaddo to ask her in person if she would write the Introduction; they'd celebrated the agreement in Saratoga Springs in the grandeur of the United States Hotel; and he was a sensitive man. *He* couldn't ask her a word about it now, either. But I could hear the groan in his words to me: "Get it out of her *now*, kid! Do you want our book *postponed*?"

It was postponed. The day the Introduction was due came and

went, and at Yaddo I had never mentioned it to Katherine Anne. But I had *been* there. And I still was there—the live-in visitor from Porlock. I think now, in this long retrospect, that she made a daily brave attempt to forget about the interfering deadline for the moment at hand, and that what I was actually doing there was helping her forget it. At any rate, *this* was a success. And though I would not have known it at the time, this Introduction was undoubtedly only one of the things Katherine Anne was being pressed to do. She was constitutionally a besieged woman.

I'd begun to realize that the summer was of a kind not unexpected by Katherine Anne. Her whole writing life was one of interruptions, and interruptions of the interruptions. I was to learn that writers do generally live that way, and not entirely without their own collusion. No help ever comes, unless in the form of still another interruption.

The one thing that was uninterrupted in her life was her seriousness of intent. And when I look back, I seem to see her surrounded entirely by papers, by pages or galley sheets, by her work—"Old Mortality," "The Leaning Tower," and, on that blue typewriter paper, stretches of the novel. It seemed then that she was always writing. *Writing*—its conception—was ever-present to her. At Yaddo, at South Hill equally; writing was the future of her house, the *intention* of her house. And writing was—yes, even for her—very hard to do.

To me it came as no shock that writing itself, the act, might always be hard. The better the writer, the harder writing knew how to be. In fact, the harder Katherine Anne's work was for her, the more exhilarated, liberated my own spirits were accordingly. What I felt able to understand for myself was that writing well was for the writer worth whatever it took. The difficulty that accompanies you is less like the dark than like a trusted lantern to see your way by. I hoped proudly for myself that acknowledging and valuing the role of difficulty in writing well would remain always with me. Katherine Anne was helping me to recognize living with difficulty as a form of passion.

Certainly I was slower in learning to know Katherine Anne than I believed I was in the summer at Yaddo. Our friendship had shown me day after day the enchanting brightness she could shed around her, but it was later, through letters she wrote when we were no longer in the same place, laughing, that I became to any degree aware of the dark, its other side, which she lived with on its own terms in equally close commune. I wondered in retrospect if hers hadn't been the sort of exultation that can arise—must arise—out of some equally intense sadness, wondered if, as South Hill was taking shape before her eyes, there wasn't also something else in the course of being left behind. She was combatting unhappiness, even desolation, I now think, through that whole summer and for times longer than that, and bravely.

John Woodburn sent me the last of his bulletins in August, to Jackson where I'd returned: "Baby: Here is the Introduction, unproofread, which I finally got out of Katherine Anne by distilling her. There was no other way. . . . "

In the end, of course, she had written her magnificent Introduction "very quickly," she told me. And all her generosity, her penetration, serenely informs it, doing everything in her power for the book and for its author, as she'd intended to do all the time.

It is time itself—there was never any use denying—that is forever the enemy. I learned in those early days that K.A.P. would always take on any enemy—and time in particular—with a deep measure of respect. The price of writing that Introduction had to have been the postponement of something else. As well we know, *Ship of Fools* suffered many another postponement to follow this, the one she assumed that summer for introducing *A Curtain of Green*.

Katherine Anne wrote to me:

Yaddo, Saratoga Springs, New York

August 27, 1941

Dear Eudora:

I go on missing you quite steadily, the whole place changed when you went, though the activities kept on. I got to Albany by bus, not too dull, and at good hours, but there was a grim air of business about the trips, no more pleasant escapade in the morning air, no unexpected finding of Hindu wool rugs, no fun, in a word. My eyes managed to give me the worst upset in my nerves of anything I have known in my life. I was almost reduced to a state of pure terror, night and day, for the better part of a week. My efforts to conceal my state made it worse; I wished to collapse, to tell my troubles, to call upon God for help. I cannot be blind, that is the one thing I would make no attempt to face . . .

. . . Far from being part of the pressure, your preface is gone, accepted, perhaps set up in galleys by now. I came home with my goggles on
fine afternoons, sat down and batted out that opus in two evenings'
very pleasant work, mailed it special delivery and received some very
kind and pleasant words of rejoicing from John Broadside; so have that
off your mind as it is off ours . . . Now of course I think of some other
things I might have said to good effect, I wish I had gone a little more
into certain stories, such as A Memory, Old Mr. Marblehall, and so on.
But I can do it later when I write about your work again in another
place. For certainly I expect to do so.

. . . I am being moved from North Farm to the Mansion for the
month of September, since a new set are going to be settled here. This
weekend must be spent packing, sending half my things to storage,
taking mss. and music with me, and all. But I shall make quick work of
it and work there as well as I can. South Hill is going faster, all at once,
the plastering is begun, I should think that is a good sign. Every time I
see it, I am pleased with it, it really is my house and just the one I
wanted. And some day we will cook our supper on a charcoal grill in
that terrace fireplace, maybe with snow outside, and the fire shining
through the windows on it . . .

. . . To work, to work. It has always been later than I thought, but
now it is later than ever . . . still I expect to make the deadline this time,
the fourth for the novel . . . it just rolls along, I don't worry about it
any more; there is this about all that space, it allows such a long line of
continuity, and time for cumulative effect; and I always did know what
I wanted to say in this book, my mind hasn't changed, and how could I
write anything that didn't belong there? I trust myself, at last.

You trust yourself, too, darling. You are as good as there is in your
time, and you have a long way to go and to grow, I can't see the end of
it, thank God . . .

With my love,
K.A.

I missed her too, and a long life of correspondence started between
us, easygoing and as the spirit moved us—about reading, recipes,
anxieties and aspirations, garden seeds and gossip. She'd never let me
thank her for the Guggenheim, or Yaddo, or possibly even the Introduction, in any proper way. But *she* was a born thanker, for any

miscellaneous trifle that might come in the mail from me, wanting to make her laugh:

Yaddo, Saratoga Springs, New York

October 7, 1941

Dear Eudora:

The sugar cane arrived in the most mysterious style, fascinating to think about: in one very short piece with the address tag on it, and a long stalk simply accompanying it, with not even a piece of string on it, unaddressed, un-everything, independent, unattached, there was nothing to stop it from going on to some destination it might have liked better, or turning in its tracks and bolting back to Mississippi again. But no, it stuck to its companion, and came in as it were under its own steam. And how good it tastes: I am still occasionally sitting down with a sharp knife and stripping off a section and gnawing away at it. My father told me once that when he was a little boy, strange and new to Texas, he and his slightly elder brother ran away to Louisiana because they were so homesick for the sight and taste of sugar cane. I put that in a story once. I know better now just how they felt, though . . .

Katherine Anne

Doubleday was giving a party for *A Curtain of Green* in November, in New York, and of course Katherine Anne's presence was called for. "I take for granted in some strange way that I am to be in New York for your party, it doesn't seem possible that I should miss it," Katherine Anne wrote from Yaddo on October 19. But on November 5, a telegram followed to tell me in New York, where I'd already arrived:

Dear Eudora, be happy and gay at your coming out party and remember me just enough to console me a little for not being there. All the good luck and reward in the world to you. You deserve everything. I hope to see you there or here before you go home. With my love, Katherine Anne.

She continued to work on restoring South Hill, and finally a letter arrived, dated August 28, 1942, on handsome letter paper only slightly different a shade of blue from her familiar typing paper, imprinted with SOUTH HILL, R.D. 3, Ballston Spa, New York. It reads in part:

Dear Eudora:

This is the very first letter on the very first page of the letter paper, and this is the first day I have been here by myself. You can hardly imagine the confusion of household gear piled up here and there, but this nice south east room upstairs is in a bare and lovely order, with my table set up and the work-lamp ready, and when I look out I see the maples and the front meadow on my left and the corner of the sun room and part of the east meadow on the right.

. . . I must get settled in before the winter closes around us. Now you can think of me as here: Caroline Slade came this morning with a big, flat basket of vegetables from her garden, beautiful as a bouquet, every little carrot and tomato and celery head all washed and polished, and I put the parsley and some celery leaves in a bottle of sauterne vinegar at once, thinking you cannot begin too early with such things.

. . . Here all is weeds and unkemptedness, but the rosa regosa and white lilacs I planted in April are flourishing, it was a lucky rainy summer for I had to leave them to their fate almost at once. They didn't mind at all. They will be strong and fine for transplanting in the spring. They started as little dry sticks and are now green full little bushes. And so other things may go as well too . . .

For a few months her letters continued to be full of pleasure and happiness and invitations. But when winter arrived and closed her in, she grew too cold, and her old enemy pneumonia caught up with her and defeated her. South Hill, like some earlier dreams, but a dream completed this time, had to be put behind her.

By December 28, 1946, she was writing to me from Santa Monica, California. "I live within six blocks of the Pacific," she says. "Sometimes at midnight I hear that desperate creature beating its brains out on the beach, but musically. At last I have some of my books and music; this little place is like a birdcage, open and round, and I have sat here on the edge of my chair for a year, thinking any minute I may find a house of my own . . . I bought a little mountain top in the Mojave desert, after selling South Hill to the Willisons—did you read his *Saints and Strangers?* a fine piece of historical writing . . . I feel well. The novel is not finished, but I think now I have my road cleared a little, there is always so much to be done about other things, other people. But it does really seem that maybe I have reached the end of that, too."

1. The use of an ellipsis in K.A.P.'s letters, when the letters appear in their entirety, is her own. When I quote segments of her letters in passing, I have indicated by ellipsis that the quote is an excerpt.

2. My literary agent in New York in the newly formed firm of Russell & Volkening. Katherine Anne was considering his offer to act as her agent. But she preferred in the end acting on her own.

3. His and Rose Russell's second child, William.

4. This short novel was later published separately by Doubleday.

1990

Elizabeth Spencer

Eudora Welty: An Introduction

I was attending a college called Belhaven in Jackson, Miss., when *A Curtain of Green* appeared. Some of us there, getting a bit weary of our relentless education in how to become ladies, had taken up with literature and were well along with our own notions about it. I myself had recently got back to where I had started in the ignorant dreams of childhood, and was now daring to say again that I was going to be a Writer, yes, indeed, which is one way to get yourself elected president of the literary society; the other members being somewhat more cautious used to say they might decide to write, if they "had time," which meant, I guess, if they didn't get married right away or find something else more important to do. Our meetings were monthly; they lagged and got boring when nobody had a new story to read, and we used to sit there eating fudge squares and complaining about routine, which dulled our inspiration and blighted our native talent.

It gave us quite a pause to read in the paper when *A Curtain of Green* appeared that there was somebody right across the street (Belhaven is bordered on the South by Pinehurst Avenue) whose inspiration had not been dulled by routine and whose native talent was unblighted. We decided we ought to call her in for advice, or at least in order to look at her close up, always taking it for granted, I guess, that she would be more than delighted to look at *us*.

How it happened I don't recall—maybe we drew straws—but it fell my lot to invite her.

As the time approached for actually doing this, I grew more and more nervous. I don't think it would have bothered any of the other members to have picked up the phone and have respectfully invited Miss Welty to a meeting of the Belhaven Literary Society. I had consented to this because it mattered, but for that very reason it got harder every minute. When I finally dialed the Welty house I had to hang on to the receiver with two hands, both trembling. One of the world's softest voices said: "Hello." (Why I thought it would say anything else, is a mystery.) Somehow I got my message out: Would she come and talk to us? Well, no, she didn't make speeches. (Oh.) But, she would love to come and just be a guest . . . Could she possibly do that? The way she said it, it seemed the favor to grant was mine.

So of course she came, and it was a spring day on a lovely campus of a girl's school in the South, and we talked and we listened and we read and she said in a phrase or so what others might have taken up a whole evening for and of course everybody was enchanted with her, the only thing that can be said about any of her appearances anywhere, from way out West to way up East, from Oxford, Mississippi, to Oxford, England, from Mexico to Maine. (I don't really know if she's ever been to Mexico, but it sounded right to say that; and I know that if she has ever been there the Mexicans were enchanted.)

In respect to this, the writer and the work are one—I mean by that, not that she writes about herself (hardly ever if at all), but that her work in every way bears her special imprint, and one hears in it the soft precision of her writing voice, no less than in her spoken one. There are astounding accuracies in her fiction—it takes a Mississippian to know that best—even if everything suddenly flies sky high or hits the ceiling in one of her grand comic explosions where everything suffers a loss of the usual gravitational center—then it can be counted on to fly sky high or hit the ceiling, according to its own nature, after its own notion. She would put it, I suspect, that "everything is in place," and so it is. But there is also something she would never mention if she wrote a dozen books of essays and criticism, and that is her own special gift. I will try to mention it now, as best I may. It operates tirelessly from first to last of just about everything she writes because there is really no first to last about it—it is simply timeless: the golden air that breathes with, suspends, her work holds it forever without seeming to do anything; this is the lens of her seeing. I think of Jinny Love Carmichael momentarily left alone in the swamp near Moon Lake, feeling the swamp "all-enveloping, dark and at the same time, vivid, alarming—it was like being inside the chest of something that breathed and might turn over." I think of the cat named Cat who jumped from the table "like milk poured out of a bottle." I think it's about three o'clock on a hot afternoon when a metronome comes sailing over the fence from the strange house next door, whence many a time the sounds of "Für Elise" have come drifting, too. I could go on with samples forever, or close to it, and all would shine with the enchantment that to me is the heart of Eudora Welty's work.

Do you want me to say that she has won literary prizes by the dozen, including the Howells' Medal for Literature for *The Ponder Heart*, the Gold Medal of the American Academy of Arts and Letters for *The Optimist's Daughter*, and the Pulitzer Prize for *The Optimist's Daughter*? She has received honorary degrees by the bucket full, been given the most coveted fellowships and grants, served for six years on the National Council for the Arts, been accorded glowing critical recognition in England as well as in this country? I think we all know that, and that we know, too, that it is far from over.

But I'm talking today just as a Mississippian about a Mississippian. She has said a lot about place and the endowment it brings to fiction. "Place endows," she has firmly stated. This is a compliment to the place she undoubtedly loves, but there is the other side of it too. Eudora Welty has, to my mind, equally endowed place. We have feelings, we have knowledge, about her places now, that we could never have felt or known without her. A writer like Miss Welty leaves things the same but different, not reformed, heaven forbid, but different, because touched by her special alchemy. This did not come from place alone, but from her own gift, which this conference so far North has gathered to honor.

1979

Eudora Welty

Foreword to
The Stories of Elizabeth Spencer

Elizabeth Spencer is from North Mississippi and I am from Central Mississippi, so there needed to be a modest coincidence to bring us together. This occurred. Elizabeth came as a student to Belhaven College in Jackson and was unerringly made president of the Belhaven Literary Society; it was the year I published my first book, and I lived right across the street facing the College. Elizabeth made a telephone call to ask if I'd please step over to a session of the Literary Society so they could meet a real writer and seek my advice. It would have been unneighborly to stay home.

I met then a graceful young woman with a slender, vivid face, delicate and clearly defined features, dark blue eyes in which, then as now, you could read that Elizabeth Spencer was a jump ahead of you in what you were about to say. She did as nice Southern girls, literary or unliterary, were supposed to do in the Forties—looked pretty, had good manners (like mine, in coming when invited), and inevitably giggled (when in doubt, giggle). But the main thing about her was blazingly clear—this girl was serious. She was indeed already a writer.

As a matter of fact, she was all but the first writer I'd ever met, and the first who was younger than I was. (The other was Katherine Anne Porter.) Elizabeth offered me my first chance to give literary advice. But my instinct protected us both. This free spirit, anybody could tell, would do what she intended to do about writing. What else, and what better, could a writer know of another writer? It was all I was sure of about myself. I imagine she was glad not to get advice.

Instead of advising each other, we became friends. To leap over something like a decade's difference in age proved no more trouble to either than crossing Pinehurst Street. It wasn't long before Elizabeth herself, with degrees from Belhaven and Vanderbilt, published her own first book, the novel *Fire in the Morning:* she'd gone right on her way as she'd known she would, and as she always has.

In the Southern branching-out way, we met each other's families; in particular, Elizabeth and I appreciated each other's mothers. In Jackson in my family home, in Carrollton in her family home, and, over the years, on the Mississippi Gulf Coast, in New York, in Florence, in London, in Montreal where she lives now, sometimes by trustworthy coincidence and sometimes by lucky planning, we'd meet, and though we might not have written each other a line, we knew right where to take up the conversation. It was as refreshing as a picnic—indeed it often *was* a picnic, and we talked over lunch on the banks of the Pearl.

Even though Elizabeth dedicated her book of stories *Ship Island* to me, I see no reason why my pride in this honor should prevent me from giving expression to my joy in the timely appearance of this full collection. It is as her fellow writer that I see so well what is *unerring* about her writing. The good South, bestowing blessings at the cradle of storytellers, touched her most tenderly with the sense of place. Elizabeth evokes place and evokes it acutely in that place's own choice terms—take, for example, her story title "First Dark." She can faultlessly set the social scene; she takes delight in making her characters reveal themselves through the most precise and telling particulars. I think she would agree that Southern writers really don't have much excuse for writing vaguely or unobservantly or without enlightenment about human relationships, when they thrive in the thick of family life. They comprehend "identity" because it's unavoidable. One reason why Elizabeth has never hesitated in her writing is that she began by knowing who she is. In her scrutiny of recalcitrant human nature there's an element of participating joy in that nature's very stubbornness, or in the way it yields every time to the same old tunes. She cannot go wrong about the absurd. All these are Southern blessings—

perhaps. But equally valuable to this writer is a gift *not* characteristic of the Southerner: this is her capacity for cool detachment.

It was never surprising that she has felt well able, early on, to strike out from her Mississippi base, to find herself new territories: her fiction has consistently reached toward its own range, found its own scope, its own depth. What she'll do next, after the broad variety of her accomplishments, is still unpredictable.

It would have been as reckless to predict for Elizabeth as it would have been to offer her advice, and for the same good reason. Indeed, how *could* I have guessed, for one thing, that a schoolgirl so fragile-looking (though she went with a determined walk that made her hair bounce) could have had so much *power* to pour into her stories? Without any sacrifice of the sensitivity and the finely shaded perceptions we expect of her, her cool deliberateness to pull no punches will time after time take the reader by surprise. Katherine Mansfield stunned readers by a like combination of means; and I should say Elizabeth Spencer has earned with these stories a place in her rare company.

1980

Anne Tyler

The Fine Full World of Welty

In Eudora Welty's small full world, events float past as unexpectedly as furniture in a flood. A lady with her neck in a noose sails out of a tree; a stabbed woman folds in upon herself in silence; a child pushed off a diving board drops upright, seeming first to pause in the air before descending; a car rolls down an embankment, rocks in a net of grapevines, and arrives on the forest floor.

All violent acts, come to think of it—but not at first glance. They are so closely observed, so meticulously described that they appear eerily motionless, like a halted film. That child falling off the diving board, for instance: The lifeguard hangs his bugle "studiously" on a tree and retrieves her from the lake. He lays her on a picnic table, alongside a basket of tin cups and cutlery, and while he resuscitates her, another child with her poison ivy patches bandaged in dazzling white, fans her with a towel, and Mrs. Lizzie Stark, Camp Mother, arrives with a little black boy bearing two watermelons like twin babies. ("You can put those melons down," Mrs. Stark tells him. "Don't you see the table's got somebody on it?")

Or a young boy, spying on a vacant house, observes the following. While the watchman sleeps upstairs, his hat upon the bedpost, a sailor and his girlfriend lie on a mattress eating pickles, and an ancient lady strings the first-floor parlor with strips of paper. At next glance, the watchman's hat is seen to have turned on the bedpost "like a weather-cock"; the sailor and his girlfriend are chasing each other in circles;

the old woman holds a candle to the strips of paper, and two passing men, after breaking through a window, take a warmup jog around the dining room table, then charge on into the fire in the parlor.

Things happen, a girl in this story observes, like planets rising and setting, or like whole constellations spinning. And the town stays unsurprised, it simply watches people come and go, only hoping "to place them, in their hour or their street or the name of their mothers' people."

Placing, naming—isn't that why these stories work so well? Firmly pinned as butterflies, Eudora Welty's characters remain vivid after 30, 40 years, every dress fold and flash of eye caught perfectly: the deaf couple waiting in a railroad station, feeble-minded Lily Daw, old Phoenix Jackson traveling her eternal path through the pines. The running boards, rusty yard pumps, butter churns and powder-flash cameras have all but disappeared, but the people themselves remain so true that this volume, held in the hands, seems teeming with life. You can imagine that it's positively noisy, ringing as it does with voices laughing and scolding and gossiping, with the farmer calling out his buttermilk song and the Powerhouse band playing "Somebody Loves Me" and Virgie Rainey tinkling away on the Bijou picture-show piano.

The present collection contains all of Eudora Welty's published stories—four volumes' worth, along with two more recent stories not previously anthologized. *A Curtain of Green,* the first volume, was written in the 1930's. It contains some of her best-known pieces: "Why I Live at the P.O.," "Petrified Man" and "A Worn Path." *The Wide Net,* published in 1943, has for its motif the Natches Trace, which runs alike through tales of the old-time outlaws who traveled it and the modern townspeople now living near it. The effect is a kind of river of time—or perhaps, more accurately, timelessness. Place (always central to Eudora Welty's writing) makes insignificant the mere passage of years.

In *The Golden Apples* (1949), place again provides the link. Morgana, Mississippi, is the setting for six of its seven stories, and even in the one exception, Morgana is a presence so haunting—at least to us, the readers—that San Francisco, where a Morgana citizen has moved, seems foreign and bizarre and jarring. What a relief, upon finishing that story, to turn the page and find ourselves back in Morgana. And how poignant and oddly satisfying to see Snowdie's pesky twin boys change to ordinary, not-very-happy men, to watch the little girls from that camp on Moon Lake grow settled and brisk and domestic, while King MacLain becomes a senile old gentleman.

The stories in *The Bride of Innisfallen* (1955) move farther afield— to New Orleans, to Circe's island, to a boat train passing through Wales and a steamer bound for Naples. It's worrisome at first (will she still be Eudora Welty? the *real* Eudora Welty?), but not for long. Just look at the title story, where on a speeding train "two greyhounds in plaid blankets, like dangerously ecstatic old ladies hoping no one would see them, rushed into, out of, then past the corrider door. . . ." Yes, it's still Eudora Welty.

In the two stories not previously anthologized—"Where Is the Voice Coming From?" and "The Demonstrators"—the movement is less in place than in time. Both deal with the racial unrest of the '60's. Introducing them, Eudora Welty says that they "reflect the unease, the ambiguities, the sickness and desperation of those days in Mississippi." They do indeed; and they prove her to be the most faithful of mirrors. She writes about what *is,* not what ought to be. The "niggers" and "colored" of her '40's stories give way to the civil-rights leaders of the '60's. It's a whole little social history, offered without comment.

Now: Is she, in fact, a Southern writer? (Someone will be bound to ask.) Well, assuming there is such a thing, I believe she qualifies—not only through accident of birth and her characters' rhythms of speech but also because, in telling a story, she concerns herself less with what happens than with whom it happens *to,* and where. Everything must have its history, every element of the plot its leisurely, rocking-chair-paced (but never dull) examination.

Unlike Flannery O'Connor, she is kind, viewing her characters with genuine sympathy and affection. Or if unkind events occur, one senses that that's simply what happened, it's not a result of any willful twist from the author. She tells stories like a friend, someone you're fond of—sitting on her porch shelling peas, you imagine, and speaking up in the South, longingly gazing over the fence at the rich, tangled lives of the Southern neighbors—Eudora Welty was a window upon the world. If I wondered what went on in the country churches and "Colored Only" cafes, her writing showed me, as clearly as if I'd been invited inside.

But what seems obvious only now, with the sum total of these collected stories, is that Eudora Welty herself must once have felt the need for such a window. The children in her stories are all eyes, soaking up other people's lives, feeling for the slightest crack that might allow them to slip into another person's existence. Over and over, they observe and conjecture and catalog, file away their mental notes, have moments when they believe they're in somebody else's skin. It's tempting to link these children directly to their creator. Such unthinking watchfulness could, years afterward, lead to some uncannily wise story-telling.

"Making the jump," she calls it in her preface. "What I do in writing of any character," she says, "is to try to enter into the mind, heart and skin of a human being who is not myself. . . . It is the act of a writer's imagination that I set most high."

A jump it may be, but she knows better than anyone that it's a jump made by very small increments, requiring supreme patience. Tirelessly, unhurriedly she assembles her details: the frazzled peacock feather dangling from a lightbulb, the lost ball on the roof, ladies' luncheons of colored cream-cheese flowers, electric fans walking across the floor, cake plates decorated with "rowdy babies." Mother's Helper paregoric bottles, Sweet Dreams mosquito repellant. And the piano recitals where "some untalented little Maloney" hands out programs, the photographer's backdrop of "unrolled, yanked-down moonlight," the name of a long-dead woman spelled out across the lawn in narcissus bulbs, the movie-theater sign requiring a deposit for coming in to talk, the saucepan of zinnias in an open mailbox with a note attached to the handle.

And if that's still not enough, she will find a way to make you see. She will spin a phrase a certain way so you have to stop dead, astonished, and then think it over and nod and agree—and thinking it over, haven't you conjured up the scene for yourself? A thorny old rose twines around a pavilion "like the initial letter in a poetry book." On a spring day, the birds are "so busy you turned as you would at people as they plunged by." A woman passing a string of abandoned, boarded-up houses remarks that she is "walking in their sleep." A country man appears "home-made, as though his wife had self-consciously knitted or somehow contrived a husband when she sat alone at night." And a hat too big for the wearer "stood up and away from his head all around, and seemed only following him—on runners, perhaps like those cartridges for change in Spight's store."

Then suddenness—an arresting incongruity—further convinces us that all this must be fact. (She couldn't just make these things up, you can hear a reader thinking.) In a crowded house where a death has occurred, a visiting relative pounces on a random child and tickles her violently—"speaking soberly over her screams, 'Now wait. You don't know who I am.'"

People are involved in strangely peripheral activities (tie-dyeing scarves, trying on lipstick) at crucial moments or are caught by irrelevant sights, like the lavender soles of the lifeguard's feet or the black family's clothesline strung with cast-offs of the observer's relatives—his sister's golfing dress, wife's duster. More real than reality, these stories fairly breathe. We're taken in completely; we don't even raise an eyebrow, finally, when events as preposterous as miracles float by on the flood of her words.

The lighter stories are very, very funny—funny in their bones, as the best humor always is, so you'd have to read the entire story aloud from start to finish if someone asked why you were laughing. But how I'd love to be asked! Like a shot, I'd read "The Wide Net" with its motley collection of ne'er-do-wells joyfully assembling to drag the river. Yet on second thought, there's an undertone of sadness to that story, as there is to much of this collection. And some of the serious pieces can break your heart—the traveling salesman seeing, all at once, the vacancies in his life, or the little girl in "A Memory" constructing for herself, with infinite care, a small circle of protection against the ugly and pathetic outside world.

A few years ago, introducing a book of photographs she'd taken during the Depression, Eudora Welty remarked that her photos must have been attended by an angel of trust. Trust did seem to shine from those subjects' faces—black and poor though most of them were. It was a mark of an innocent time, she suggested; but of course, it was more than that. People know, somehow, whom to open up to, and imaginary people know as surely as real ones. In Eudora Welty's stories, characters present themselves hopefully and confidingly, believing that she'll do right by them. Their faith is not misplaced. Eudora Welty is one of our purest, finest, gentlest voices and this collection is something to be treasured.

1980

Anne Tyler

A Visit with Eudora Welty

She lives in one of those towns that seem to have outgrown themselves overnight, sprouting—on reclaimed swampland—a profusion of modern hospitals and real estate offices, travel agencies and a Drive-Thru Beer Barn. (She can remember, she says, when Jackson, Miss., was so small that you could go on foot anywhere you wanted. On summer evenings you'd pass 'the neighbors' lawns scented with petunias, hear their pianos through the open windows. Everybody's life was more accessible.) And when her father, a country boy from Ohio, built his family a house back in 1925, he chose a spot near Belhaven College so he'd be sure to keep a bit of green around them, but that college has added so many parking lots, and there are so many cars whizzing by nowadays.

Still, Eudora Welty's street is shaded by tall trees. Her driveway is a sheet of pine needles, and her house is dark and cool, with high ceilings, polished floors, comfortable furniture and a wonderfully stark old kitchen. She has lived here since she was in high school (and lived in Jackson all her life). Now she is alone, the last of a family of five. She loves the house, she says, but worries that she isn't able to keep it up properly: A porch she screened with $44 from the Southern Review, during the Depression, needs screening once again for a price so high that she has simply closed it off. One corner of the foundation has had to be rescued from sinking into the clay, which she describes as "shifting about like an elephant's hide."

148

But the house seems solid and well tended, and it's clear that she has the vitality to fill its spare rooms. Every flat surface is covered with tidy stacks of books and papers. A collection of widely varied paintings—each with its own special reason for being there—hangs on wires from the picture rails. One of them is a portrait of Eudora Welty as a young woman—blond-haired, with large and luminous eyes.

Her hair is white now, and she walks with some care and wears an Ace bandage around her wrist to ease a touch of arthritis. But the eyes are still as luminous as ever, radiating kindness and . . . attention, you would have to call it; but attention of a special quality, with some gentle amusement accompanying it. When she laughs, you can see how she must have looked as a girl—shy and delighted. She will often pause in the middle of a sentence to say, "Oh, I'm just enjoying this so much!" and she does seem to be that rare kind of person who takes an active joy in small, present moments. In particular, she is pleased by *words*, by ways of saying things, snatches of dialogue overheard, objects' names discovered and properly applied. (She likes to read technical manuals and diagrams with the parts labeled. Her whole face lights up when she describes how she heard a country woman confess to a "gnawing and a craving" for something. "Wasn't that a wonderful way of putting it?" she asks. "A gnawing and a craving.")

Even in conversation, the proper word matters deeply to her and is worth a brief pause while she hunts for it. She searches for a way to describe a recent heat wave: The heat, she says, was like something waiting for you, something out to *get* you; when you climbed the stairs at night, even the stair railing felt like, oh, like warm toast. She shares my fear of merging into freeway traffic because, she says, it's like entering a round of hot-pepper in a jump-rope game: "'Oh well,' you think, 'maybe the next time it comes by. . . .'" (I always did know freeways reminded me of something; I just couldn't decide what it was.) And when she re-read her collected stories, some of which date back to the 1930's: "It was the strangest experience. It was like watching a negative develop, slowly coming clear before your eyes. It was like recovering a memory."

A couple of her stories, she says, she really had wished to drop from the collection, but was persuaded not to. Others, the very earliest, were written in the days before she learned to rewrite ("I didn't know you *could* rewrite"), and although she left them as they were, she has privately revised her own printed copies by hand. Still others continue to satisfy her—especially those in "The Golden Apples"—and she laughs at herself for saying how much she loves "June Recital" and "The Wanderers." But her pleasure in these stories is, I think, part and parcel of her whole attitude toward writing: She sees it as truly, joyful work, as something she can hardly wait to get down to in the mornings.

Unlike most writers she imposes no schedule on herself. Instead she waits for things to "brood"—usually situations from her own life which, in time, are alchemized into something entirely different, with different characters and plots. From then on, it goes very quickly. She wakes early, has coffee and sets to work. She writes as long as she can keep at it, maybe pausing for a brief tomato sandwich at noon. (And she can tell you exactly who used to make the best tomato sandwiches in Jackson, back during her grade-school days when everybody swapped lunches. It was Frances MacWillie's grandmother, Mrs. Nannie MacWillie.)

What's written she types soon afterward; she feels that her handwriting is too intimate to re-read objectively. Then she scribbles revisions all over the manuscript, and cuts up parts of pages and pins them into different locations with dressmakers' pins—sometimes moving whole scenes, sometimes a single word. Her favorite working time is summer, when everything is quiet and it's "too hot to go forth" and she can sit next to an open window. (The danger is that any passing friend can interrupt her: "I saw you just sitting at your typewriter. . . .")

Describing the process of writing, she is matter-of-fact. It's simply her life's work, which has occupied her for more than 40 years. She speaks with calm faith of her own instincts, and is pleased to have been blessed with a visual mind—"the best shorthand a writer can have." When she's asked who first set her on her path (this woman who has, whether she knows it or not, set so many later writers on *their* paths), she says that she doesn't believe she ever did get anything from other writers. "It's the experience of living," she says—leaving unanswered, as I suppose she must, the question of just how she, and not some next-door neighbor, mined the stuff of books from the ordinary experiences of growing up in Jackson, Miss., daughter of an insurance man and a schoolteacher; of begging her brothers to teach her golf; bicycling to the library in two petticoats so the librarian wouldn't say, "I can see straight through you," and send her home; and spending her honor roll prize—a free pass—to watch her favorite third baseman play ball.

And where (she wonders aloud) did she get the idea she was bound to succeed as a writer, sending off stories on her own as she did and promptly receiving them back? How long would she have gone on doing that?

Fortunately, she didn't have to find out. Diarmuid Russell—then just starting as a literary agent—offered to represent her. He was downright *fierce* about representing her, at one time remarking that if a certain story were rejected, the editor "ought to be horsewhipped." (It wasn't rejected.) And there were others who took a special interest in her—notably the editor John Woodburn, and Katherine Anne Porter. (Katherine Anne Porter invited her to visit. Eudora Welty was so overwhelmed that she only got there after a false start, turning back at Natchez when her courage failed.) A photo she keeps from around this period shows a party honoring the publication of her first book: a tableful of admiring editors, a heartbreakingly young Diarmuid Russell, and in their midst Eudora Welty, all dressed up and wearing a corsage and looking like a bashful, charming schoolgirl. She does not admit to belonging to a literary community, but what she means is that she was never part of a formal circle of writers. You sense, in fact, that she would be uncomfortable in a self-consciously literary environment. (Once she went to the writers' colony at Yaddo but didn't get a thing done, and spent her time attending the races and "running around with a bunch of Spaniards." She'd suspected all along, she says, that a place like that wouldn't work out for her.)

Certainly, though, she has had an abundance of literary friendships, which she has preserved and cherished over the years. She speaks warmly of Robert Penn Warren; and she likes to recall how Reynolds Price, while still a Duke student, met her train in a pure white suit at 3 A.M. when she came to lead a workshop. But some other friends are

gone now. Elizabeth Bowen was especially dear to her. Katherine Anne
Porter's long illness and death have left her deeply saddened. And
Diarmuid Russell, she says, is someone she still thinks of every day of
her life.

In a profession where one's resources seem likely to shrink with
time (or so most writers fear), Eudora Welty is supremely indifferent
to her age. She says, when asked, that it does bother her a little that
there's a certain depletion of physical energy—that she can't make
unlimited appearances at colleges nowadays, much as she enjoys
doing that, and still have anything left for writing. (Colleges keep
inviting her because, she claims, "I'm so well-behaved, I'm always on
time and I don't get drunk or hole up in a motel with my lover.") But
it's plain that her *internal* energy is as powerful as ever. She credits the
examples she's seen around her: Elizabeth Bowen, who continued full
of curiosity and enthusiasm well into her 70's; and V. S. Pritchett, now
80, whose work she particularly admires. In fact, she says, the trouble
with publishing her collected stories is the implication that there won't
be any more—and there certainly will be, she says. She takes it as a
challenge.

She does not, as it turns out, go to those ladies' luncheons with the
tinted cream cheese flowers that she describes so well in her stories.
(I'd always wondered.) Her life in Jackson revolves around a few long-
time friends, with a quiet social evening now and then—somebody's
birthday party, say. Her phone rings frequently just around noon,
when it's assumed that she's finished her morning's work. And one
friend, an excellent cook, might drop off a dish she's prepared.

Nor is she entirely bound to Jackson. She loves to travel, and she
positively glows when describing her trips. "Oh, I would hate to be
confined," she says. Her only regret is that now you have to take the
plane. She remembers what it was like to approach the coast of Spain
by ship—to see a narrow pink band on the horizon and then hear the
tinkling of bells across the water.

When she talks like this, it's difficult to remember that I'm supposed
to be taking notes.

Is there anything she especially wants known about herself—anything she'd like a chance to say? Yes, she says, and she doesn't even

have to think about it: She wants to express her thankfulness for all those people who helped and encouraged her so long ago. "Reading my stories over," she says, "brings back their presence. I feel that I've been very lucky."

1980

Alice Walker

Eudora Welty: An Interview

It is a hot summer day in Jackson—97 degrees. In Eudora Welty's front yard the tallest oak tree I have ever seen in a yard covers the whole house with shade. It was planted by her father when she was a child. Inside, in the room she has chosen for this interview, a coolness comes from an air conditioner in the window, but also from the cool neutral colors of the room: white, eggshell, beige—dark brown floors and picture frames. There is solid quiet here, and space and light.

When we face each other, talking at first in starts, I think how odd it is that I feel entirely relaxed, entirely comfortable. Considering how different we are—in age, color, in the directions we have had to take in this life. I wonder if my relaxation means something terrible. For this *is* Mississippi, U.S.A., and black, white, old, young, Southern black and Southern white—all these labels have meaning for a very good reason: they have effectively kept us apart, sometimes brutally. So that, although we live in the same town, we inhabit different worlds. This interview itself is an accidental meeting. Though we are both writers, writing in some cases from similar experiences, and certainly from the same territory, we are more strangers, because the past will always separate us; and because she is white and not young, and I am black and not old. Still, I am undaunted, unafraid of discovering whatever I can.

She is modest, shy, quiet, and strong as the oak tree out in the yard. Life has made a face for her that concentrates a beauty in her eyes.

They light with directness, and will not be moved downward or to the side. She speaks softly and says she is hard of hearing. When the tape recorder collects nothing after spinning pleasantly for half an hour, she is sympathetic. Her understanding helps me recover from embarrassment. We go over, as best we can, the parts the tape recorder missed.

How many books have you written?
Well, I believe I've written eleven, counting the collections of short stories.

Do you write mostly short stories? Novels? Which do you like to write best?
I think I'm more of a natural short story writer. I've written many more short stories. In fact, the novels I've written usually began as short stories. And I then realized they were developing beyond the bounds of a story.

Do you feel that all short stories are potential novels?
No, they are two different things. I think that one of my faults as a novelist is that I don't think as a novelist does. I think the short story is a sustained thing, all in one piece, and compact. You don't have any of the expansion and scope that the novel can have. So any time I've made the mistake of writing a short story that became a novel I've had to go back and start at the beginning again. It's like starting for the long jump or the short hop. You don't have the same impulse.

Do you ever write poems?
No.

Never? Not any? Not even one or two?
Oh, maybe one. I don't think I count as a poet. I think poetry takes a very special gift. I do think the lyric impulse which is in poetry, is also in the other form.

Do you like any poets?
Oh yes, I do. I'm not too up on the new ones, although I've read a good many of the new ones. But I mostly turn to poets I've liked all

my life, such as Yeats, John Donne . . . I tend to go back to them, no matter what else I read.

How long did you live in New York City, and when was that?
Well, I went to school there for a year, at Columbia, which was the longest I've ever been there. And I have gone up and stayed many times for several weeks. Then one summer I worked on the *New York Times Book Review* for about three months; that was the longest time I've been there since I began working for my living.

You know Langston Hughes spent a year at Columbia too, in the twenties; one year. He hated it. He said the teachers were dull and the buildings looked like factories. Did you like it?
Oh, I enjoyed it. What I really went for was to learn my way around New York. I was taking a business course which took up almost no time and so I could go to the theatre every night!

A business course! I don't understand. Why did you take a business course?
Well, I'm glad I did. My father, when he learned I wanted to be a writer, very wisely said that I could never hope to earn a living at it, which turned out to be absolutely true. He said I should learn a business or profession that would keep me going. When I came home during the Depression I got a job at the radio broadcasting station and I also worked for the WPA.

And you took the pictures you collected in One Time, One Place *while working for the WPA?*
Yes. My father died that same year. I was thankful to get a job. Of course I was writing, at the same time. But although my stories from the first were given an encouraging welcome in college quarterlies and the so-called "little" magazines, they took six years of trying to find a place in a magazine of national circulation. It wasn't until the *Atlantic* took two and published them that the charm was broken. After that, some of the same stories that had been rejected by magazines before were accepted by those same magazines. Over all, I've always been lucky in publishing—in the people I've worked with, I mean, especially.

What did your parents think about you going to New York?
They knew it was what I wanted to do. They'd always believed in the value of gaining new experience. They were extraordinarily sympathetic parents both of them.

Did you think there was anything wrong with Mississippi [in terms of race] in those days, when you were young? Did you see a way in which things might change?
Well, I could tell when things were wrong with people, and when things happened to individual people, people that we knew or knew of, they were very real to me. It was the same with my parents. I felt their sympathy, I guess it guided mine, when they responded to these things in the same way. And I think this is the way real sympathy *has* to start—from direct feeling for something present and known. People are first and last individuals, and I don't think of them in the mass when I feel for them most.

How does living in Jackson affect your writing?
It's where I live and look around me—it's my piece of the world—it teaches me. Also as a domestic scene it's completely familiar and self-explanatory. It's not everything, though—it's just a piece of everything, that happens to be my sample. It lets me alone to work as I like. It's full of old friends with whom I'm happy to be. And I'm not stuck, either, not compelled to stay here—I'm free to leave when I feel like it, which makes me love it more, I suppose.

What do your friends think of your writing? Do they read it? Do any of them ever creep into your fiction?
Oh yes. They do read it. But they don't creep in. I never write about people that I know. I don't want to, and couldn't if I did want to. I work entirely in terms of the imagination—using, of course, bits and pieces of the real world along with the rest.

Do you write every day?
No, I don't write every day—I write only when I'm in actual work on a particular story. I'm not a notebook keeper. Sustained time is what I fight for, would probably sell my soul for—it's so hard to manage that. I'd like to write a story from beginning to end right through without having to stop. Where I write is upstairs in my bedroom.

In bed?
Oh no, I write at a desk. I have a long room with six big windows in it, and a desk and typewriter at one end.

What does it overlook? A garden? Trees?
It overlooks the street. I like to be aware of the world going on while I'm working. I think I'd get claustrophobic sitting in front of a blank wall with life cut off from view.

Do you have a "Philosophy of Life"? Some pithy saying that you quote to yourself when you seem inundated with troubles?
No. I have work in place of it, I suppose. My "philosophy" is like the rest of my thinking—it comes out best in the translation of fiction. I put what I think about people and their acts in my stories. Of course back of it all there would have to be honesty.

Many modern writers don't seem overly concerned with it.
It's noticeable. Truth doesn't seem to be the thing they're getting at, a good deal of the time.

In fact, much popular poetry, some of it black, engages in clever half-truths, designed to shock only. Or to entertain.
Some of the black poets I've read I have not been able to understand. It hasn't so far as I know anything to do with race. I don't quite under-stand the virtue of the idiom they strain so over, the language—I don't see the good of it. I feel *tactics* are being used on me, the reader—not the easiest way to persuade *this* reader. It's hard to see the passion behind it.

Oh, I understand the idiom and the language; I can see the passion behind it and admire the rage. My question is whether witty half-truths are good for us in the long run, after we've stopped laughing. And whether poetry shouldn't stick to more difficult if less funny ground, the truth.
That's its real business. I don't believe any writing that has falsity in it can endure for very long. It's end will take care of itself.

Let's hope. What are your thoughts on the Women's Movement?
Well, equal pay for equal work, and so on, fine. But some of the other stuff is hilarious.

*Hilarious? Oh, you mean "the lunatic fringe," the flamboyant stances
used to attract attention.*
Some of the effervescences. Of course, I haven't any bones to pick,
myself. A writer never has the problem to face. Being a woman has
never kept me from writing or from finding publication for my work.

*That's interesting. In the course I teach on black women writers I find
that in critical studies black women writers are always given scant
attention and sometimes none. They may have published with ease, as
Zora Hurston did, but later they were forgotten. Until quite recently,
of course. Of course to many women your life would seem ideal, you
have your work, which is substantial, both in what it gives you and
what it gives others. You have a house of your own—a lovely one—
and all the freedom you want. You are rare, a successful writer who is
a woman!*
Well, I do have freedom. The successful part is not so much to the
point. I think that any artist has it over other people.

*Well, some women artists feel that when they marry they must share
too much of their time with their husbands and children. They feel
they lose single-mindedness, energy they need to put into their own
work.*
That of course I couldn't say—about husbands and children, I mean.
But my tendency is to believe that all experience is an enrichment
instead of an impoverishment. My own relationships with people are
the things that mean the most to me. I couldn't say what marriage and
childbearing would do, of course.

*But have you regretted not having been married and not having chil-
dren?*
Oh, I would have been glad if it had come along. Yes I would have. Of
course. It wasn't a matter of choosing one thing in place of the other. I
think the more things the better.

*Over the years have you known any black women? Really known
them?*
I think I have. Better in Jackson than anywhere, though only, as you'd
expect, within the framework of the home. That's the only way I'd

have had a chance, in the Jackson up until now. Which doesn't take away from the reality of the knowledge, or its depth of affection—on the contrary. A schoolteacher who helped me on weekends to nurse my mother through a long illness—she was beyond a nurse, she was a friend and still is, we keep in regular touch. A very bright young woman, who's now in a very different field of work, began in her teens as a maid in our house. She was with us for ten years or more. Then she went on to better things—her story is a very fine one. She's a friend, and we are in regular touch too. Of course I've met black people professionally, in my experience along the fringes of teaching. Lecturing introduced us. The first college anywhere, by the way, that ever invited me to speak was Jackson State—years ago. I read them a story in chapel, as I remember. Now I don't count meeting people at cocktail parties in New York—black or any other kind—to answer the rest of your question. But I do know at least a few black people that mean a good deal to me, and I think they like me too.

Have any of them ever crept into your fiction?
No. As I said before, I never write about real people. You know, human beings are incapable of being made into characters, as is. They are so much more fluid, and so opaque in places where they need to be transparent and so transparent in places where they need to be opaque. But I think that what I put into a short story in the form of characters might be called certain *qualities* of people in certain situations—no, pin it down more—some quality that makes them unique. I try to dramatize something like this in a way that can show it better than life shows it. Better picked out.

Has it ever been assumed that because you were born and raised in Mississippi your black characters would necessarily suffer from a racist perspective?
I hardly see how anyone could claim that. Indeed to my knowledge no one ever has. I see all my characters as individuals, not as colors, but as people, alive—unique.

Have you ever been called a Gothic Writer?
They better not call me that!

No?
Yes, I have been, though. Inevitably, because I'm a Southerner. I've

never had anybody call me that to my face. I've read that I'm Gothic, or I get asked by students to explain why I am.

Why do they try to put all Southern writers in that mold?
I don't know. It's just easy.

I was never even sure of what it meant, exactly.
I'm not sure either. When I hear the word I see in my mind a Gustave Dore illustration for "The Fall of the House of Usher." Anyway it sounds as if it has nothing to do with real life, and I feel that my work has something to do with real life. At least I hope it has.

Do you do much publicity for your books?
No, I don't do any. Never have done. I've had sympathetic editors who wouldn't try to get me to "appear."

Did you ever meet Langston Hughes?
No. I guess he would have been before my day, really.

But he just died in 1967. He was sixty-five, but he never grew old.
I wish I had. He was the first, one of the first, poets, I ever read, down here at the library, and I loved his work.

What are you working on now?
Well, I'm not doing anything except thinking. I haven't got anything on paper yet. I've got many things that I want to write, and expect to write.

How long does it take you to write a novel like Losing Battles?
Different things take different lengths of time. It took me a long time to write *Losing Battles* . . .

It's a long book.
. . . and I was doing a lot of other things too. I do rewrite a good deal and I write carefully and I'm not satisfied with things for a long time. Maybe I keep things too long. You have to know when to quit, you know. That's one of the things I'm least sure about in my work, one of the most important things.

Are you leaving your books and papers and manuscripts to a school?
Well, the Department of Archives and History here in Jackson has everything. I started giving them my papers a long time ago. That

bunch of stuff over there on the table is on its way to them. I like having my things in Mississippi. Of course many universities do try to collect a writer's papers and books, and that's a good thing. I think the important thing is to try to have everything in one place. Think about Mr. Faulkner, whose work is spread from one end of the country to the other.

Yes. Or of Richard Wright, whose work is spread all over this country and France too, from what I hear.
Or many others.

Was The Optimist's Daughter, *the whole thing, in the* New Yorker *before it became a book?*
It was the finished story, but I later worked on it some more. I mean I didn't take out any of the book to publish it in the *New Yorker*. I wrote it first just as it came out in the magazine. But I still had that feeling that I didn't want to let it go. I added a little to it, eventually expanded it—in the interests of precision, really. It's the same story, just more so. And I suppose too there are millions, well, hundreds, of small changes that nobody would know but me. Maybe just a modification of a word, the transposition of a sentence—important to the author, though.

Have you gotten many awards and grants?
Yes. I've been lucky that way, which is a fine thing. Now, I think, authors get paid tremendous sums—I don't mean writers like us (laughter) . . . but you know it was a great help back in the forties, fifties and sixties too, to have a grant. What it meant was that that year you wouldn't have to teach a class or give lectures or something. It buys you time. And anything that buys you time is God-given. God-sent.

Are you able to support yourself entirely by your writing?
At the present I am. Because this last book (*The Optimist's Daughter*), and the one before that (*Losing Battles*) did very well—I'm still speaking in terms of the kind of writer I am, not as a "seller." I just mean that I can get along all right this year. I think. Touch wood. But I hope to keep on, selling stories . . . writing.
I think it's possible to support yourself by writing, but it is the most

precarious livelihood in the world. Of course my father couldn't have been more right. For example, I said that my novel, *Losing Battles,* did very well, but I suppose it represents eight or ten years of work. During which time you don't get anything. You get a lump sum of money for a novel but that could be five years of working during which you have to support yourself, so it really isn't a way to earn a living.

Did you teach at a local college at one time?
At Millsaps. I asked them for a job, because it was when my mother was ill and I couldn't leave home to do lectures. I needed a job of that same sort that I could do and still live at home. So it was *just* wonderful.

They must have been delighted to get you.
Well, *I* was delighted. I had a grand class. Just grand. I had about sixteen students. And I still see lots of them, too. They look me up when they come through town. One of them brings me a big watermelon from Smith County every summer. That makes a writer feel good!

1973

Alice Walker

Zora Neale Hurston:
A Cautionary Tale and a Partisan View

I became aware of my need of Zora Neale Hurston's work some time before I knew her work existed. In late 1970 I was writing a story that required accurate material on voodoo practices among rural Southern blacks of the thirties; there seemed none available I could trust. A number of white, racist anthropologists and folklorists of the period had, not surprisingly, disappointed and insulted me. They thought blacks inferior, peculiar, and comic, and for me this undermined, no, *destroyed,* the relevance of their books. Fortunately, it was then that I discovered *Mules and Men,* Zora's book on folklore, collecting herself, and her small, all-black community of Eatonville, Florida. Because she immersed herself in her own culture even as she recorded its "big old lies," i.e., folk tales, it was possible to see how she and it (even after she had attended Barnard College and become a respected writer and apprentice anthropologist) fit together. The authenticity of her material was verified by her familiarity with its context, and I was soothed by her assurance that she was exposing not simply an adequate culture but a superior one. That black people can be on occasion peculiar and comic was knowledge she enjoyed. That they could be racially or culturally inferior to whites never seems to have crossed her mind.

The first time I heard Zora's *name,* I was auditing a black-literature class taught by the great poet Margaret Walker, at Jackson State College in Jackson, Mississippi. The reason this fact later slipped my mind was that Zora's name and accomplishments came and went so fast. The class was studying the usual "giants" of black literature: Chestnutt, Toomer, Hughes, Wright, Ellison, and Baldwin, with the hope of reaching LeRoi Jones very soon. Jessie Fauset, Nella Larsen, Ann Petry, Paule Marshall (unequaled in intelligence, vision, craft by anyone of her generation, to put her contributions to our literature modestly), and Zora Neale Hurston were names appended, like verbal footnotes, to the illustrious all-male list that paralleled them. As far as I recall, none of their work was studied in the course. Much of it was out of print, in any case, and remains so. (Perhaps Gwendolyn Brooks and Margaret Walker herself were exceptions to this list; both poets of such obvious necessity it would be impossible to overlook them. And their work—owing to the political and cultural nationalism of the sixties—was everywhere available.)

When I read *Mules and Men* I was delighted. Here was this perfect book! The "perfection" of which I immediately tested on my relatives, who are such typical black Americans they are useful for every sort of political, cultural, or economic survey. Very regular people from the South, rapidly forgetting their Southern cultural inheritance in the suburbs and ghettos of Boston and New York, they sat around reading the book themselves, listening to me read the book, listening to each other read the book, and a kind of paradise was regained. For what Zora's book did was this: it gave them back all the stories they had forgotten or of which they had grown ashamed (told to us years ago by our parents and grandparents—not one of whom could *not* tell a story to make you weep, or laugh) and showed how marvelous, and, indeed, priceless, they are. This is not exaggerated. No matter how they read the stories Zora had collected, no matter how much distance they tried to maintain between themselves, as new sophisticates, and the lives their parents and grandparents lived, no matter how they tried to remain cool toward all Zora revealed, in the end they could not hold back the smiles, the laughter, the joy over who she was showing them to be: descendants of an inventive, joyous, courageous, and outrageous people; loving drama, appreciating wit, and, most of all, relishing the pleasure of each other's loquacious and *bodacious* company.

This was my first indication of the quality I feel is most charac-

teristic of Zora's work: racial health; a sense of black people as complete, complex, *undiminished* human beings, a sense that is lacking in
so much black writing and literature. (In my opinion, only Du Bois
showed an equally consistent delight in the beauty and spirit of black
people, which is interesting when one considers that the angle of his
vision was completely the opposite of Zora's.) Zora's pride in black
people was so pronounced in the ersatz black twenties that it made
other blacks suspicious and perhaps uncomfortable (after all, they
were still infatuated with things European). Zora was interested in
Africa, Haiti, Jamaica, and—for a little racial diversity (Indians)—
Honduras. She also had a confidence in herself as an individual that
few people (anyone?), black or white, understood. This was because
Zora grew up in a community of black people who had enormous
respect for themselves and for their ability to govern themselves. Her
own father had written the Eatonville town laws. This community
affirmed her right to exist, and loved her as an extension of its self. For
how many other black Americans is this true? It certainly isn't true for
any that I know. In her easy self-acceptance, Zora was more like an
uncolonized African than she was like her contemporary American
blacks, most of whom believed, at least during their formative years,
that their blackness was something wrong with them.

On the contrary, Zora's early work shows she grew up pitying
whites because the ones she saw lacked "light" and soul. It is impossible to imagine Zora envying anyone (except tongue in cheek), and
least of all a white person for being white. Which is, after all, if one is
black, a clear and present calamity of the mind.

Condemned to a desert island for life, with an allotment of ten
books to see me through, I would choose, unhesitatingly, two of
Zora's: *Mules and Men,* because I would need to be able to pass on to
younger generations the life of American blacks as legend and myth;
and *Their Eyes Were Watching God,* because I would want to enjoy
myself while identifying with the black heroine, Janie Crawford, as she
acted out many roles in a variety of settings, and functioned (with
spectacular results!) in romantic and sensual love. *There is no book
more important to me than this one* (including Toomer's *Cane,* which
comes close, but from what I recognize is a more perilous direction).

Having committed myself to Zora's work, loving it, in fact, I became curious to see what others had written about her. This was, for the young, impressionable, barely begun writer I was, a mistake. After reading the misleading, deliberately belittling, inaccurate, and generally irresponsible attacks on her work and her life by almost everyone, I became for a time paralyzed with confusion and fear. For if a woman who had given so much of obvious value to all of us (and at such risks: to health, reputation, sanity) could be so casually pilloried and consigned to a sneering oblivion, what chance would someone else—for example, myself—have? I was aware that I had much less gumption than Zora.

For a long time I sat looking at this fear, and at what caused it. Zora was a woman who wrote and spoke her mind—as far as one could tell, practically always. People who knew her and were unaccustomed to this characteristic in a woman, who was, moreover, a. sometimes in error, and b. successful, for the most part, in her work, attacked her as meanly as they could. Would I also be attacked if I wrote and spoke my mind? And if I dared open my mouth to speak, must I always be "correct"? And by whose standards? Only those who have read the critics' opinions of Zora and her work will comprehend the power of these questions to riddle a young writer with self-doubt.

Eventually, however, I discovered that I repudiate and despise the kind of criticism that intimidates rather than instructs the young; and I dislike fear, especially in myself. I did then what fear rarely fails to force me to do: I fought back. I began to fight for Zora and her work; for what I knew was good and must not be lost to us.

Robert Hemenway was the first critic I read who seemed indignant that Zora's life ended in poverty and obscurity; that her last days were spent in a welfare home and her burial paid for by "subscription." Though Zora herself, as he is careful to point out in his book *Zora Neale Hurston: A Literary Biography,* remained gallant and unbowed until the end. It was Hemenway's efforts to define Zora's legacy and his exploration of her life that led me, in 1973, to an overgrown Fort Pierce, Florida graveyard in an attempt to locate and mark Zora's grave. Although by that time I considered her a native American genius, there was nothing grand or historic in my mind. It was, rather, a duty I accepted as naturally mine—as a black person, a woman, and a writer—because Zora was dead and I, for the time being, was alive.

Zora was funny, irreverent (she was the first to call the Harlem Renaissance literati the "niggerati"), good-looking, sexy, and once sold hot dogs in a Washington park just to record accurately how the black people who bought the hot dogs talked. (A letter I received a month ago from one of her old friends in D.C. brought this news.) She would go anywhere she had to go: Harlem, Jamaica, Haiti, Bermuda, to find out anything she simply had to know. She loved to give parties. Loved to dance. Would wrap her head in scarves as black women in Africa, Haiti, and everywhere else have done for centuries. On the other hand, she loved to wear hats, tilted over one eye, and pants and boots. (I have a photograph of her in pants, boots, and broadbrim that was given to me by her brother, Everette. She has her foot up on the running board of a car—presumably hers, and bright red—and looks racy.) She would light up a fag—which wasn't done by ladies then (and, thank our saints, as a young woman she was never a lady) on the street.

Her critics disliked even the "rags" on her head. (They seemed curiously incapable of telling the difference between an African-American queen and Aunt Jemima.) They disliked her apparent sensuality: the way she tended to marry or not marry men, but enjoyed them anyway—while never missing a beat in her work. They hinted slyly that Zora was gay, or at least bisexual—how else could they account for her drive? Though there is not, perhaps unfortunately, a shred of evidence that this was true. The accusation becomes humorous—and of course at all times irrelevant—when one considers that what she did write was one of the sexiest, most "healthily" rendered heterosexual love stories in our literature. In addition, she talked too much, got things from white folks (Guggenheims, Rosenwalds, and footstools) much too easily, was slovenly in her dress, and appeared maddeningly indifferent to other people's opinions of her. With her easy laughter and her Southern drawl, her belief in doing "cullud" dancing authentically, Zora seemed—among these genteel "New Negroes" of the Harlem Renaissance—*black*. No wonder her presence was always a shock. Though almost everyone agreed she was a delight, not everyone agreed such audacious black delight was permissible, or, indeed, quite the proper image for the race.

Zora was before her time, in intellectual circles, in the life style she chose. By the sixties everyone understood that black women could wear beautiful cloths on their beautiful heads and care about the authenticity of things "cullud" and African. By the sixties it was no longer a crime to receive financial assistance—in the form of grants and fellowships—for one's work. (Interestingly, those writers who complained that Zora "got money from white folks" were often themselves totally supported, down to the food they ate—or, in Langston Hughes's case, *tried* to eat, after his white "Godmother" discarded him—by white patrons.) By the sixties, nobody cared that marriage didn't last forever. No one expected it to. And I do believe that now, in the seventies, we do not expect (though we may wish and pray) every black person who speaks *always* to speak *correctly* (since this is impossible): and if we do expect it, we deserve all the silent leadership we are likely to get.

During the early and middle years of her career Zora was a cultural revolutionary simply because she was always herself. Her work, so vigorous among the rather pallid productions of many of her contemporaries, comes from the essence of black folk life. During her later life she became frightened of the life she had always dared bravely before. Her work too became reactionary, static, shockingly misguided and timid. (This is especially true of her last novel, *Seraphs on the Sewannee*, which is not even about black people, which is no crime, but *is* about white people for whom it is impossible to care, which is.)

A series of misfortunes battered Zora's spirit and her health. And she was broke.

Being broke made all the difference.

Without money of one's own in a capitalist society, there is no such thing as independence. This is one of the clearest lessons of Zora's life, and why I consider the telling of her life "a cautionary tale." We must learn from it what we can.

Without money, an illness, even a simple one, can undermine the will. Without money, getting into a hospital is problematic and getting out without money to pay for the treatment is nearly impossible. Without money, one becomes dependent on other people, who are likely to be—even in their kindness—erratic in their support and despotic in their expectations of return. Zora was forced to rely, like Tennessee Williams's Blanche, "on the kindness of strangers." Can anything be more dangerous, if the strangers are forever in control? Zora, who worked so hard, was never able to make a living from her work.

She did not complain about not having money. She was not the type. (Several months ago I received a long letter from one of Zora's nieces, a bright ten-year-old, who explained to me that her aunt was so proud that the only way the family could guess she was ill or without funds was by realizing they had no idea where she was. Therefore, none of the family attended either Zora's sickbed or her funeral.) Those of us who have had "grants and fellowships from 'white folks' " know this aid is extended in precisely the way welfare is extended in Mississippi. One is asked, *curtly,* more often than not: How much do you need *just to survive?* Then one is—if fortunate—given a third of that. What is amazing is that Zora, who became an orphan at nine, a runaway at fourteen, a maid and manicurist (because of necessity and not from love of the work) before she was twenty—with one dress—managed to become Zora Neale Hurston, author and anthropologist, at all.

For me, the most unfortunate thing Zora ever wrote is her auto-biography. After the first several chapters, it rings false. One begins to hear the voice of someone whose life required the assistance of too many transitory "friends." A Taoist proverb states that *to act sincerely with the insincere is dangerous.* (A mistake blacks as a group have tended to make in America.) And so we have Zora sincerely offering gratitude and kind words to people one knows she could not have respected. But this unctuousness, so out of character for Zora, is also a result of dependency, a sign of her powerlessness, her inability to pay back her debts with anything but words. They must have been bitter ones for her. In her dependency, it should be remembered, Zora was not alone—because it is quite true that America does not support or honor us as human beings, let alone as blacks, women, and artists. We have taken help where it was offered because we are committed to what we do and to the survival of our work. Zora was committed to the survival of her people's cultural heritage as well.

In my mind, Zora Neale Hurston, Billie Holiday, and Bessie Smith form a sort of unholy trinity. Zora *belongs* in the tradition of black women singers, rather than among "the literati," at least to me. There were the extreme highs and lows of her fire, her undaunted pursuit of adventure, passionate emotional and sexual experience, and her love of freedom. Like Billie and Bessie she followed her own road, believed in her own gods, pursued her own dreams, and refused to separate herself from "common" people. It would have been nice if the three of them had had one another to turn to, in times of need. I close my eyes and imagine them: Bessie would be in charge of all the money; Zora would keep Billie's masochistic tendencies in check and prevent her from singing embarrassing anything-for-a-man songs, thereby preventing Billie's heroin addiction. In return, Billie could be, along with Bessie, the family that Zora felt she never had.

We are a people. A people do not throw their geniuses away. And if they are thrown away, it is our duty *as artists and as witnesses for the future* to collect them again for the sake of our children, and, if necessary, bone by bone.

1979

Alice Walker

Beyond the Peacock:
The Reconstruction
of Flannery O'Connor

It was after a poetry reading I gave at a recently desegregated college in Georgia that someone mentioned that in 1952 Flannery O'Connor and I had lived within minutes of each other on the same Eatonton-to-Milledgeville road. I was eight years old in 1952 (she would have been 28) and we moved away from Milledgeville after less than a year. Still, since I have loved her work for many years, the coincidence of our having lived near each other intrigued me, and started me thinking of her again.

As a college student in the sixties I read her books endlessly, scarcely conscious of the difference between her racial and economic background and my own, but put them away in anger when I discovered that, while I was reading O'Connor—Southern, Catholic, and white—there were other women writers—some Southern, some religious, all black—I had not been allowed to know. For several years, while I searched for, found, and studied black women writers, I deliberately shut O'Connor out, feeling almost ashamed that she had reached me first. And yet, even when I no longer read her, I missed her, and realized that though the rest of America might not mind, having endured it so long, I would never be satisfied with a segregated literature. I would have to read Zora Hurston *and* Flannery O'Connor, Nella Larsen *and* Carson McCullers, Jean Toomer *and* William Faulkner, before I could begin to feel *well* read at all.

I thought it might be worthwhile, in 1974, to visit the two houses,

Flannery O'Connor's and mine, to see what could be learned twenty-two years after we moved away and ten years after her death. It seemed right to go to my old house first—to set the priorities of vision, so to speak—and then to her house, to see, at the very least, whether her peacocks would still be around. To this bit of nostalgic exploration I invited my mother, who, curious about peacocks and abandoned houses, if not about literature and writers, accepted.

In her shiny new car, which at sixty-one she has learned to drive, we cruised down the wooded Georgia highway to revisit our past.

At the turnoff leading to our former house, we face a fence, a gate, a NO TRESPASSING SIGN. The car will not fit through the gate and beyond the gate is muddy pasture. It shocks me to remember that when we lived here we lived, literally, in a pasture. It is a memory I had repressed. Now, for a moment, it frightens me.

"Do you think we should enter?" I ask.

But my mother has already opened the gate. To her, life has no fences, except, perhaps, religious ones, and these we have decided not to discuss. We walk through pines rich with vines, fluttering birds, and an occasional wild azalea showing flashes of orange. The day is bright with spring, the sky cloudless, the road rough and clean.

"I would like to see old man Jenkins [who was our landlord] come bothering me about some trespassing," she says, her head extremely up. "He never did pay us for the crop we made for him in fifty-two."

After five minutes of leisurely walking, we are again confronted with a fence, fastened gate, POSTED signs. Again my mother ignores all three, unfastens the gate, walks through.

"He never gave me my half of the calves I raised that year either," she says. And I chuckle at her memory and her style.

Now we are facing a large green rise. To our left calves are grazing; beyond them there are woods. To our right there is the barn we used, looking exactly as it did twenty-two years ago. It is high and weathered silver and from it comes the sweet scent of peanut hay. In front of it, a grove of pecans. Directly in front of us over the rise is what is left of the house.

"Well," says my mother, "it's still standing. And," she adds with wonder, "just look at my daffodils!"

In twenty-two years they have multiplied and are now blooming from one side of the yard to the other. It is a typical abandoned sharefarmer shack. Of the four-room house only two rooms are left; the others have rotted away. These two are filled with hay.

Considering the sad state of the house it is amazing how beautiful its setting is. There is not another house in sight. There are hills, green pastures, a ring of bright trees, and a family of rabbits hopping out of our way. My mother and I stand in the yard remembering. I remember only misery: going to a shabby segregated school that was once the state prison and that had, on the second floor, the large circular print of the electric chair that had stood there; almost stepping on a water moccasin on my way home from carrying water to my family in the fields; losing Phoebe, my cat, because we left this place hurriedly and she could not be found in time.

"Well, old house," my mother says, smiling in such a way that I almost see her rising, physically, above it, "one good thing you gave us. It was right here that I got my first washing machine!"

In fact, the only pleasant thing I recall from that year was a field we used to pass on our way into the town of Milledgeville. It was like a painting by someone who loved tranquillity. In the foreground near the road the green field was used as pasture for black-and-white cows that never seemed to move. Then, farther away, there was a steep hill partly covered with kudzu—dark and lush and creeping up to cover and change fantastically the shapes of the trees. . . . When we drive past it now, it looks the same. Even the cows could be the same cows—though now I see that they *do* move, though not very fast and never very far.

What I liked about this field as a child was that in my life of nightmares about electrocutions, lost cats, and the surprise appearance of snakes, it represented beauty and unchanging peace.

"Of course," I say to myself, as we turn off the main road two miles from my old house, "that's Flannery's field." The instructions I've been given place her house on the hill just beyond it.

There is a garish new Holiday Inn directly across Highway 441 from Flannery O'Connor's house, and, before going up to the house, my mother and I decide to have something to eat there. Twelve years ago I could not have bought lunch for us at such a place in Georgia, and I feel a weary delight as I help my mother off with her sweater and hold out a chair by the window for her. The white people eating lunch all around us—staring though trying hard not to—form a blurred backdrop against which my mother's face is especially sharp. *This* is the proper perspective, I think, biting into a corn muffin; no doubt about it.

As we sip iced tea we discuss O'Connor, integration, the inferiority of the corn muffins we are nibbling, and the care and raising of pea-cocks.

"Those things will sure eat up your flowers," my mother says, explaining why she never raised any.

"Yes," I say, "but they're a lot prettier than they'd be if somebody human had made them, which is why this lady liked them." This idea has only just occurred to me, but having said it, I believe it is true. I sit wondering why I called Flannery O'Connor a lady. It is a word I rarely use and usually by mistake, since the whole notion of ladyhood is repugnant to me. I can imagine O'Connor at a Southern social affair, looking very polite and being very bored, making mental notes of the absurdities of the evening. Being white she would automatically have been eligible for ladyhood, but I cannot believe she would ever really have joined.

"She must have been a Christian person then," says my mother. "She believed He made everything." She pauses, looks at me with tolerance but also as if daring me to object: "And she was *right,* too."

"She was a Catholic," I say, "which must not have been comfortable in the Primitive Baptist South, and more than any other writer she believed in everything, including things she couldn't see."

"Is that why you like her?" she asks.

"I like her because she could *write,*" I say.

"'Flannery' sounds like something to eat," someone said to me once. The word always reminds me of flannel, the material used to make nightgowns and winter shirts. It is very Irish, as were her ancestors. Her first name was Mary, but she seems never to have used it. Certainly "Mary O'Connor" is short on mystery. She was an Aries, born March 25, 1925. When she was sixteen, her father died of lupus, the disease that, years later, caused her own death. After her father died,

O'Connor and her mother, Regina O'Connor, moved from Savannah, Georgia, to Milledgeville, where they lived in a townhouse built for Flannery O'Connor's grandfather, Peter Cline. This house, called "the Cline house," was built by slaves who made the bricks by hand. O'Connor's biographers are always impressed by this fact, as if it adds the blessed sign of aristocracy, but whenever I read it I think that those slaves were some of my own relatives, toiling in the stifling middle-Georgia heat, to erect her grandfather's house, sweating and suffering the swarming mosquitoes as the house rose slowly, brick by brick.

Whenever I visit antebellum homes in the South, with their spacious rooms, their grand staircases, their shaded back windows that, without the thickly planted trees, would look out onto the now vanished slave quarters in the back, this is invariably my thought. I stand in the backyard gazing up at the windows, then stand at the windows inside looking down into the backyard, and between the me that is on the ground and the me that is at the windows, History is caught.

O'Connor attended local Catholic schools and then Georgia Women's College. In 1945 she received a fellowship to the Writer's Workshop at the University of Iowa. She received her M.A. in 1947. While still a student she wrote stories that caused her to be recognized as a writer of formidable talent and integrity of craft. After a stay at Yaddo, the artists' colony in upstate New York, she moved to a furnished room in New York City. Later she lived and wrote over a garage at the Connecticut home of Sally and Robert Fitzgerald, who became, after her death, her literary executors.

Although, as Robert Fitzgerald states in the preface to O'Connor's *Everything That Rises Must Converge,* "Flannery was out to be a writer on her own and had no plans to go back to live in Georgia," staying out of Georgia for good was not possible. In December of 1950 she experienced a peculiar heaviness in her "typing arms." On the train home for the Christmas holidays she became so ill she was hospitalized immediately. It was disseminated lupus. In the fall of 1951, after nine wretched months in the hospital, she returned to Milledgeville. Because she could not climb the stairs at the Cline house her mother brought her to their country house, Andalusia, about five miles from town. Flannery O'Connor lived there with her mother for the next thirteen years. The rest of her life.

The word *lupus* is Latin for "wolf," and is described as "that which eats into the substance." It is a painful, wasting disease, and O'Connor suffered not only from the disease—which caused her muscles to weaken and her body to swell, among other things—but from the medicine she was given to fight the disease, which caused her hair to fall out and her hipbones to melt. Still, she managed—with the aid of crutches from 1955 on—to get about and to write, and left behind more than three dozen superb short stories, most of them prizewinners, two novels, and a dozen or so brilliant essays and speeches. Her book of essays, *Mystery and Manners,* which is primarily concerned with the moral imperatives of the serious writer of fiction, is the best of its kind I have ever read.

"When you make these trips back south," says my mother, as I give the smiling waitress my credit card, "just what is it exactly that you're looking for?"

"A wholeness," I reply.

"You look whole enough to me," she says.

"No," I answer, "because everything around me is split up, deliberately split up. History split up, literature split up, and people are split up too. It makes people do ignorant things. For example, one day I was invited to speak at a gathering of Mississippi librarians and before I could get started, one of the authorities on Mississippi history and literature got up and said she really *did* think Southerners wrote so well because 'we' lost the war. She was white, of course, but half the librarians in the room were black."

"I bet she was real old," says my mother. "They're the only ones still worrying over that war."

"So I got up and said no, 'we' didn't lose the war. '*You all*' lost the war. And you all's loss was our gain."

"Those old ones will just have to die out," says my mother.

"Well," I say, "I believe that the truth about any subject only comes when all the sides of the story are put together, and all their different meanings make one new one. Each writer writes the missing parts to the other writer's story. And the whole story is what I'm after."

"Well, I doubt if you can ever get the *true* missing parts of anything away from the white folks," my mother says softly, so as not to offend the waitress who is mopping up a nearby table; "they've sat on the truth so long by now they've mashed the life out of it."

"O'Connor wrote a story once called 'Everything That Rises Must Converge.'"

"What?"

"Everything that goes up comes together, meets, becomes one thing. Briefly, the story is this: an old white woman in her fifties—"

"That's not old! I'm older than that, and I'm not old!"

"Sorry. This middle-aged woman gets on a bus with her son, who likes to think he is a Southern liberal . . . he looks for a black person to sit next to. This horrifies his mother, who, though not old, has old ways. She is wearing a very hideous, very expensive hat, which is purple and green."

"Purple and green?"

"Very expensive. *Smart.* Bought at the best store in town. She says, 'With a hat like this, I won't meet myself coming and going.' But in fact, soon a large black woman, whom O'Connor describes as looking something like a gorilla, gets on the bus with a little boy, and she is wearing this same green-and-purple hat. Well, our not-so-young white lady is horrified, out*done.*"

"I *bet* she was. Black folks have money to buy foolish things with too, now."

"O'Connor's point exactly! Everything that rises, must converge."

"Well, the green-and-purple-hats people will have to converge without me."

"O'Connor thought that the South, as it became more 'progressive,' would become just like the North. Culturally bland, physically ravished, and, where the people are concerned, well, you wouldn't be able to tell one racial group from another. Everybody would want the same things, like the same things, and everybody would be reduced to wearing, symbolically, the same green-and-purple hats."

"And do you think this is happening?"

"I do. But that is not the whole point of the story. The white woman, in an attempt to save her pride, chooses to treat the incident of the identical hats as a case of monkey-see, monkey-do. She assumes she is not the monkey, of course. She ignores the idiotic-looking black woman and begins instead to flirt with the woman's son, who is small and black and *cute*. She fails to notice that the black woman is glowering at her. When they all get off the bus she offers the little boy a 'bright new penny.' And the child's mother knocks the hell out of her with her pocketbook."

"I bet she carried a large one."

"Large, and full of hard objects."

"Then what happened? Didn't you say the white woman's son was with her?"

"He had tried to warn his mother. 'These new Negroes are not like the old,' he told her. But she never listened. He thought he hated his mother until he saw her on the ground, then he felt sorry for her. But when he tried to help her, she didn't know him. She'd retreated in her mind to a historical time more congenial to her desires. 'Tell Grand-papa to come get me,' she says. Then she totters off, alone, into the night."

"Poor *thing*," my mother says sympathetically of this horrid woman, in a total identification that is *so* Southern and *so* black.

"That's what her son felt, too and *that* is how you know it is a Flannery O'Connor story. The son has been changed by his mother's experience. He understands that, though she is a silly woman who has tried to live in the past, she is also a pathetic creature and so is he. But it is too late to tell her about this because she is stone crazy."

"What did the black woman do after she knocked the white woman down and walked away?"

"O'Connor chose not to say, and that is why, although this is a good story, it is, to me, only half a story. *You* might know the other half. . . ."

"Well, I'm not a writer, but there *was* an old white woman I once wanted to strike . . ." she begins.

"Exactly," I say.

I discovered O'Connor when I was in college in the North and took a course in Southern writers and the South. The perfection of her writing was so dazzling I never noticed that no black Southern writers were taught. The other writers we studied—Faulkner, McCullers, Welty—seemed obsessed with a racial past that would not let them go. They seemed to beg the question of their characters' humanity on every page. O'Connor's characters—whose humanity if not their sanity is taken for granted, and who are miserable, ugly, narrow-minded, atheistic, and of intense racial smugness and arrogance, with not a graceful, pretty one anywhere who is not, at the same time, a joke—shocked and delighted me.

It was for her description of Southern white women that I appreciated her work at first, because when she set her pen to them not a whiff of magnolia hovered in the air (and the tree itself might never have been planted), and yes, I could say, yes, these white folks without the magnolia (who are indifferent to the tree's existence), and these black folks without melons and superior racial patience, these are like Southerners that I know.

She was for me the first great modern writer from the South, and was, in any case, the only one I had read who wrote such sly, demythifying sentences about white women as: "The woman would be more or less pretty—yellow hair, fat ankles, muddy-colored eyes."

Her white male characters do not fare any better—all of them misfits, thieves, deformed madmen, idiot children, illiterates, and murderers, and her black characters, male and female, appear equally shallow, demented, and absurd. That she retained a certain distance (only, however, in her later, mature work) from the inner workings of her black characters seems to me all to her credit, since, by deliberately limiting her treatment of them to cover their observable demeanor and actions, she leaves them free, in the reader's imagination, to inhabit another landscape, another life, than the one she creates for them. This is a kind of grace many writers do not have when dealing with representatives of an oppressed people within a story, and their insistence on knowing everything, on being God, in fact, has burdened us with more stereotypes than we can ever hope to shed.

In her life, O'Connor was more casual. In a letter to her friend Robert Fitzgerald in the mid-fifties she wrote, "as the niggers say I have the misery." He found nothing offensive, apparently, in including this unflattering (to O'Connor) statement in his Introduction to one of her books. O'Connor was then certain she was dying, and was in pain; one assumes she made this comment in an attempt at levity. Even so, I do not find it funny. In another letter she wrote shortly before she died she said: "Justice is justice and should not be appealed to along racial lines. The problem is not abstract for the Southerner, it's concrete: he sees it in terms of persons, not races—which way of seeing does away with easy answers." Of course this observation, though grand, does not apply to the racist treatment of blacks by whites in the South, and O'Connor should have added that she spoke only for herself.

But *essential* O'Connor is not about race at all, which is why it is so refreshing, coming, as it does, out of such a *racial* culture. If it can be said to be "about" anything, then it is "about" prophets and proph-ecy, "about" revelation, and "about" the impact of supernatural grace on human beings who don't have a chance of spiritual growth with-out it.

An indication that *she* believed in justice for the individual (if only in the corrected portrayal of a character she invented) is shown by her endless reworking of "The Geranium," the first story she published (in 1946), when she was twenty-one. She revised the story several times, renamed it at least twice, until, nearly twenty years after she'd origi-nally published it (and significantly, I think, after the beginning of the Civil Rights Movement), it became a different tale. Her two main black characters, a man and a woman, underwent complete meta-morphosis.

In the original story, Old Dudley, a senile racist from the South, lives with his daughter in a New York City building that has "niggers" living in it too. The black characters are described as being passive, self-effacing people. The black woman sits quietly, hands folded, in her apartment; the man, her husband, helps Old Dudley up the stairs when the old man is out of breath, and chats with him kindly, if condescendingly, about guns and hunting. But in the final version of the story, the woman walks around Old Dudley (now called Tanner) as if he's an open bag of garbage, scowls whenever she sees him, and "didn't look like any kind of woman, black or white, he had ever seen." Her husband, whom Old Dudley persists in calling "Preacher" (under the misguided assumption that to all black men it is a courtesy title), twice knocks the old man down. At the end of the story he stuffs Old Dudley's head, arms, and legs through the banisters of the stairway "as if in a stockade," and leaves him to die. The story's final title is "Judgment Day."

The quality added is rage, and, in this instance, O'Connor waited until she saw it *exhibited* by black people before she recorded it.

She was an artist who thought she might die young, and who then knew for certain she would. Her view of her characters pierces right through to the skull. Whatever her characters' color or social position she saw them as she saw herself, in the light of imminent mortality. Some of her stories, "The Enduring Chill" and "The Comforts of Home" especially, seem to be written out of the despair that must, on occasion, have come from this bleak vision, but it is for her humor that she is most enjoyed and remembered. My favorites are these:

> Everywhere I go I'm asked if I think the universities stifle writers. My opinion is that they don't stifle enough of them. There's many a best-seller that could have been prevented by a good teacher.
>
> —*Mystery and Manners*

> She would of been a good woman, if it had been somebody there to shoot her every minute of her life.
>
> —"The Misfit," *A Good Man is Hard to Find*

> There are certain cases in which, if you can only learn to write poorly enough, you can make a great deal of money.
>
> —*Mystery and Manners*

> It is the business of fiction to embody mystery through manners, and mystery is a great embarrassment to the modern mind.
>
> —*Mystery and Manners*

It mattered to her that she was a Catholic. This comes as a surprise to those who first read her work as that of an atheist. She believed in all the mysteries of her faith. And yet, she was incapable of writing dogmatic or formulaic stories. No religious tracts, nothing haloed softly in celestial light, not even any happy endings. It has puzzled some of her readers and annoyed the Catholic church that in her stories not only does good not triumph, it is not usually present. Seldom are there choices, and God never intervenes to help anyone win. To O'Connor, in fact, Jesus was God, and he won only by losing. She perceived that not much has been learned by his death by crucifixion, and that it is only by his continual, repeated dying—touching one's own life in a direct, searing way—that the meaning of that original loss is pressed into the heart of the individual.

In "The Displaced Person," a story published in 1954, a refugee from Poland is hired to work on a woman's dairy farm. Although he speaks in apparent gibberish, he is a perfect worker. He works so assiduously the woman begins to prosper beyond her greatest hopes. Still, because his ways are not her own (the Displaced Person attempts to get one of the black dairy workers to marry his niece by "buying" her out of a Polish concentration camp), the woman allows a runaway tractor to roll over and kill him.

"As far as I'm concerned," she tells the priest, "Christ was just another D.P." He just didn't fit in. After the death of the Polish refugee, however, she understands her complicity in a modern crucifixion, and recognizes the enormity of her responsibility for other human beings. The impact of this new awareness debilitates her; she loses her health, her farm, even her ability to speak.

This moment of revelation, when the individual comes face to face with her own limitations and comprehends "the true frontiers of her own inner country," is classic O'Connor, and always arrives in times of extreme crisis and loss.

There is a resistance by some to read O'Connor because she is "too difficult," or because they do not share her religious "persuasion." A young man who studied O'Connor under the direction of Eudora Welty some years ago amused me with the following story, which may or may not be true:

"I don't think Welty and O'Connor understood each *other*," he said, when I asked if he thought O'Connor would have liked or understood Welty's more conventional art. "For Welty's part, wherever we reached a particularly dense and symbolic section of one of

O'Connor's stories she would sigh and ask, 'Is there a Catholic in the class?'"

Whether one "understands" her stories or not, one knows her characters are new and wondrous creations in the world and that not one of her stories—not even the earliest ones in which her consciousness of racial matters had not evolved sufficiently to be interesting or to differ much from the insulting and ignorant racial stereotyping that preceded it—could have been written by anyone else. As one can tell a Bearden from a Keene or a Picasso from a Hallmark card, one can tell an O'Connor story from any story laid next to it. Her Catholicism did not in any way limit (by defining it) her art. After her great stories of sin, damnation, prophecy, and revelation, the stories one reads casually in the average magazine seem to be about love and roast beef.

Andalusia is a large white house at the top of a hill with a view of a lake from its screened-in front porch. It is neatly kept, and there are, indeed, peacocks strutting about in the sun. Behind it there is an unpainted house where black people must have lived. It was, then, the typical middle-to-upper-class arrangement: white folks up front, the "help," in a far shabbier house, within calling distance from the back door. Although an acquaintance of O'Connor's has told me no one lives there now—but that a caretaker looks after things—I go up to the porch and knock. It is not an entirely empty or symbolic gesture: I have come to this vacant house to learn something about myself in relation to Flannery O'Connor, and will learn it whether anyone is home or not.

What I feel at the moment of knocking is fury that someone is paid to take care of her house, though no one lives in it, and that her house still, in fact, stands, while mine—which of course we never owned anyway—is slowly rotting into dust. Her house becomes—in an instant—the symbol of my own disinheritance, and for that instant I hate her guts. All that she has meant to me is diminished, though her diminishment within me is against my will.

In Faulkner's backyard there is also an unpainted shack and a black caretaker still lives there, a quiet, somber man who, when asked about Faulkner's legendary "sense of humor" replied that, as far as he knew, "Mr. Bill never joked." For years, while reading Faulkner, this image of the quiet man in the backyard shack stretched itself across the page.

Standing there knocking on Flannery O'Connor's door, I do not think of her illness, her magnificent work in spite of it; I think: it all comes back to houses. To how people live. There are rich people who own houses to live in and poor people who do not. And this is wrong. Literary separatism, fashionable now among blacks as it has always been among whites, is easier to practice than to change a fact like this. I think: I would level this country with the sweep of my hand, if I could.

"Nobody can change the past," says my mother.

"Which is why revolutions exist," I reply.

My bitterness comes from a deeper source than my knowledge of the difference, historically, race has made in the lives of white and black artists. The fact that in Mississippi no one even remembers where Richard Wright lived, while Faulkner's house is maintained by a black caretaker is painful, but not unbearable. What comes close to being unbearable is that I know how damaging to my own psyche such injustice is. In an unjust society the soul of the sensitive person is in danger of deformity from just such weights as this. For a long time I will feel Faulkner's house, O'Connor's house, crushing me. To fight back will require a certain amount of energy, energy better used doing something else.

My mother has been busy reasoning that, since Flannery O'Connor died young of a lingering and painful illness, the hand of God has shown itself. Then she sighs. "Well, you know," she says, "it is true, as they say, that the grass is always greener on the other side. That is, until you find yourself over there."

In a just society, of course, clichés like this could not survive.

"But grass *can* be greener on the other side and not be just an illusion," I say. "Grass on the other side of the fence might have good fertilizer, while grass on your side might have to grow, if it grows at all, in sand."

We walk about quietly, listening to the soft sweep of the peacocks' tails as they move across the yard. I notice how completely O'Connor, in her fiction, has described just this view of the rounded hills, the tree line, black against the sky, the dirt road that runs from the front yard down to the highway. I remind myself of her courage and of how much—in her art—she has helped me to see. She destroyed the last vestiges of sentimentality in white Southern writing; she caused white women to look ridiculous on pedestals, and she approached her black characters—as a mature artist—with unusual humility and restraint. She also cast spells and worked magic with the written word. The magic, the wit, and the mystery of Flannery O'Connor I know I will always love, I also know the meaning of the expression "Take what you can use and let the rest rot." If ever there was an expression designed to protect the health of the spirit, this is it.

As we leave O'Connor's yard the peacocks—who she said would have the last word—lift their splendid tails for our edification. One peacock is so involved in the presentation of his masterpiece he does not allow us to move the car until he finishes with his show.

"Peacocks are inspiring," I say to my mother, who does not seem at all in awe of them and actually frowns when she sees them strut, "but they sure don't stop to consider they might be standing in your way."

And she says, "Yes, and they'll eat up every bloom you have, if you don't watch out."

1975

Lisa Alther

Introduction to *A Good Man Is Hard to Find* by Flannery O'Connor

Flannery O'Connor had a deep suspicion of people who tried to label her writing. In a letter she said of a reporter, "He wanted me to characterize myself so he would have something to write down. Are you a Southern writer? What kind of Catholic are you? etc." Well, I too need "something to write down" about this author whose fiction has startled and entertained me for years. And in fact she *was* a Southerner, a Catholic, and a woman. And each hated category has its bearing on her writing.

Born in Georgia in 1925, she died there of lupus thirty-nine years later, having been out of the state only long enough to attend the writers' school at the University of Iowa; to live briefly at the artists' colony, Yaddo; in New York City, and in Connecticut with friends; to take a trip to Lourdes; and to lecture at various American colleges. Her characters are the poor whites of piedmont Georgia and east Tennessee, descendants of the rowdy Scotch-Irish who flowed down the Shenandoah Valley of Virginia from Pennsylvania, and of renegades of various kinds who escaped over the mountains from the more "civilized" coastal areas of the South. Her South is not the South of decaying mansions and fallen dynasties. She sometimes seems to go out of her way to undercut the myths of Southern gentility and beleaguered aristocracy with her dirt farmers and crazed backwoods prophets. Her South concerns unsophisticated people on remote farms and in isolated cabins.

Someone like me who grew up in this region reads Flannery O'Connor's work with great admiration for her ability to capture the behavior and attitudes of these people, her ability to differentiate between the almost identical speech patterns of the blacks and whites. In addition, she is very funny, deflating the platitudes I grew up surrounded by. In a story in this volume called "Good Country People", a woman says with piety, "Carramae said when her and Lyman was married Lyman said it sure felt sacred to him. She said he said he wouldn't take five hundred dollars for being married by a preacher."

"How much would he take?" asks another character sourly.

When a woman wrote to Flannery O'Connor saying that one of her books "left a bad taste in my mouth", Flannery O'Connor wrote back, "You weren't supposed to eat it."

Outsiders sometimes regard Flannery O'Connor's characters as grotesques and freaks, similar to those caught in the photographs of Diane Arbus. But what some label "grotesque" is simply reality to others. A man in my east Tennessee home town used to sleep in his coffin every night to get used to it. I played tennis on courts next to a Holy Roller church; our calls of "forty-love" were often drowned out by shrieks and wails from the church, where the God-besotted were speaking in tongues and convulsing in the aisles.

Flannery O'Connor herself once said, "I hate to think that in twenty years Southern writers too may be writing about men in gray flannel suits and may have lost their ability to see that these gentlemen are even greater freaks than what we are writing about." This remark is typical of Southern writers, many of whom have harbored a contempt for the bland secular materialism of the nation of which we are a sometimes reluctant part. For all its failings, the South at its best has always encouraged a certain stubborn and prickly individualism, humility and awe in the face of nature, a reverence for ritual and good manners, a concern for spiritual and aesthetic and interpersonal values over and above the production and acquisition of goods. Often Flannery O'Connor's stories involve the clash as her characters in their untested simplicity confront representatives from the amoral exploitative urban world. She once explained, "The anguish that most of us have observed for some time now has been caused not by the fact that the South is alienated from the rest of the country, but by the fact that it is not alienated enough, that every day we are getting more and more like the rest of the country, that we are being forced out, not only of our many sins, but of our few virtues."

The South also breeds in its children a suspicion of the glib rationalism of our more "progressive" countrymen. Southerners, for better or worse, tend to reaction rather than reflection. Flannery O'Connor's fiction embodies this bent, being replete with concrete objects and vivid physical details, and short on analysis. (To many this is the prime characteristic of good fiction.) Like a visual artist, she strives for effect, mood, atmosphere, revelation through action rather than through explanation. Sometimes this action is violent and grisly—murder, fatal accidents, thievery or deceit. Statistically the South is more violent than the rest of the United States. My brother, a sociology professor, once remarked on this fact in a speech in Alabama. A stranger phoned him that night and said it wasn't true that the South was more violent, and if he didn't get out of town he'd be sorry. Much of the violence in Flannery O'Connor's stories stems from characters thwarting or repressing or distorting their spiritual impulses until those impulses explode into consciousness with the force of fire bombs. (Similarly, much of the violence in the South at large stems from the thwarting of hostile impulses by rigorous codes of manners, until the codes collapse and all hell breaks loose.)

If Flannery O'Connor were just a documentor of a particularly distinctive part of the United States, though, she would be of little interest beyond the confines of her region. Yet many critics and readers feel she is one of the best short story writers of our time. (Though she also wrote two fine novellas, *Wise Blood* and *The Violent Bear It Away,* her short stories are generally considered her more impressive work.) The physical deformity and material poverty of her characters are intended to function beyond the level of documentary to indicate a more general spiritual deformity, a poverty of the soul not confined to any one geographical region.

"The only thing that keeps me from being a regional writer," she wrote, "is being a Catholic, and the only thing that keeps me from being a Catholic writer (in the narrow sense) is being a Southerner." This is the kind of split vision that produces either a writer or a schizophrenic, or both. The majority religion of her South and of her characters is a primitive apocalyptic Protestantism, perhaps closest in Britain to the dissenting Puritan tradition, or to Scottish Pres- byterianism. Its emotional fervor, its preoccupation with humanity's fall and its hunger for salvation are congenial to Flannery O'Connor's Catholicism. The primary difference lies in the do-it yourself mentality of Southern fundamentalism, the tradition of the individual in the wilderness struggling in isolation. Flannery O'Connor delights in showing the myriad ways this attitude can lead believers astray.

"Whenever I'm asked why Southern writers particularly have a penchant for writing about freaks, I say it is because we are still able to recognize one. To be able to recognize a freak, you have to have some conception of the whole man," she wrote. Her Catholicism gives her this standard against which to measure the failings and flailings of her characters. Yet she acknowledged the difficulty of applying this standard in the face of readers who don't share it. "The novelist with Christian concerns will find in modern life distortions which are re- pugnant to him, and his problem will be to make these appear as distortions to an audience which is used to seeing them as natural; and he may well be forced to take ever more violent means to get his vision across to this hostile audience . . . to the hard of hearing you shout, and for the almost-blind you draw large and startling figures." Just as Catholicism tries to translate its spiritual institutions into worldly terms through its rituals and through the person of Christ— "the Word made flesh"—so does Flannery O'Connor try to incorpo- rate her transcendent concerns in concrete situations involving very distinctive characters. The South—with its actual history of slavery, devastation in war, humiliation and poverty, with its struggle to regain self-respect and atone for past sins—provides a natural arena for her exploration of the individual soul, fallen from grace and mired down in sin, simultaneously yearning for and fighting against salvation.

Flannery O'Connor once referred to this volume, *A Good Man is Hard to Find*, as "nine stories about original sin." The sin is usually some form of vanity or self-love. There is, in each story, a moment of grace or revelation or retribution, often violent, during which a char- acter accepts or fails to accept enlightenment about the paucity of his or her existence and the need for reformation. But description does very little for the stories. Like bad dreams, they have to be experienced for their full impact to be felt. Flannery O'Connor said, "The meaning in a story can't be paraphrased and if it's there it's there, almost more as a physical than a intellectual fact."

Regarding her identity as a woman writer, Flannery O'Connor wrote in a letter, "I just never think . . . of qualities which are specifically feminine or masculine. I suppose I divide people into two classes: the Irksome and the Non-Irksome, without regard to sex." Nevertheless, she was writing in and of a culture that was and is somewhat matriarchal. Historically the South has been agrarian, a frontier tamed by pioneers, and women played an important part in the domestic economy. The stereotype of the languid Southern Belle notwithstanding, my childhood was filled with energetic women who usually got their own way, however limited the options. And so are Flannery O'Connor's stories filled with such women—and with shadowy men, ineffectual or roguish. Flannery O'Connor lived most of her life with her mother, who ran a dairy farm, and many of the stories involve mother-daughter or parent-child relationships, though with no specifically feminist overtones. The stories also often feature a relationship between two middle-aged women, employee and employer, both thoroughly formidable. These women are indomitable, terrifying, not at all "feminine." No one would want to butt heads with them. In portraying their interactions Flannery O'Connor melds traditionally "female" subject matter (life in the kitchen and drawing room) with traditionally "male" thematic concerns (the larger meaning of life). In doing so, she lends a dignity and lofty significance to female experience that have sometimes escaped other writers.

Girls growing up in the South have had very few socially acceptable outlets for this ambitiousness and aggressiveness inherited from a frontier past, other than cheerleader or beauty queen, housewife and mother and clubwoman. But those of us who liked to read soon noticed that much of the finest American literature was written by Southerners, many of them women. Kate Chopin, Flannery O'Connor, Eudora Welty, Carson McCullers and Katherine Anne Porter performed the same function for young Southern women that Jane Austen, the Brontës and George Eliot have no doubt performed for generations of English women.

The rest of the United States—subconsciously guilty about the devastation of the Civil War, justifiably critical of the South's racial situation, and loathing the failure and poverty the South embodied—informed us that the South and its inhabitants were backward and Christ-haunted, just as the English have the Irish. But like the Irish, because of our writers like Flannery O'Connor, we knew better: we were just different, not inferior; we had different traditions and values and capacities. In some cases we even came to see these differences as virtues.

The charge most often levelled at Flannery O'Connor's work concerns its "narrowness," its limited range of settings and subject matter. But to me this makes about as much sense as calling Jane Austen's work narrow. It's true that physically you rarely leave Georgia and Tennessee when reading her work. But the social interactions and psychological processes she illuminates are of universal concern, or should be. But I refer you to these amazing stories. As Flannery O'Connor herself said, "The meaning of a piece of fiction only begins where everything psychological and sociological has been explained . . . Too much interpretation is certainly worse than too little."

1980

Shirley Ann Grau

Introduction to *Cross Creek*
by Marjorie Kinnan Rawlings

Few regional writers in the U.S. have had the gift of looking beyond regionalism. Marjorie Kinnan Rawlings was one of those who not only made a minute section of the landscape her own, but made it universal as well. As she put it, "A man may learn a deal of the general from studying the specific, whereas it is impossible to know the specific by studying the general. For that reason, our philosophers are usually the most unpractical of men, while very simple folk may have a great deal of wisdom."

Before Mrs. Rawlings began writing about her neighbors, the land she cultivated and the simple people she celebrated were all but unknown to American readers. When she first arrived, in 1928, Cross Creek was no more than "a bend in a country road" in the heart of Florida's scrub country. It was not easy to reach in those days, and few strangers had reason to stop there. To a transplanted Yankee, even the local language seemed alien: it was not easy at first to comprehend the cracker idiom—sometimes Chaucerian or Elizabethan—of the proud, good-natured backwoodsmen who lived there. Yet Mrs. Rawlings was aware from the first that isolation had conferred special blessings on these country folk. Civilization, she observed, "had remained too remote, physically and spiritually, to take from them something vital." She sensed "a primal quality" about the people living amid the moss-hung silence of the scrub country.

To be sure, Cross Creek was no demi-Eden. Mrs. Rawlings was

terrified of its snakes, victimized by lazy and murderous field hands, driven close to ruin by the frost and pestilence that forever threatened her orange crop. She was oppressed by termites, mosquitoes, roaming cattle, poison ivy and neighborhood feuds. Yet, she soon came to agree with Martha Mickens, the wise old matriarch of the Creek's Negro community, when she said, "To get yo' grease an' grits in the place you enjoys gettin' 'em, ain't that makin' a livin'?"

By today's standards, Cross Creek folk would be considered piteously underprivileged, a blot on the affluent society. But Mrs. Rawlings, no lover of "wanton orderliness," saw in its very shabbiness and poverty a spur to extraordinary neighborliness. This was something that, after years of city life, she could never take for granted. "The Creek doesn't amount to anything," allowed one resident. "The people don't amount to anything. But if you're sick and have no money, they'll cook for you and fetch it to you, and they'll doctor you, and if you get past their doctoring, they'll send for a doctor and pay his bill. And if you die, they'll take up a collection and bury you. I figure it's just as close to Heaven here as any other place."

Before she settled in the scrub country, Marjorie Rawlings had been a newspaperwoman in Louisville, Kentucky, and Rochester, New York. Tiring of a life that seemed "scrappy and always in a hurry," she turned her hand unsuccessfully to short-story writing. She had almost given up when, at 32, she used a small legacy to buy her 72-acre orange grove at Cross Creek. The people and the country inspired her to continue writing. Increasingly, her fiction reflected her deepening knowledge of her chosen patch of earth. Two prizewinning stories were followed by two highly praised novels; her third novel, *The Yearling,* won its author a Pulitzer Prize and a delighted following the world over.

It was not until 1942, fourteen years after she had settled there, that Mrs. Rawlings published *Cross Creek*. Part georgic, part autobiography, it is perhaps her most enduring work, shorn of the sentiment that marked her earlier writing, enriched with an extraordinary feeling for the flora and fauna of the rural South. In *Cross Creek* Marjorie Rawlings gave full expression to her deep, near-mystical love for nature. She knew the names of plants and insects that native Southerners commonly overlooked, as Shirley Ann Grau points out in her new introduction to this special edition. No American writer has ever been closer to the fierce, furtive Florida earth, to its pine woods and gallberry flats, and the bears, "toady-frogs, lizards, antses, and varmints" that inhabit them.

In writing this book, she sensed also that "human life in such a place must share the interest of its background." If at times the unpredictable Creek folk seem downright deranged, the author reasons, it is because "madness is only a variety of mental nonconformity and we are all individualists here."

Cross Creek has no dearth of such distinctive characters. There is old Martha, whose "inviolable sense of proportion" the author attributes to the rare gift of seeing people as they are. Illiterate, unfailingly generous, possessed of exquisite courtesy, Martha raised a dynasty of daughters and sons. ("I was a fast-breedin' woman.") Others of Martha's family worked in Mrs. Rawlings' house or grove, but none more memorably than the girl named Adrenna. Adrenna was a *femme fatale;* nevertheless, she could not seem to capture a husband. The trouble, author Rawlings admits, was that Adrenna's choice would have to serve two women—to "provide her with whatever she wanted of a husband, and me with a good grove and yard man. Adrenna and I fell constantly between the upper and the nether millstone."

No less forceful is Mrs. Rawlings' portrait of 'Geechee, a murderous-looking, one-eyed girl from the Ogeechee River region of Georgia (where the Negroes, according to the author, are descended from an exceptionally violent African tribe and have somehow retained much of their strong genetic heritage). 'Geechee showed up one day when Mrs. Rawlings had almost despaired of getting help. "I hear tell you want a girl," she said fiercely. "You take me." From dawn to dusk, 'Geechee tore through the house, cleaning it from rafters to rugs; she once pursued a stain clear through the kitchen floor. She made herself so much a part of the house that Mrs. Rawlings began to feel "it was not she who was serving me, but I who was destined to serve her." And so it turned out.

'Geechee's man, Leroy, was serving a 20-year sentence for manslaughter, and the girl persuaded Mrs. Rawlings to seek his release. The state prison, it seemed, was only too glad to be rid of Leroy.

Within two weeks the author was begging the prison superintendent to take his charge back, only to be told: "We have absolutely no room for him." Leroy was sent packing.

Not long afterward the author discovered two kegs of moonshine, half emptied. 'Geechee did not deny filching the liquor. "It's the onliest way I can make out," she sighed. "It's the onliest thing lifts my heart up, times I think I'm jus' obliged to die." In the end Mrs. Rawlings had to fire the girl, but 'Geechee returned once a year for a visit, always a little drunk.

One of the most comic accounts in the book describes the complicated social and economic ritual Mrs. Rawlings had to go through after shooting a young hog bent on devouring her cherished petunias. The dead pig's owner, a trigger-tempered neighbor named Mr. Martin, was particularly outraged by reports that the author had celebrated her coup with "a drunken party—and *ate* it." It took a delicate three-way barter deal conducted by a middleman before Mr. Martin weeks later took her hand and announced: "Mis' Rawlings, the pig is paid for."

Cross Creek celebrates the virtues and quirks of many another local figure, black and white. Living among these people, Mrs. Rawlings learned to cherish their way of life. After a while she even learned to enjoy such exotic backwoods delicacies as turtle eggs and bear steaks, fresh-water blue crab and alligator tail; the reader is offered not only descriptions of these dishes but also the recipes.

Cross Creek is filled with the sound of redbirds and whippoorwills, the smell of cypress water and magnolias; it notes the dispassionate cold stars of a winter's night, the long, sweet, lazy summer days, the hardship and hopes of the people. No individual in the book catches this latter mood better than Mrs. Rawlings' friend Fred Tompkins, who recited before every meal an oddly moving and possibly immemorial backwoodsman's grace:

> Good God, with a bounty
> Look down on Alachua County,
> For the soil is so po' and so awful rooty, too,
> I don't know what to God the po' folks gonna do.

Marjorie Rawlings stayed on at her beloved Cross Creek for more than 10 years. Though often alone, she was seldom lonely in this land of insistent, savage beauty. She shared the comforting vision of old Martha Mickens: "I'se seed the grove freeze to the ground. I'se seed it swivvel in a long drought. But Sugar, they was grove here before my folks crossed the big water. . . . And they'll be grove here right on, after you and me is forgotten."

"It seems to me," the author wrote, "that the earth may be borrowed but not bought. It may be used, but not owned. It gives itself in response to love and tending, offers its seasonal flowering and fruiting. But we are tenants and not possessors, lovers and not masters."

This view encompassed the people, with their fast-vanishing way of life, as well as the land. Marjorie Rawlings did not write of poor Southerners with the irony of an Erskine Caldwell or the sardonic pessimism of a William Faulkner. She depicted them with sympathy, humor and a tough-minded respect for the complicated traditions by which they lived. Although her neighbors looked upon her as a Yankee to the end, she forged a distinctively regional style, laying the groundwork for a later generation of women writers who emerged from the South.

Cross Creek was written back in 1942. The more famous novel *The Yearling* is even older, and Marjorie Kinnan Rawlings, who was no young woman when she wrote either book, has been dead since 1953. The Southerners and the South she wrote about have undergone a radical change, a bloodless revolution, economically and socially. It is really extraordinary that after all these years, all this change, *Cross Creek* still stands as a memorial to all that is good and admirable and beautiful in the South.

And there *are* things that are enduringly good and lovely in the South—though non-Southerners tend to forget this sometimes. Perhaps *Cross Creek* will remind them.

This is essentially a Southern *Walden*, a people-filled *Walden*, a very personal record of a woman's love affair with the country and the people of north-central Florida.

Marjorie Rawlings was first, last and always a nature writer. She took the trouble to learn the names and the ways of the Southern flora and fauna—perhaps because she was not a native Southerner. (She was born in Washington, D.C., went to college in Wisconsin, worked in New York.) I, for example, was born and raised in the Deep South, and there are plenty of flowers and grasses whose names I don't know.

They are always there, always within my sight, and it has never occurred to me to ask about them, to look closely at them. Like the tree frogs. I've always heard them called rain frogs, because they call for a shower and then sing themselves silly after it falls—I've seen them now and again, and their little suction-cupped feet have passed over my hands. They are a flash, identified but not studied. They were there when I was born, they will be there when I die. They are permanent, but not interesting to me.

Marjorie Rawlings, who had not seen them nearly so often, looked at them long and hard and found them fascinating. She transmits her enthusiasm to the reader.

The pages of *Cross Creek* are filled with a careful, meticulous detailing of the superb Southern countryside and its ways. It is all there: the heat and the cold, the shiver of the grasses in the wind, the fierce frightening storms, the unbelievable pleasure of a hunt, the great satisfaction of listening to a good pack of dogs work, of being able to single out the voices. It was a wonderful life that she wrote about— simple but not primitive, so full of excitements that every day glistens and sparkles.

Rural Southerners are not by and large very articulate. They are shy and slow in expression, but they have a feeling for the earth that I've never seen matched elsewhere. One old Mississippian put it this way (and years later I remember his words): "You live on this land year after year, and you live on it month after month, and it's never hidden from you by snow, nor sleet. In summer it's pretty and soft, and in winter, leaves gone and nothing to hide behind, it's open and sweet."

And the Alabama girl who once told me, as we walked across the smooth stretch of white frost, "I hate to step on it, hate to spoil it, it being so smooth like a table cloth."

I feel it sometimes myself, this tug of the land which all Southerners have. "Hunter's moon" was the phrase I always heard for it: nights when the moon was full and you had to be outside, moving around restlessly with all the varmints.

Where fiction writers say this obliquely, Marjorie Rawlings says it directly. This is the very essence of the Southern spirit, this closeness to the land and identification with it.

What emerges clearly from these pages is the fact that Marjorie

Rawlings loved the land and the people—and yet (as you read you will see this) she remained a foreigner, an outsider. The Southern word for this is "Yankee." The community considered her so when she arrived, and she never was able to change their minds. She stayed a Yankee. Not because—as she thought—she had come to Cross Creek from New York. The small community's horizons were much narrower than that. She was a Yankee because she came from some place north of them—Virginia or South Carolina would have been the same. She was a stranger because she was not born there, and because she was not related to anybody who was. Blood is so very, very important in that part of the world. I have been treated hospitably by Southerners to whom my political and social convictions must have been utterly repellent—for one and only one simple reason: I could claim a distant blood relationship. In some small towns I've had unknown people address me by name as "Barbara's cousin," and when I asked how they knew, they shrugged and said, "You had the family look about you."

If the Southerner is willing to count you in, he is also willing to count you eternally out, eternally a stranger. Once in Lake City, a tiny town not too far from Cross Creek, I heard a youngster say of one of the houses in town: "Yankee lives there." I asked about the Yankee and found that he had indeed come from the North, but he'd come 40 years before.

Ironically enough, the woman who did most to explain the customs and habits of Florida remained an interested outsider in her own chosen community. That's the way of this part of the country.

In addition to being a portrait of a region, *Cross Creek* is the portrait of a woman. Her writing is plain, flat and quite un-Faulknerian. It's perfectly suited to the homey day-by-day housekeeping account of her life. As you read, bit by bit the character of the author emerges. A complex, curious woman. A woman who loved the earth and the little creatures on it with the intensity of a Francis of Assisi. A woman who could be incredibly patient with drunken Negro hands, trusting them with more responsibility than they could bear. A woman who could turn into a busybody, a bluenosed meddler, insisting on court justice in a jealousy shotgunning, insisting on the inevitable travesty of a trial that everyone else wanted to avoid. A woman who is stubborn, senti-mental, kind; at once perceptive and foolish, spiritually troubled, searching for personal contentment. In a way *Cross Creek* is the chronicle of a modern woman coming to terms with her existence.

But *Cross Creek* is no new book anymore. Is it still true? Or is it the evocation of a wonderful world that has since disappeared? A bit of both, I suppose.

It is almost as true today as it ever was.

About the time *Cross Creek* was written, I was living in Alabama, in country not too unlike the Florida woods. I have known many people from north Florida. And I think we all agree on one thing: *Cross Creek,* for all its accuracy, is only part of the picture.

Today my conservative segregationist friends often point to this book as an example of the idyllic days before the present confusion. And certainly in *Cross Creek* there is no indication of any sort of racial restlessness. In its pages black and white live harmoniously together without a ripple of discontent. There is even a kind of romantic ap-proach to the widespread and bitter poverty, rather like another book published at about the same time, James Agee's *Let Us Now Praise Famous Men.* Perhaps by the end of the Depression (and the Deep South was still very much in the Depression when this book was written) we had begun to be resigned to poverty, and had begun perversely to find virtues in it.

Nothing in my experience makes me agree with Marjorie Rawlings' gentle picture of the poor white. I've known them—the crackers, the rednecks, the wool-hat boys. And I've found little to admire, a lot to pity.

But the South *is* changing. There is more money, more education, and above all there is more sense of the great outside world. It's a mighty poor family that doesn't have television now, and the old folkways are being forgotten. People are becoming healthier and bet-ter fed. They're losing their uniqueness and becoming more like the rest of the country. There are few places progress has not reached.

There are of course people who wonder whether this direction does indeed represent progress. I'll pass that question. There is no doubt that, for better or worse, the South has been revolutionized since *Cross Creek* was written.

The most startling change for a Southerner is with the Negro. The Negro revolution has penetrated into the most backward, most remote parts of the South. It isn't always overt, it doesn't always take the form of voter-registration marches. It is subtle, this resistance, it is difficult to put your finger on. It is a look, a glance, a bearing. I'll quote one of my many cousins: "If I knew what they were doing, I'd tell them to stop it. But I don't ever seem to find out what it is." However you put it, it comes to this: the traditionally placid social structure of the South (if it ever existed) is gone.

People have changed. And the land has changed too. I wonder if Marjorie Rawlings would recognize her Florida today. All through those central counties, citrus groves stretch endlessly in neat, precise rows. It's still the same risky business it was in *Cross Creek;* there are just infinitely more trees. In other places the sandy soil has been cleared and turned over to pasture. Sleek cattle move slowly over brilliant green grass. The country has an openness that it lacked before.

And then of course there are the towns. For example, Gainesville, which appears occasionally in the pages of *Cross Creek,* was then a small, sleepy place. Today, with the enormous expansion of the state university, it has become a prosperous small city. Streets of new houses stretch out in all directions under the tall, slender pines.

And—biggest change of all—the retirement towns. The tract houses, the tremendous developments built since World War II. They seem more grim somehow in the north part of Florida than they do farther south. Perhaps because this is not quite tropical country, and it retains the scars of the bulldozers and the land-graders for a long time.

In all this change, there are still Cross Creeks. There are still worlds unaffected by time and change and circumstance. There are not too many, especially not in Florida, but they do exist, the exceptions, the backwaters.

I was in one not long ago. Its name wasn't Cross Creek but it certainly could have been. Four houses and a little grocery. The outside wall of the grocery was decorated with the skulls of bass, little silent white rows of them. And the grocery owner wore the eternal black hat, the badge of the poor whites, the wool-hat boys. Lanky, loose-jointed Negroes moved silently in the background. Except for our cars it could have been any time during the last century. Soon we were far out of sight of any house, with only the timeless, busy silence of the country all around us. The endless, endlessly fascinating panorama of woods and swamps: the mark of a bear at a honey tree; the baleful stare of sleeping 'gators. And overhead that great soaring bird I've always heard called The Lord God Bird. There was one thing missing that trip—something I heard years ago and not often then: the scream of a panther. No other sound like that—I dream about it occasionally. It's the essence of wildness and the essence of beauty. It exists in far-off corners if you have the patience to find it.

These are the communities where time really seems to have no meaning, where the only movement is the slow progression of the gentle seasons. When you've been in them for a bit, it hurts to leave. And when they are gone—and all the Cross Creeks will go eventually—something fundamental and valuable will go with them.

1966

Lee Smith

The Voice Behind the Story

When I first began writing in my college days, nothing I wrote was very good. I was taking the introductory creative writing course at Hollins College, and my average was a B−. Sometimes I got a C+.

The problem was that I thought I had to think up something exciting, something glamorous, to write about. One of my early main characters, I remember, was a stewardess in Hawaii named Cecile. Or occasionally I came up with a story strong in theme—which, in my case, meant sappy and melodramatic. I am reminded of my story about the whole family that died in a fire on Christmas Eve and when the rescue squad arrived, the only thing left intact was a little music box among the ashes playing "Silent Night." C− for that one.

My teachers kept telling me, "Write what you know" but I didn't know, for a long time, what that was.

Then, in Louis Rubin's southern literature class, I came upon the stories of Eudora Welty and Flannery O'Connor. It was as though a literal light bulb snapped on in my head, exactly the way it happens in cartoons, because I realized that these writers hadn't been anywhere I hadn't been, and didn't know anybody I didn't know. Now that was arrogant, but when you're eighteen years old you *are* arrogant, and anyway it didn't matter. For the first time I began to have a sense of what I knew, of what my subject might be. I remembered a man in Grundy, up in the mountains where I'm from, telling me how, if you buy a woman a set of new teeth, she'll leave you every time. I remembered ladies sitting on the front porch engaged in endless discussions about whether somebody did or did not have colitis. I began to think I might have something to say. Something about families, and about daily life, and small towns, and kids, and about expectations and reality and that point where they collide, because that's the point—I realized this much later—where the story happens.

I've heard Max Steele say that nothing is ever finally fiction. If it didn't happen to us, he says, then it might have, or it might have happened to a friend of ours, or at least it *should* have, or maybe it happened to us in some other life, or it might as well have. I think this is true. Every event we think we make up corresponds to an emotional reality, or to a psychological reality, or to an experience we have dreamed.

I am reminded of Anne Tyler, who once said, "I write because I want to have more than one life." This is the point: it's ALL US, finally, in some awful and wonderful way. The trick is to find a means to handle the material so that it will be true and meaningful for us, yet in such a way that we can feel free to juggle the facts and conditions in order to achieve the maximum aesthetic effect.

Real life, of course, is chaos. Cause and effect are crazy. Often it all seems entirely whimsical, or tragic, or ridiculous—at best, arbitrary. What the writer does is impose an order on all this chaos. That's what plot is about. But to do this most effectively, this drawing order out of chaos, we have to be neither too close to nor too far from our chosen—or given—material.

This appropriate distance can best be achieved, I think, through choosing the right point of view for any given story. If I want to write a story based on something that really happened to me, for instance, I will usually put it in the third person point of view and change the character radically so I can feel free enough of it to maintain aesthetic control. But all writers have to figure out for themselves how to manipulate point of view in their own best interests. In any case, here are a few things to consider in choosing the angle of narration.

By using the first-person point of view, with a reliable narrator, a very special kind of closeness can be achieved almost immediately with the reader. The main character is easily developed because he or she is speaking, and it's easy to control plot—you can only tell whatever the main character sees or thinks or hears. On the negative side, this can be severely limiting. But first person is not restricted to the reliable narrator; we can have an unreliable narrator, too, like Sister in "Why I Live at the P.O." The unreliable speaker often reveals things to the reader of which he or she is unaware, adding a whole level of complexity to the story. This makes the reader work harder, and the reader loves to work.

Or we can have a first-person narrator who is telling a story about somebody else. Good examples are John Cheever's story "Torch Song" and Melville's "Bartleby the Scrivener." This is a tricky point of view in one respect because, at the end, the inevitable question comes up: exactly why has this narrator told us this story? What does it mean to the narrator? And we have to deal with that.

If we use the close third-person point of view, we can have the main advantage of the first-person narrator—open access to one character's consciousness—with the added advantage of being able to tell many things about our main character which he would not tell about himself. What he's wearing, for instance, or how he walks across a room.

The other option is the omniscient—the most flexible, the most unrestricted and the hardest, finally, for me, because it offers too many options.

But the writer's voice is really what we're talking about here. Having found the subject and the point of view necessary to distance the material, the writer has already gone a long way toward finding a voice. Because the writer's voice will always be heard. Sometimes the whole process of contemporary literature seems to me to be a voyage into narcissism: in, in, down further and further into consciousness, with the writer intruding more and more into the work. The writer has become less concerned with the grand design, with the whole of society, and has become more and more focused upon the individual consciousness, and upon himself. This is partly because our real world has become so fragmented and diffuse and confusing that we feel we can't attempt to see it whole and partly because we have moved, it seems to me, farther away from our old beliefs and closer to the contemplation of our own psyches as the ultimate reality. This trend reached a kind of apogee, I think, with the publication of D. M. Thomas's extraordinary novel *The White Hotel,* in which Thomas attempts to set up Freudian analysis as the sustaining myth of our time.

In any case, the writer will be heard. Let's explore that for a second. What is the "voice" I'm talking about? How is it established? From what does it derive? First, from exactly that idea of *subject* I mentioned earlier. What does a writer write about? What is the world of the fiction? What kind of people typically inhabit it? When I think of Walker Percy, for instance, a visual image immediately springs to mind: it is a large, well-kept southern golf course, with pine trees in the rough and exceptional water hazards. This is his fictional terrain, just as John Cheever inhabited upper-class suburbia and John Updike inhabits any house in any middle-class neighborhood. Here, for an example, is what I'm talking about, the Third World milieu of V. S. Naipaul, at the beginning of *Guerillas:*

> The sea smelled of swamp; it barely rippled, had glitter rather than color, and the heat seemed trapped below the pink haze of bauxite dust from the bauxite loading station. After the market, where refrigerated trailers were unloading; after the rubbish dump burning in the remnant of mangrove swamp, with black carrion corbeaux squatting hunched on fence posts or hopping about on the ground; after the built-up hillsides; after the new housing estates, rows of unpainted boxes of concrete and corrugated iron already returning to the shantytowns that had been knocked down for this development; after the naked children playing in the red dust of the straight new avenues, the clothes hanging like rags from backyard lines; after this, the land cleared a little. And it was possible to see over what the city had spread; on one side, the swamp, drying out to a great plain; on the side, a chain of hills, rising directly from the plain.
>
> The openness didn't last for long. Villages had become suburbs. Sometimes the side wall of a concrete house was painted over with an advertisement. In the fields that had survived there were billboards. And soon there was a factory area. It was here that the signs for Thrushcross Grange began: the name, the distance in miles, a clenched fist emblematically rendered, the slogan For the Land and for the Revolution, and in a strip at the bottom the name of the firm that had put the sign up. The signs were all new. The local bottlers of Coca-Cola had put one up; so had the American Bauxite Co., a number of airlines, and many stores in the city.
>
> Jane said, "Jimmy's frightened a lot of people."

So we have the writer's fictional terrain to consider, and often we have a particular kind of character who turns up again and again because he's at home there. Here are two paragraphs from the beginning of Raymond Carver's story, "Mr. Coffee and Mr. Fixit." Carver frequently uses first-person narrators.

> I've seen some things. I was going over to my mother's to stay a few nights. But just as I got to the top of the stairs, I looked and she was on the sofa kissing a man. It was summer. The door was open. The TV was going. That's one of the things I've seen.
>
> My mother is sixty-five. She belongs to a singles club. Even so, it was hard. I stood with my hand on the railing and watched as the man kissed her. She was kissing him back, and the TV was going.

Carver characters are somewhat similar to Barry Hannah's characters, except that Hannah is wackier and darker. Here's the narrator of Hannah's story "Love Too Long," telling us about himself:

> My head's burning off and I got a heart about to bust out of my ribs. All I can do is move from chair to chair with my cigarette. I wear shades. I can't read a magazine. Some days I take my binoculars and look out in the air. They laid me off. I can't find work. My wife's got a job and she takes flying lessons. When she comes over the house in her airplane, I'm afraid she'll screw up and crash.
>
> I got to get back to work and get dulled out again. I got to be a man again. You can't walk around the house drinking coffee and beer all day, thinking about her taking her brassiere off. We been married and divorced twice. Sometimes I wish I had a sport. I bought a croquet set on credit at Penny's. First day I got so tired of it I knocked the balls off in the weeds and they're out there rotting, mildew all over them, I bet, but I don't want to see.

After the place and the people, we come inevitably to the question of *tone:* what attitude is the writer taking toward this material. Is it ironic? Are we meant to believe it? or what? Sometimes this is easy, as when we pick up a story by Donald Barthelme and begin to read about angels.

But sometimes the question is more complicated, as in *The French Lieutenant's Woman,* when the intrusive narrative voice continually reminds us that there is a writer manipulating these characters: and forcing us finally to choose the ending. Are we to believe, or not believe? We are meant, I think, to do something rather more complex, just as we are meant to respond to certain South American writers— as we are meant to respond to Tim O'Brien's novel *Searching for Cacciato*, in which the author sets up, in effect, alternate—yet equally believable—realities.

Of course, ambivalence of tone is not new to American writing, but goes way back to the writer's search for an American language that might combine all the old eloquence, all the grand themes, of English literature with the raw new vernacular of our country and with the kind of people who have lived here. Nothing, especially tone, is ever separate from language, either, and we can trace this combination of the high-falutin' and the mundane back to Twain, to Whitman, and especially to William Faulkner. I would like to cite a brief section from *As I Lay Dying*. This is Darl's point of view.

> "If you see a good-sized can, you might bring it," I say. Dewey Dell gets down from the wagon, carrying the package. "You had more trouble than you expected, selling these cakes in Mottson," I say. How do our lives ravel out into the no-wind, no-sound, the weary gestures wearily recapitulant; echoes of old compulsions with no-hand on no-strings: in sunset we fall into furious attitudes, dead gestures of dolls. Cash broke his leg and now the sawdust is running out. He is bleeding to death is Cash.
> "I wouldn't be beholden," pa says. "God knows."

So we frequently find, in contemporary writing, an ambiguity of tone, a blend of realism with surrealism or hyperbole, and often a return to mythic elements. Here's the end of Eudora Welty's story "The Wanderers." An old beggar woman has just sat down next to Virgie Rainey on the stile.

> Occasional drops of rain fell on Virgie's hair on her cheek, or rolled down her arm, like a cool finger; only it was not, as if it had never been, a finger, being the rain out of the sky. October rain on Mississippi fields. The rain of fall, maybe on the whole South, for all she knew on the everywhere. She stared into its magnitude.
> She smiled once, seeing before her, screenlike, the hideous and delectable face Mr. King McClain had made at the funeral, and when they all knew he was next, even he. Then she and the old beggar woman, the old black thief, were there alone and together in the shelter of the big public

tree, listening to the magical percussion, the world beating in their ears. They heard through falling rain the running of the horse and bear, the stroke of the leopard, the dragon's crusty slither, and the glimmer and the trumpet of the swan.

Thinking about Eudora Welty reminds me of how crucial these points of style become for those of us who are from the South, and who are writing about the South. We don't have any new material. We all have doomed cousins who are still going to Sweetbriar and crazy uncles who still live in their mothers' back rooms. A lot of the land is the same. Maybe we don't have the degree of racial guilt, but there's always plenty of general southern guilt to go around. So what are we going to do? How are we going to write about what we know, yet keep it from being trite—keep it from being a bad imitation of those writers we most admire, Faulkner and Eudora Welty and Flannery O'Connor, all those people who have "done" southern so well?

The best we can hope for, since we can't just wish away all those givens we have to work with, is to make it new *through language*—through point of view, through tone, through style. And this is happening all over the place. Bobbie Ann Mason throws all the hyperbole out the window and deals with her people—people who drive school buses and who say Datsun dog, for instance—with a clear, direct, unsentimental precision. It would be so easy to romanticize her people, yet she never does. Walker Percy's ironic detachment; Cormac McCarthy's lush yet enigmatic fables; the way Barry Hannah uses all the old Southern elements but stands them on their heads; Breece Pancake's dark vision; Anne Tyler's abiding sense of magic and the deep mystery at the heart of family life—all these are stylistic approaches, really, to making it brand new.

Even the small considerations of language contribute to any writer's voice: such prosaic questions as the length of the sentences, the favored grammatical constructions, the imagery, or the lack of imagery. All these are points of style, and it is only through style finally—through language—that any writer can be original. All the themes are old.

So we come to the quality of the prose. Is it lean, spare, and reductive, like, say the work of Joan Didion or Grace Paley? Is it lush, full, almost overblown, like that of Joyce Carol Oates? What degree of development is given? How much detail is given, and what kind of detail? Ann Beattie, for instance, rarely gives a physical description of any of her characters. Many contemporary writers write in the present tense and avoid referring to the past at all in the way in which we have traditionally used it, to illuminate character in the present moment of the story.

And a final thought in determining any writer's voice: how present is the author in the work?

Although I had been writing for a long time, I had never, it seemed to me, been able to deal with some of my best material—mostly, the things having to do with my growing up in the mountains. I couldn't write it straight, was the problem. I still felt all the old ambivalence you feel about the place you grew up in. So one day I was kind of messing around, and I wrote the beginning of a story:

> Geneva moves through a dream these days. Right now she sits in a straightback kitchen chair on the front porch, stringing pole beans on a newspaper on her lap and looking up every now and then at the falling-down sidetrack up on the mountain across the road, at the dusty green leaves the way they curl up in the heat, at nothing. It is real hot. The black hair on Geneva's forehead sticks to her skin and she keeps on pushing it back. She strings the beans and breaks them in two and drops them into the pot by her side without once looking down. She feels a change coming on. Geneva has known that something is up ever since last Wednesday night when she hollered out in church.

As soon as I wrote that, I felt the most enormous sense of relief. All of a sudden I was using the way the characters spoke *in the narrative voice,* which plenty of other writers have done, but which had never really occurred to me. This sounds minor, perhaps, but it freed me up enormously. Now I felt that I could write about my characters without writing down to them, because I was using their words, but I wasn't restricted to their words, either. I was using what Tom Wolfe has called the *downstage narrative voice.* All the ambivalence I felt could be contained stylistically. It would even be part of the story, so I could tell what I wanted to tell. Suddenly I could tell things—revivals and beauty contests and first dates and 4-H potato salad-making contests—which I had not been able to tell before.

Since then I've become more and more intrusive, and the writing has come more and more easily. In a short story named "Cakewalk," for instance, I amazed myself by breaking into the narrative with this comment straight from me, the writer—there is not really any narrator in this story.

> There comes a time in a woman's life when the children take over, and what you do is what you have to, and it seems like the days go by so slow while you're home with them, and nothing ever really gets done around the house before you have to go off and do something else which doesn't ever get done either, and it can take you all day long to hem a skirt. Every day lasts a long, long time. But then before you know it, it's all over, those days gone like a fog on the mountain, and the kids are all in school and there you are with this awful light empty feeling in your stomach like the beginning of cramps, when you sit in the chair where you used to nurse the baby and listen to the radio news.

I can't say whether it's good or bad that I have fallen upon this kind of an intrusive, down-home narrative voice. I don't even know that it works. But it has made it possible for me to write about what I want to write about right now—the people I'm interested in, their lives and times.

1985

Anne Tyler

The South without the Scent
of Lavender

Review of *The Collected Stories of Caroline Gordon*

Caroline Gordon published her first story in 1929. In the half-century since, she has produced nine novels, two short-story collections, two books of criticism and (with her husband, Allen Tate) an anthology of fiction. Her territory is the South—specifically Kentucky, in that time not so long ago when families still kept track of first cousins twice removed, and when the men spent their days hunting while the women, left behind, sat langorously on the gallery.

The extraordinary vigor of her "Collected Stories" arises from the fact that Caroline Gordon's heart lies more with the hunters than with those women on the gallery. No scent of faded lavender drifts from these pages. Instead, there's the smell of frost and blood and wood smoke. Dogs bay at possums, hooves clatter past, a child calls, "Honey, Honey, Bee Ball. . . . I cain't see y'all. . . . " There's the taste of home-cured ham, the sight of fish dimpling the water and the baited pause while a bird climbs toward a perfectly aimed shot.

Professor Aleck Maury (whom some may recognize from the novel "Aleck Maury, Sportsman") charges through many of these stories in his hunting coat, brandishing rifle or fishing rod. A recurring theme in the Maury stories is his preference for freedom, however painful or dangerous, over domestication, and the loss of that freedom with the passage of time. Aleck Maury will sacrifice much for the sake of a good hunt. Abandoning an attractive new woman acquaintance when he hears of a run of bass on the Suwannee River, he tosses a line of poetry over his shoulder: "And snatch'd his rudder and shook out more sail." He is contemptuous of his mother-in-law when she asks if time hangs heavy on his hands:

"*Time,* he thought, *time!* They were always mouthing the word, and what did they know about it? Nothing in God's world! He saw time suddenly, a dull, leaden-colored fabric depending from the old lady's hands, from the hands of all of them, a blanket that they pulled about between them, now here, now there, trying to cover up their nakedness. Or they would cast it on the ground and creep in among the folds, finding one day a little more tightly rolled than another, but all of it everywhere the same gray substance. But time was a banner that whipped before him always in the wind! He stood on tiptoe to catch at the bright folds, to strain them to his bosom."

In "Old Red," Aleck Maury, feeling the first pangs of age, dreams he is the wily fox who always eludes his pursuers. In "One More Time," a fishing companion from his past, now terminally ill, drowns himself in the pool where Maury has been casting for bream. "The Last Day in the Field" describes Maury's farewell hunting trip, using the last dogs trained by a man now dead. And in "The Presence," Maury, restricted finally to his boarding house in the company of women and children, watches as a younger man carries on the reckless life that Maury once enjoyed.

The effect of the Maury stories—which are interspersed with others, unrelated—is gradual and cumulative, much like seeing an acquaintance at wide intervals, watching him grow old by fits and starts and feeling, in the end, a sense of sorrow at what he has become. Taken as a whole, these stories are perhaps the most successful, and certainly the most illustrative of Caroline's Gordon's crisp vitality and her constant alertness to the natural world. But she is capable, as well, of quieter subjects—as in "One Against Thebes," a mesmerizing piece in which an ordinary child's daily life takes on the tone of a fairytale:

"A woman is sitting in a rocking chair on the porch and she gets up when she sees them and comes and stands on the top steps and smiles as she takes the basket of peaches from Aunt Maria's hand, then smiles again and, descending a step, lays her hand lightly on the child's shoulder and makes a gesture toward the rear of the house, uttering the words the child has heard every time she has come to this house."

This woman's words—a simple directive to pay respects to an old lady—are implied by subsequent action but never quoted to us outright. The result is that soundless, underwater quality found in dreams.

Dreamlike, too, are the Civil War stories—vividly evocative of the desolate landscape and the crushing exhaustion of the South in its defeat. And for sheer atmosphere, nothing can match "The Olive Garden," in which a man returns to the France of his youth and, without encountering anything from his past but a handful of inanimate objects (a dry fountain, a window, a potting shed), enlists us in his feelings.

There are some failures here—especially in pieces dealing with blacks, where an "I'segwine" tone prevails, and hangings, hauntings and crimes of passion tend to define the characters. And in a few cases there is confusion as to the sex of the narrator, so that we're brought up short and forced to reorient ourselves several pages into the story. But for the most part, Caroline Gordon writes with uncommon probity and assurance. As Robert Penn Warren points out in his introduction, she displays that "solidity of specification" so valued by Henry James. These stories are indeed solid, and indeed specific, and in most instances so real as to make us believe that we ourselves have whistled up our dogs and joined the hunt.

1981

Kaye Gibbons

Planes of Language and Time:
The Surfaces of the Miranda Stories

In 1939 the embryologist Ernest Everett Just published *The Biology of the Cell Surface*, a pioneer study of the relationship between the cellular membrane and the cellular surface. Had Just not been a black scientist working independently in Charleston, South Carolina, during the early decades of the twentieth century, his extraordinary accomplishments might have earned him appropriate renown. He explained, before the invention of an electron microscope that would validate his deduction, that the cellular substance is an active participant in cell activities:

> The surface cytoplasm cannot be thought of as inert or apart from the living cell substance. The ectoplasm [Just's name for the surface material] is more than a barrier to stem the rising tide within the active cell substance; it is more than a dam against the outside world. It is a living mobile part of the cell. . . . It stands guard over the peculiar form of the living substance, is buffer against the attacks of the surroundings and means of communication with it.
>
> —*The Biology of the Cell Surface*

Just might have tested his cell surface hypothesis on the literature of Katherine Anne Porter and observed the same principles of life science at work flawlessly, harmoniously, quietly in the Miranda stories. Correspondences between the life of a cell and the life of these stories order the forces of memory and time that churn beneath calm narrative surfaces.

215

Porter's language, for all its superficial simplicity, pulls the reader vertically towards submerged meanings and horizontally backward through time and memories. Just as the cell surface regulates the cell's internal environment, so does the surface of the Miranda stories transmit the messages of a fictional nucleus to the reader. The relationships between past and present, interior and exterior, symbolic values and superficiality are analogous to Just's cellular theory, unifying the stories into a tightly organized, closed system. This system is framed by young Miranda's initial enchantment with "living memory" ("Old Mortality") and by the reanimation of the past through sensuous memory, the final scene of "The Grave."

Understanding the role of surfaces in the Miranda stories depends on acceptance of the presence of the adult Miranda as their narrator. Her maturity and her distance from her early community are necessary as she views the past with the objectivity of a theater critic, her job in "Pale Horse, Pale Rider." Memories and familial ties, however, soften an unemotional glance backward, pulling her past in so close that Amy's passion and young Miranda's curiosity seem immediate and real.

The experienced Miranda of "Pale Horse, Pale Rider" is privy to the lessons of "ruin" and time. She knows the quest of the "pale rider," and she intrudes throughout "Old Mortality" as if "she were an elder admonishing some younger misguided creature" ("Old Mortality"). Near the beginning of this story the older Miranda, the narrator, interrupts young Miranda's barrage of questions about Aunt Amy with a revelatory assessment of her life: "Ruin has taught me thus to ruminate, that time will come and take my love away" ("Old Mortality"). Time, the immutable cycle that Porter outlines, does eventually take away Miranda's love. At the close of "The Grave" Miranda's credibility as narrator, as the interpreter of her past, is firmly established, for here she gains the artistic insight that embraces sentiment without nostalgia and distance without dispassion.

Miranda's skill as arbiter of conflicts between the "abyss of complaining darkness" and her "reasoning coherent self" ("Pale Horse, Pale Rider") and between her past and present does not compromise her ability to survey exteriors. Visions of a dress or a room are substantial and satisfying, even when the visionary implications are not explored. Bizarre details accumulate on a lively surface that might feature Amy waltzing with a "young man in Devil costume, including ill-fitting scarlet cloven hoofs" or Gabriel standing "fairly shriveled in his blue satin shepherd's costume" ("Old Mortality").

However, Miranda is not content to leave zany details swirling unorganized in her memory. At the close of "Old Mortality" she presses her intellect to assign truths, meanings, to memories recounted to her and to a past she has seen relived scene by scene, tableau-fashion, "peering in wonder like a child at a magic-lantern show" ("Old Mortality"). She does not yet know that she cannot reorder the past nor order her future by an act of will. She needs something closer to an act of faith. In order to discern the truths that flicker beneath that lantern show and behind the illusions of the past, she must gain an unclouded vision of the past.

This sort of vision has nothing to do with will, intellect, or conscious decisions to destroy "distorted images and misconceptions" ("Old Mortality"). Rather, it involves the re-creation of time, and it will not tolerate interference from the intellect. She achieves her goal through no effort of her own, for she finally rushes backward through barriers of contrived meanings, on downward into places where a coffin screw can be a "shining silver dove" and further on down where beauty and pain lay twisted together under a "thin scarlet veil" ("The Grave"). Like Whitman's speaker in "Out of the Cradle Endlessly Rocking," Miranda could also thank a bird:

> Never again leave me to be the peaceful child I was
> before what there in the night,
> By the sea under the yellow and sagging moon,
> The messenger there arous'd, the fire, the sweet hell within,
> The unknown want, the destiny of me.

The stories about Miranda track her growth from childhood to womanhood, marking significant leaps from innocence to experience. Viewed superficially, her struggles are neither extraordinary nor metaphoric. Many girls have spent Saturday mornings waiting for someone to bail them out of boarding school, and many more have held antique photographs and wondered about the past. Miranda's growth, however, is in preparation for her emergence as an artist, for her view of what another Southern writer, Eudora Welty, has termed "sky, water, birds, light, and confluence" (*The Optimist's Daughter*). Porter leaves Miranda poised on a pivotal point of confluence, but when the vision fades away she will click back into time, into a "strange city of a strange country" ("The Grave"), better equipped to understand the world.

The story entitled "The Witness" is the starting point, a story in which themes are sketched out and ordered in planes above and below the narrative surface. Porter achieves distance between exterior description and interior meaning by manipulating simple tones, by working basic colors in a method used and explained by Vincent Van Gogh in a letter to his brother:

> What is called black and white is in fact "painting in black." Painting in this respect, one gives in a drawing the depth of effect, the richness of tone value which must be in a picture. Every colorist has his own peculiar scale of colors. This is also the case in black and white: One must be able to go from the highest light to the deepest shadow, and this with only a few simple ingredients.
> —*Dear Theo: The Autobiography of Vincent Van Gogh*

In "The Witness" Porter goes from "highest light to the deepest shadow" with young Miranda as a fledgling guide to both levels. Miranda, the "little quick one who wanted to know the worst" about slavery ("The Witness"), will someday want to know the worst about war, Aunt Amy, and where baby rabbits come from. Like an inquisitive reader of John Crowe Ransom's poem "Captain Carpenter" or Eudora Welty's *Delta Wedding*, Miranda must ask whether the story is just a good tale or whether it contains memories of personal, passionate involvement in the past. She wonders about the old ex-slave Uncle Jimbilly's connection with history: "Did they act like that to you, Uncle Jimbilly?" ("The Witness"). Because of his emotional involvement, stories about black men dying "by de thousands and tens upon thousands" will never be told with the objectivity of a Ransom or a Welty. For those writers, like Miranda, were part of a new generation of Southern storytellers who could only listen to memories of what older men and women witnessed and lived.

Miranda continues checking beneath surfaces in another story, "The Circus," and everything she finds there sends her screaming home with Dicey, "chilled with a new kind of fear" ("The Circus"). Although a circus is a fine thing for most children to see, Miranda, like Welty's Laura McRaven in *Delta Wedding,* looks past illusion to learn that "sweetness could be the visible surface of profound depths—the surface of all the darkness that might frighten her" (*Delta Wedding*). The acrobatic act pleases her as long as she thinks it is only magic: "Miranda thought at first he was walking on air, or flying, and this did not surprise her" ("The Circus"). When she sees the wire, she understands that the potential for danger exists, for the acrobat is not a magician flying but a man walking on a very thin wire. His fall breaks the spell, the consensus that the show is all illusion and that death could not be part of his act. Miranda's reaction anticipates the fear of Welty's Moon Lake campers in *The Golden Apples* as they watch Loch Morrison hunting for the orphan girl, Easter. Like the circus, childhood in general, a Moon Lake is supposed to be magic, a place to play under the "light, light, light, light, light of the silvery moon." When Easter falls from the diving board like one "hit in the head by a stone from a sling," time that was suspended at Moon Lake is forced back into cyclical reality. Loch Morrison knows about this cycle, and when Miranda stops fearing it, she will understand it, too.

The grimacing dwarf at the circus adds insult to Miranda's injury. She will not accept him as a little odd man, for she senses something terribly wrong with him. After she swats at him, she sees that he is "really human." Once at home, the other children chide Miranda for her foolishness, cataloging all the splendid sights she missed. Miranda's memories are different, for while the others recall a delightful acrobat and a "funny old clown," Miranda recalls the threats beneath the comical surfaces:

> She fell asleep, and her invented memories gave way before her real ones, the bitter terrified face of the man in the blowsy white falling to his death—ah, the cruel joke!—and the terrible grimace of the unsmiling dwarf. She screamed in her sleep and sat up crying for deliverance from her torments.
>
> —"The Circus"

In "The Fig Tree" language creates a calm exterior, a surface as smooth as the earth Miranda pats down over the chicken grave. The process she follows in burying her chicken recalls Hemingway's Nick

Adams's care in selecting grasshoppers, or handling a trout carefully so "he would not disturb the delicate mucus that covered him" ("Big Two-Hearted River"). Miranda wraps her "slimpsy chicken in tissue paper, trying to make it look pretty" ("The Fig Tree"). Both Miranda and Nick respect nature and would agree that consideration should be shown for its cycles. Such concern connects them both in the progression of life and time. Welty's Loch Morrison falls into this same rhythmic progression as he resuscitates Easter.

Although Miranda buries her chicken, a telltale "weep-weep" torments her: "But oh, what had made that funny sound? Miranda's ears buzzed and she had a dull round pain in her just under her front ribs" ("The Fig Tree"). Her fear strikes her with the same "real pain" she felt when the acrobat dangled from his wire. She thinks she has done something horrible when she hears a "little crying voice from the smothering earth, the grave" ("The Fig Tree"). She imagines the chicken clawing and pecking its way through the tissue paper she lovingly wrapped it in. She sees tragedy beneath the surface, and she feels responsible. However, a half-dead chicken is not yelping in its grave, for tree frogs are singing "weep-weep" not in pain but in anticipation of rain. Just as in "The Witness" and "The Circus," Miranda expects to find the worst meanings underneath surfaces. She considers the likeliest hiding places as she searches for hidden messages: behind Uncle Jimbilly's tale, inside the dwarf's "horrid grimace," and under the soil she piles over a dead chicken, packed neatly in a "nice mound, just like people's."

In "Old Mortality" surfaces expand, covering past realities with a "romantic haze" that Miranda will first embrace, then finally destroy. Encountered on a train en route to a family funeral, Cousin Eva pierces this haze, inverting Miranda's sense of order and wrecking the set pieces she has fixed in her imagination. Cousin Eva's vitriolic assertion of her version of the truth about Amy's romantic escapades discounts surfaces, the rhetoric of legend and memory. She has no patience with romance, for she knows the reality of life without illusion and beauty. She has not been able to hide her deformity the way that Amy could adjust her bodice and skirt to hide or reveal cleavage or her tempting white ankles. Cousin Eva knows that reality cannot be decorated and made acceptable by taking a tuck in the truth here and there. Surface illusions have not been kind to Eva, and she denies her traditional role. Whereas Miranda negotiates surfaces while recognizing the "terrors and darkness" beneath ("Old Mortality"), she needs the chinless suffragette to force her into those frightening places. She runs from the circus, but she stands resolute at the close of "Old Mortality," making promises about the future "in her hopefulness, her ignorance." She is bound to fail in her attempt to "always know the truth about what happens" to her because, as the scientist Lewis Thomas explains in *Some Late Night Thoughts on Listening to Mahler's Ninth Symphony:*

> The human mind is not meant to be governed, certainly not by any book of rules not yet written; it is supposed to run itself, and we are obliged to follow it along trying to keep up with it as best we can. It is all very well to be aware of your awareness, even proud of it, but never try to operate it. You are not up to the job. . . . Attempting to operate one's own mind, powered by such a magical instrument as the human brain, strikes me as rather like using the world's biggest computer to add columns of figures, or towing a Rolls-Royce with a nylon rope.

Miranda aims to live without illusions of the sort that her cousin has just swiftly dismantled. She takes Eva's stricture to heart: "Knowledge can't hurt you. You mustn't live in a romantic haze about life" ("Old Mortality"). This forced denial of superficial understanding, of agreed-upon ways of thinking about the past, will frustrate Miranda until she releases control of her mind, letting sensuous memory recreate time for her.

"Pale Horse, Pale Rider" features Miranda living the way she decided to live, and she is miserable. The war forces a wide gulf between reality and the rhetoric that Miranda has just decided to do without. She abides only truth, and she finds plenty behind Adam's eyes and deep within the feverish "whirlpool of gray water turning upon itself for all eternity" ("Pale Horse, Pale Rider").

When Miranda starts rebelling against the community's codes, she echoes Cousin Eva's bitterness. This community calls for rituals, for ways of managing wartime fear and pain, just as the people of Eudora Welty's Morgana need their funeral rites. Miranda's reaction against talking and singing that try to gentle pain rivals her cousin's. Rhetoric, Miranda knows, does not admit Uncle Jimbilly's pain or Adam's fate:

And what are we going to sing this time, "Tipperary" or "There's a Long, Long Trail"? Oh, please let the show go on and be over with. I must write a piece about it before I can go dancing with Adam and we have no time. Coal, oil, iron, gold, international finance, why don't you tell us about them, you little liar?

—"Pale Horse, Pale Rider"

A fever sends Miranda beneath the surface of her consciousness, but nursing brings her back up into the "dull world to which she was condemned" ("Pale Horse, Pale Rider"). She cannot stay submerged, communing with that wonderful light she sees, and she cannot conjure Adam up out of his grave by a "mere act of will" ("Pale Horse, Pale Rider"). By the close of this story Miranda realizes that the promise she made to herself at the close of "Old Mortality" is impossible to keep. Strong and intelligent though Miranda is, she does not see that images are created and re-created in the imagination, not in the calculating, willful intellect. She sees only the ghost of Adam, nothing as real and satisfying as the sight of her brother turning a tiny object over in his hand.

By the close of "The Grave," Miranda has tried many times and in many ways to get beneath surfaces and find beauty there. She realized truths about her family and hated them. She found out the dwarf was human and struck at him. Although the chicken was indeed dead and not struggling in its grave, Miranda imagined its agony so intensely that the chicken might as well have been buried alive. In all the time that Miranda digs beneath surfaces, she does not realize that the very act of digging will destroy anything of value she might find on her way down through layers of meaning or time. Miranda and Paul do not dig the graves in which they find the ring and the coffin screwhead. They were already dug. What they can do is to eye them adventurously and jump in, feeling "nothing except an agreeable thrill of wonder: they were seeing a new sight, doing something they had not done before" ("The Grave").

When Miranda is not trying, when she is not digging graves searching for happiness, she sees what she needs to see and the sight does not terrify her. It fills her again with the "agreeable thrill of wonder" she felt when she and Paul hopped in the open pits. At the close of "The Grave" her vision is restored just as the crumb of Madeleine re-creates

Combray for Proust. Surfaces expand and fold over to create a new vision of something very old. Miranda's sudden memory of Paul proves that up until then she had been poking and prodding at surfaces of time and memory to gain admittance, that she had been using the wrong digging tool all along. She did not even need to work. All she needed was imagination enough to allow a visitation by sensuous memory. Things erupt through surfaces by no act of will, and the memory is no more a locked vault than a cell wall is only a "barrier to stem the rising tide within the cell substance."

1988

Dialogues

The story of shared experience forms the foundation of all communities. Indeed, any sense of community emerges through conversation and dialogue. In a world that is increasingly complex and distant yet closely knit together through the immediacy of technology and transportation systems, such interaction now requires new forms. Women who might have shared their troubles and triumphs at quilting bees or at church, for example, take to the telephone or the airlines. Even those inclined to write letters, a traditional way of staying in touch, employ, as often as not other, quicker ways of communicating.

Throughout this century, however, writers have maintained one form of conversation that serves to bind them together in a loose but largely supportive community. Through reviews of one another's works they have established a public dialogue, and through that dialogue they have created a sense of common experience. Doris Betts, for instance, has written many times on the works of Anne Tyler; Tyler has in turn reviewed the works of Betts. Tyler has also written on the fiction of Mary Lee Settle, as have Betts and Gail Godwin. Their reviews appear in all manner of styles and publications, although largely in newspapers. They represent not so much an academic or scholarly form of literary criticism as an engagement in the work of one another and an effort to share that engagement with the larger community. Not confined solely to the private interactions of individual writers, these reviews demonstrate a remarkable degree of insight, candor, and empathy—essential qualities of friendship and sympathy.

Elizabeth Spencer

Douglas Book Is "Good and Courageous"

Review of *Apostles of Light* by Ellen Douglas

"Apostles of Light" by Ellen Douglas is a good and courageous book. At times it achieves brilliance. It addresses itself, without apology, to one of the knottier problems of our society: the plight of the aged. Yet Miss Douglas has by intelligence and talent avoided writing the sort of social protest novel in which the characters have no life outside the author's purpose. The people in it for the most part, are real in themselves, and she has given us at least two splendidly realized figures who will not fade when her story ends.

Her title is savagely ironic, as is made plain by the opening quotation from the Bible. These 'apostles' are disguised emissaries of Satan. They are those do-gooders we all know so well, spiritual Snopses whose 'helping' others is always mixed in with helping themselves. In this story we observe how they treat the old and for what reasons. There is every shading of attitude toward age here; no line is arbitrarily drawn, and it would be a conscienceless reader indeed who did not at times find his own guilt in these pages. Much of this, Miss Douglas is fair enough to make plain, relates simply to the human predicament. Who wants age, who wants to die? The old make all too plain to the young a disagreeable reality. So, little at a time, damage, like flood water, finds its crevices. Pretty soon we are up to our necks. We are seeing at first hand those who put the old away, tidily tranquilize their human anguish, deny them their dignity, their right to decision, their identity; who do not in the long run even hear them, for to say a person is getting 'senile' is a way of saying that nothing he utters is of any validity.

For all her deceptively quiet manner and muted tone, Miss Douglas' own perception is fierce. If purists complain that novels should not be used to express social problems, let them first dismiss Dickens and Zola; they will have, I think, to come to terms.

The method of the book is extremely interesting, and I urge readers not to be misled by the overleaf, which says, 'Miss Douglas's work lies in the main tradition of the English novel from George Eliot to Eudora Welty,' whatever that means. (There are similarities in literature, but family trees, though often claimed, are seldom seen.) At the present moment in fiction, it's every writer for himself; a general free-for-all exists. We long, as in a children's game, to make everybody freeze for better determining what they're up to. When Miss Douglas's novel, after what seemed to me in the early pages a kind of hesitance, finally strikes free and runs on its own, the method is that of Greek drama. The book discovers this when it finds its true protagonist, Lucas Alexander, a local doctor long known as an eccentric, principally it seems, because he isn't interested in money. A "home" for older citizens has been made from the lovely old family residence of Lucas's lifelong sweetheart, a retired schoolteacher, Martha Clarke. He goes there himself to live, mainly to be near her. Thus he learns firsthand what is going on and it is the gradual unfolding of this situation to his fine intelligence and conscience that generates both pity and terror. True, a sense of doom has been everywhere from the very beginning, though at first only in normal forms—in Martha's sister's death, for instance, in the human plight of aging at all, in Martha's haunted dreams. But it becomes specific and even Satanic in the sinister intrigues and outrageous cruelties of the nursing home scene. So the net is woven. It is finally Lucas' choice, after his long losing battle to expose the truth, to accept doom supinely or to choose his own doom, and his decision is heroic.

Set against Lucas for dramatic contrast, a method which is obvious but which works effectively in this writer's hands, is a selfeducated black man, Matthew Harper. Harper was once Martha Clarke's butler, later a servant in the 'home.' As an intellectual hobby, Harper has devoted himself through the years to finding out all the ways in which human beings have slaughtered each other down through the centuries. This long passage is brilliantly done. It gives a needed dimension, a sort of backdrop, to the book, and it even shines at times with a peculiar charm and humor, though in this story we can't ever feel very confident about laughing. No fictional diversion is this pursuit of Harper's; he, a despised member of society just as are the old, has figured out what to do when the time comes and they are trying to get rid of you; survival is all; forget the 'community'; go and hide. Seeing Lucas's plight at the end leads Harper to try to persuade Lucas to see life in the same way—the old, like blacks, are discards. Mere survival for Lucas and Martha seems in Harper's terms, to be all that is possible. He offers to help them escape and hide. This scene is dramatically fine, perhaps the finest in the book. It maintains an impeccable intellectual tension—its pathos is almost unbearable.

Miss Douglas refuses to overwrite; she is at times too terse. Though the ruthless nurse Miss Crawley is fully realized, a crucial character Howie Snyder does not, it seems to me, reach any rich fictional ambience. An important dimension is missing when Miss Douglas does not explore more deeply the relationship of Lucas and Martha. There is also some spareness in the rendering of lesser characters. These are minor flaws, however, when placed against the rewards of this novel.

1973

Gail Godwin

Review of *Celestial Navigation* by Anne Tyler

Anne Tyler is especially gifted in the art of freeing her characters and then keeping track of them as they move in their unique and often solitary orbits. Her fiction is filled with displaced persons who persist stubbornly in their own destinies. They are "oddballs," visionaries, lonely souls, but she has a way of transcribing their peculiarities with such loving wholeness that when we examine them we keep finding more and more pieces of ourselves.

The hero of her fifth novel is a real artist with real artist's problems. Jeremy Pauling, a 38-year-old bachelor who lives with various boarders in a shabby Baltimore house left to him by his mother, makes sculptures of what his dealer calls "simple humanity." But he is so overcome by the complexity and untidiness and depressing aspects of this same humanity that he suffers nausea and vertigo whenever he ventures as far as the corner grocery store. ("The old ladies were rude and sniveling, the men lacked solidity somehow, and the children seemed to carry a threat of violence.")

He is awed when his dealer, Brian, tells of his plans to sail his new boat by celestial navigation, though, as Miss Vinton, a boarder, observes to herself: "Oh Jeremy . . . you too sail by celestial navigation and it is far more celestial than Brian's." Jeremy makes his sculptures the way other men make maps, "setting down the few fixed points that he knows, hoping they will guide him as he goes floating through this unfamiliar planet."

"Humanity" at last overwhelms Jeremy in the form of a mysterious young woman who comes to live, with her child, in his boarding house. Mary Tell is an unlikely blend of Earth Mother and Maverick. She has a voracious need to give birth to as many children as possible. She also wishes she could climb inside every passing person, learn everything about their lives, "see how and who their friends were, what they fought about." She and Jeremy have five children, though Jeremy can never quite believe he had a part in it.

He is baffled and a little frightened by these fearless creatures who shout and cheer and throw oranges and—unlike himself—brave the teeming streets. Like a man who foresees what is inevitable to himself, he commits them to memory, "preparing for some moment in the future when he could sit down alone and finally figure them out." When this sad moment does come, it is a tribute to the author's gentle genius in preserving the integrity of her people that we do not hate Mary Tell. And she succeeds in convincing us that Jeremy Pauling's first and final act of heroism—taking a bus across Baltimore to visit Mary and his children—is more valiant and terrifying for him than blasting off to Venus would be for an astronaut.

1974

Gail Godwin

An Epic of West Virginia

Review of *The Killing Ground* by Mary Lee Settle

The Killing Ground opens with novelist Hannah McCarkle returning home to the mining town of Canona, West Virginia, where she has been invited to lecture on her work at the old country club on the hill. Though a pariah in the eyes of "the best people" among whom she was raised (Hannah marched against the war in Vietnam; worse, she "exposed" her family and region in her novels), she is "the only famous person" who will consent to be the star attraction for this important fundraiser for the town's new art museum. "All that's left to us is the arts," bewails one member of the hanging committee, as the four ladies drive Hannah to her lecture. "You have to understand . . . that this audience is not really intellectual or literary like you're used to," the same lady tells Hannah as the Cadillac climbs the hill and we, the readers, receive capsule histories of the "pathetic, redundant" lives of these four women who do hope Hannah will keep her remarks light and amusing. On the drive, Hannah sits rather grudgingly and compares her companions to herself and to the land around them:

> They carry in themselves the residue of old-needs and fears which have been composted into prejudice. The origins are buried in their minds as deeply as the spearhead was buried under [Hannah's ancestor's] tree, for they fear the exposure of facts as I fear the isolation of illusion.

These women are, Hannah concludes to herself, in a little ecstasy of hatred, "in one of the bloodiest centuries of the Christian era, women to whom nothing has happened that is not personal."

But personal things have a way of happening whenever Hannah comes home, and this time is no exception. While she is presenting a high-minded and technically sophisticated lecture on how she went about tracing the history of this community through novels (which, incidentally, have the same titles as Mary Lee Settle's Beulah Quintet, of which *The Killing Ground* is the conclusion), word spreads round the hall that a popular bachelor in town has hanged himself. The crowd disperses with alacrity; the dinner party for Hannah is canceled on the spot as the "hanging committee" transfers its interest from art to the deceased. The personal has, if you will, avenged itself on Hannah, who is left alone with her memories of another homecoming, eighteen years ago, when she arrived just in time for the freakish death of another popular Canona bachelor: her beloved brother Johnny.

The circumstances surrounding this death, caused by a blow from a resentful hill kin's fist against the face of white-dinner-jacketed Johnny during a Saturday night sojourn in the jailhouse drunk tank, were what galvanized Hannah McCarkle into becoming a novelist. Before that, she had lived

> of course, in New York, a socialist in Bonnie Cashin leather, a radical with a guest list that consisted always of one or two understanding friends from Sweet Briar . . . one black Ph.D. from Columbia, two beats, a junkie, somebody from the UN . . . and, of course, the friends who mirrored what I was, thirty-year-old, carefully-brought-up rebellious children.

The impact of her promising, attractive brother's wasteful death, and the social and historical questions that lie behind it, impel Hannah to begin a fictional quest that will take her all the way back to 1649 to an ancestor, also named Johnny, a soldier in Cromwell's army who is shot for refusing to doff his hat to authority. From England she will begin her imaginative recreation of the collective consciousness of the people who settled the hills and valleys of Canona, instilling into their descendants a "genetic sense of loss," some dim racial memory of being kicked out, of having to leave home. Through four novels, Hannah will trace the paradoxical, ornery seam that runs through her people or perhaps all Americans, making them fight their oppressors to the death for freedom, yet imitate the pretensions of these oppressors once they've got it. It is this central paradox that provides the themes and the tensions in Hannah's (and Mary Lee Settle's) Beulah books: we see generation after generation struggling out of poverty, anonymity, danger, only to achieve the house on the hill and start aping the very oppressors who threw out their ancestors.

Until her ill-fated lecture at the old country club, Hannah thought her project was almost done: *Prisons, O Beulah Land, Know Nothing,* and *The Scapegoat* were to be the great act of imagination which would set her free to live in the present. Now she realizes that the quartet must be a quintet, and the last book must deal with what's closest to home: *The Killing Ground* will be the personal story behind the historical, fictionalized ones. In it, Hannah must come full circle back to her own time, her immediate family, the wasted Johnny of her own generation, and her own struggle to leave home without getting trapped by the old fears and hatreds.

It is perhaps Hannah's grimness as she shoulders the last burden of this huge, protracted task she has set for herself that gives this final volume of the series its joyless, duty-ridden tone. ("My God, I have traced us through four books, and still it wasn't over, paid my dues and been charged again.") Unfortunately, this tone of a writer/protagonist being overawed by her own Grand Design interferes with the enjoyment of the work. Every time we begin to be eased into the stream of fiction, the voice of Hannah pulls us back with an interpretation of the events we are witnessing, the characters we are getting to know, quite well, on our own. Settle ought to trust her vivid, discriminating eye, her accurate ear more: what people do and how they express themselves reveal much in this society Settle evokes for us, where young women keep fox heads in the deep freeze, and uncles name their dogs Calhoun and Jubal, and a young man in a dinner jacket smirks sarcastically at a redneck inferior and says, "*Thank you,*" after the redneck's fist had dealt his killing blow. But Hannah is too often at our elbow, reminding us how these people are generic as well as personal, or assuring us, mid-description, how much she condemns them, even though she is one of them.

> He never did an evil thing. He was honored by everyone who had ever known him, mild anti-semite, racist; he stood for everything I hated. I

was at war with the love I bore him. . . . His imitators, the wild, peripheral men we bred, in their pickup trucks and with their gun racks,
who were our own distant blood, acted out dreams for him he didn't
know he had. He made jokes. They acted on them.

Here a startling insight into kindly Uncle Ephraim, the gentleman
farmer, loses half its impact because of Hannah's untimely infusion of
hate. It's hard to see a character clearly when you are rushing to his
defense. Just as, when Hannah brought the weight of the Christian
centuries down on those ladies with their spotted hands in the Cadillac, I felt suddenly more sympathetic toward them than I'm sure
Hannah meant me to feel.

Maybe it was part of Mary Lee Settle's plan to make Hannah, her
mouthpiece and alter ego, difficult to like; perhaps she thought it
would be unfair, making "herself" lovable while drawing such re-
lentlessly devastating portraits of Hannah's family and friends.
(Hannah's mother is a monster of Southern respectability; her sister a
cornucopia of small-minded bitcheries.) Whatever happened here, Settle is capable of creating more appealing heroines: the headstrong,
passionate Lily Lacey, the mine owner's daughter in *The Scapegoat,*
who was, like Hannah, an idealist, an activist, but also charming. I'm
also thinking of that tough, brave, elegant young woman in *All the
Brave Promises,* Settle's fascinating and moving memoir of her time in
the Royal Air Force in World War II. It is because I loved this book so
much that I felt so impatient with the voice in *The Killing Ground.*
The voice of the memoir is compassionate, perceptive, warm. I kept
wondering why Settle had denied her alter ego in *The Killing Ground*
a fuller range of the tones she had in her to draw on.

Although I could not love the book, or lose myself in it, I was
compelled, with Hannah, to pursue the "mystery" of brother Johnny's
needless death. It is a mystery in the philosophical sense. We know
who felled this last male hope of the McCarkles, but we must learn,
through Hannah's tireless researches into family secrets, what it is in a
society that breeds dangerous "feral twins." Hannah finally tracks
down her brother's destroyer on a final trip home to the funeral of an
eccentric old aunt who has been sitting on the information Hannah
needs for her epilogue. It is with a grudging acceptance that Hannah

has been right all along in her thesis that we discover Johnny's killer diligently struggling up through the layers of Canona society—trying to become Johnny.

During her country club lecture, Hannah tells her Canona audience that she has been trying

> to trace the clues to both the failure of a dream and its persistence in our innate dissatisfaction with things as they are, that is our constant under-current, and breaks sometimes into revolt . . .

She accomplishes this task to her own satisfaction at the end of *The Killing Ground*. As her plane circles higher above Canona, she feels she carries away something deeper than the land whose history and people have enthralled her for so long. The single legacy she chooses to keep from her heritage is "the choice to choose, to be singular, burn bridges, begin again, whether in a new country or a new way of seeing or a new question. . . ."

We come away admiring her ambitious undertaking and her stamina to complete it; we cannot help but hope her future choices will earn her that eventual larger freedom whose ripest fruit is compassion.

1982

Anne Tyler

Stories of Escape and Love

Review of *Beasts of the Southern Wild* by Doris Betts

The title story in Doris Betts' new collection concerns an unhappily married woman who, in moments of privacy, leads a fantasy life as a black man's concubine. It is fitting that it *should* be the title story, for much of the book deals with people straining toward some sort of release, either real or imaginary, from their present situations. A scarred and ugly girl journeys to a faith healer for the gift of beauty. A woman commuting to a tedious job heads her car off a bridge and floats downstream, evolving from driver to hitchhiker on a dreamlike river. A boy who is badgered by his half-mad mother descends into a secret world of horror where he plots his route to freedom.

The lives that the characters try to flee from are generally not so much tragic as bleak. The true evils are dullness, lovelessness, narrowness of spirit. In "The Glory of His Nostrils," one of Miss Betts' comic pieces, a widow bewails the hardships her late husband had to endure and walks the streets reading Job aloud; but the pestilences that plagued *her* Job were bank errors, canceled appointments, and dented fenders. She is rescued by a larger-than-life man, a self-confessed abortionist who persuades her to dye her hair bright red. Her escape route is a physical one, out of town by railroad, and she is last seen rubbing noses with her rescuer in a lighted train window "like a speechless Eskimo in a flaming parka."

Most of the escapes in these stories, however, are the sort that occur only in the imagination. Like the woman commuter, Doris Betts often starts on prosaic ground and floats off into dreams and nightmares and fantasies and myths. She has an especially deft touch when it comes to madness—a form of departure that is used several times.

In "The Spider Gardens of Madagascar," for instance, we learn every facet of the disturbed mother's erratic behavior, her whining, her reproachful speeches. Beginning reasonably, she suggests to her son that they start a new life together; when he agrees, she wonders why he isn't more enthusiastic; she accuses him of being disinterested, then unloving; she ends up in tears, wishing she were dead. Her gradual slipping across the line between logic and illogic is precisely recorded, and as with most of these stories, the structure is almost seamless. It has been built up layer by layer, detail by detail, until it forms a solid whole that is a pleasure to read.

The style here is more angular, harder-edged, than in the author's previous collection. In stories about unlikable people or unpleasant situations, there is a brittleness than can be uncomfortable. This is most apparent in "Burning the Bed," a characterization of a woman grudgingly tending her dying father, or in "Hitchhiker," with its slick description of hangovers and cocktail-party chitchat. It is only when Miss Betts deals with positive situations—places you imagine she would like to be herself, characters she feels close to—that she really draws the reader in with her.

She is unsurpassed, for instance, when writing about love (surely the most difficult subject around, in spite of all the people who attempt it), and she proves it here in "The Mother-in-Law," a long meditation on family love and its responsibilities and failures. It is the most moving story in the book. A household comes beautifully to life—effortlessly, you might say, but that is only proof of how well Miss Betts can write.

1974

Doris Betts

More Like an Onion than a Map

Review of *The Odd Woman* by Gail Godwin

Because Gail Godwin's complicated third novel, *The Odd Woman,* is shaped more like an onion than a map, it may help to peel off three major themes before trying to reconstruct its plot.

The first theme involves the narrator, Jane Clifford, an unmarried teacher of women's studies at a Midwestern university. She is "odd" like a single glove or a left shoe; in society's eyes, she is the loose half of an unknown but presumably matched male-female pair. Lacking what Webster's might call her "complementary mate," Jane almost literally invents one in the person of Gabriel Weeks, only to learn in seven hectic days how little the actual man ever resembled the angelic image she had ascribed to him.

Around this single life radiate the lives of other women who offer Jane alternatives and against whom she measures her life. Like her, these women have also given their lives to imagined men, wasted their fears on dreamed villains, or married "ideal" husbands and pretended idyllic bliss for years.

Enveloping the whole is a larger and more pessimistic theme: though Jane wakes up from her dream of Gabriel, she never fully awakes from the confusion that caused it—that reality becomes the lie we imagine it to be. As if to illustrate Jane's steady measure of life against books, Godwin compares her characters with invented ones in the Victorian novel Jane will teach. *The Odd Women,* written in 1893 by George Gissing.

Confusing? So does the novel seem at first, but its intelligence and verbal richness make the thematic convolutions worthwhile.

As the book opens, Jane Clifford, 32, liberated but romantic, lies insomniac in the night beside her clock, inscribed *Tempus Fugit*. She calls it "old T.F." She is meditating on the power of words as well as on her course in visionary literature, beyond words. She prefers reflections on Dante, Donne, and Rilke to considering two frightening realities: (1) that her beloved grandmother, Edith, is dying this same night in North Carolina, and (2) that she may at any moment be attacked by the local night prowler, the Enema Bandit.

The Enema Bandit is real; lately he has terrorized Jane's college community by entering unlocked apartments and giving enemas to women only, though he does no further harm. Indeed, as bandits go, he is surprisingly gentle. We all know the stuff that enemas remove: the operative, foreshadowing metaphor seems to be that many women could stand its loss. A week later, in Chapter 18, the novel ends with Jane thinking she has heard the Bandit outside her own window, and perhaps she has "unlocked" her life to his entry. Between these opening and closing metaphors, seven days and 50-odd years of the lives of many women pass through Jane's experience and memories; the link between all their stories is always the gap between what women dream and how they must actually live. Jane almost becomes an "enema bandit" herself; she grows so relentless in her search to eliminate wasted falsehood in favor of truth. Eventually her own gut is the last one left to clean.

The women involved are: her grandmother, Edith Dewar Barnstorff; her mother, Kitty Sparks; her long-dead aunt, Cleva Dewar; and her best friend, Gerda.

It is Edith's death that calls her home to Asheville. Here she recalls the Southern lady grandmother who reared her on outdated principles, whose favorite saying was "life is a disease," and who claimed she married the one man who would save her from it. Edith continued revering that husband's memory long after much memory could have lasted, and he had become only a ghost.

After the funeral, Jane stays on to help her mother, Kitty—also a teacher—settle the estate. Kitty's second husband is Ray Sparks, who once studied Keats in her class and called her his "Belle Dame sans

Merci." She has not retained that role; Ray has grown into such a merciless, mercenary, overbearing husband that Kitty has now jilted him for God and the mystics. The original attraction between them was sexual, and Kitty chose flesh over spirit while still dreaming of her secret, never consummated love for a professor at Tulane. Now she has escaped entirely to Jesus, as other women in the novel choose to worship whatever is absent from their daily experience.

Among Edith's possessions, Jane and Kitty find old papers referring to Aunt Cleva Dewar, who in 1905 ran away with a traveling actor in a melodrama, died in childbirth, and left a baby daughter to be sent home South and reared on new distortions of reality. Aunt Cleva met her villain between acts, a parallel for the fragmentary lives most of Godwin's women lead with other part-time men. Later in New York, Jane, reading his name in an old theater program, decides to search for the real man whom she has always imagined as a destroyer of young virgins, and whose melodramatic seduction still fascinates her.

At this point, the themes of Jane's current love affair and Aunt Cleva's old one join. Jane has gone to New York to meet Gabriel Weeks and to re-create and reject his love. Here she also finds Aunt Cleva's actor-lover, now in his nineties, and either he's forgotten he ever fathered a child, or else the Dewars have had the villain's name wrong for years.

The theme of most dramatic interest, Jane Clifford and Gabriel Week's relationship, is assembled by hindsight. Jane has loved him sporadically and abstractly for two years. Having met the "bringer of good news" at a Modern Language Association meeting, Jane knows him largely through letters, and from puzzling through his scholarly art-history work on the Pre-Raphaelites. They have met very seldom. (Gerda, the realistic friend, counting their clandestine meetings in various hotels, dismisses the two-year devotion as "fourteen furtive fucks.") By the time they meet in New York, Jane has been so steadily involved in the struggles between literary/mundane, abstract/concrete, and romantic/realistic that she—who makes up prayers while making love—is forced to see that her married lover is not the angelic man she imagined.

They quarrel and separate. Jane, disillusioned with the realities of both her lover and the 19th-century villain, flees to Chicago to her friend Gerda, who edits the magazine *Feme Sole* (Old French: "Woman Alone"). There Jane finds that Gerda and the women on her staff are also tilting at male windmills of their own invention. In her own bed again at the novel's end, still sleepless, Jane will end as she must, "trying to organize the loneliness and the weather and the long night into something of abiding shape and beauty."

Even this sketchy summary is necessary before we place Godwin's novel in the context of Gissing's, which Jane Clifford is reading while we read this one. Gissing's grim view of Victorian life focused, in *The Odd Women,* on the despair of poor, uneducated, and unmarried women, making vivid his belief that "misery is the keynote of modern life." As Jane reads, she attempts to direct her own years like a penlight along that Aristotelian plot line she admires: from Possibility to Probability to Necessity. Gissing's five biographies of women measure the shadows cast by herself and other living and dead women. Nor is it accident that Aunt Cleva, exposed to the pretend world of the stage, became a melodramatic figure herself. Melodrama, the 90-year-old actor tells Jane, is the naturalism of the dream world. Jane, who begins by wanting her life "to make sense to the careful reader," is left in the end like Gissing's women, trying to make sense of it to herself. Gissing "let his characters think," Jane concludes, "and though all came to horrible ends, they kept track of themselves so beautifully along the way."

The weakness of Godwin's novel derives directly from its strength. Concentrating as she must on false female images of men and the collapse of the images, Godwin operates solely within the subjectivity of her narrator. Jane's is a strong, word-loving, intelligent subjectivity. Within Jane's mind, male characters float away, dematerialized, and that steady flotation is part of the writer's intention. Yet, by missing their reality, we readers become locked into Jane Clifford's exact position: we seek in the novel some image of maleness with which no women can live. A more realistic writer would have chosen to show the contrast, perhaps, by introducing a male character who *was* real, and permitting him to enact the contrast Jane can only meditate upon.

Readers who do not savor inner denouements, or enjoy watching multiple themes become gradually manifest through skillful language, will find Jane Clifford solipsistic. Such readers may feel they have driven for a week inside a closed car with Jane, all windows misted shut to close off the larger world.

Other readers, facing the much-feared Enema Bandit again in the last chapter, will suddenly sense how many circles of plot and theme come together at that moment, and will turn back—as I did—to read the novel again.

1975

Anne Tyler

Mary Lee Settle: Mining a Rich Vein

Review of *The Scapegoat* by Mary Lee Settle

At 3 o'clock on a June afternoon in 1912, the scene at a West Virginia mine owner's house is a "regular tableau vivant," as one of the daughters describes it. Papa is down at the tennis court, Mother overseeing her three girls, the girls themselves lolling in their white summer dresses among a trio of admiring young men. But these young men are armed detectives, sent to guard against striking miners; and when Althea, the family coquette, poses for her picture on the rose-covered porch, it's with a machine gun standing next to her, and when she flirts with her favorite beau she gets gun grease on her lace peplum.

What a perfect opening for *The Scapegoat*! Leisurely and richly detailed, this book takes its time, sets the handcarved furniture just so, lovingly arranges its languid, elegant characters—while all around swarms harsh reality, in the form of rebellious miners and homesick immigrant strikebreakers shipped in from out of state.

It's Mary Rose, the youngest daughter, who introduces us to the family in its initial repose. Mary Rose's chattery voice, hovering dangerously on the edge of cuteness, sets up a faint distrust in the reader, but other voices soon take over to speak with more depth and passion—the detectives, the dying mine owner, an Italian laborer's wife, and the "Miners' Angel," Mother Jones, among others. Althea the coquette, now grown old and bitter, looks back upon that summer and reminisces sadly: "Oh I was the loveliest thing when I was a girl. Mother had brought me a hat in the Via Condotti in Rome. It was the loveliest thing you ever saw and it cost the earth, pale gray clouds of georgette with pink rosebuds . . ." And Lily, the troublemaker of the daughters, crusades for women's voting rights and rages against the capitalist mine bosses. "Lily," says one of her sisters, "has an ironing-board body and a critical soul. . . . She has always refused to let us *not* notice things."

This refusal of Lily's is what saves *The Scapegoat* from being merely a period piece. It gives the novel its tension, its twist of events that keeps the reader's interest, Lily is a perfect example of the naive do-gooder—morally indignant, with ease, from the safety of her dotted Swiss world. You can't help liking her—there's no doubt about her earnestness—but at the same time you groan and wince for her. Entering a miners' gathering after pointlessly crawling through a mine shaft, Lily is proud that "the dirt of the people" covers her hands and her dress. "She hadn't noticed that the women inside were all as clean as new pins." When she wants to arrange a meeting with a laborer in order to enlighten him with passages from Montaigne, she ties hand-kerchiefs to trees—a signal learned from some swashbuckling book. "So much of it was games," the laborer reflects, "—games with real people and real blood. Jesus."

Real people and real blood win out, of course, in the end. Lily unwittingly causes more violence on her own than any capitalist mine boss would have. Her games backfire, although Lily herself (in a brown silk hat with her ivory wool because "ladies don't wear black with white") slips away scot-free, or almost free.

Mary Lee Settle's last novel, *Blood Tie,* won the National Book Award in 1978. The prize was well-deserved, but *The Scapegoat* is, I think, an even better book. Like *Blood Tie,* it shows the inner workings of a prodigious variety of people, but these people are somehow closer to us, less brittle, more genuine, their contradictions and self-delusions more subtly dealt with. Hard-bitten Mother Jones ("sitting there dumpy like a sweet little old lady, about the shape of a keg of dynamite") grows as familiar to us as our own grandmothers. We see into the very soul of Annunziata Pagano as she coolly, firmly summons the Italian-mama hysteria that will help her control a crisis. We know first-hand that Captain Dan Neill, so worshipped by his men, owes his calm and silence not to courage but to despair; and that the genteel mine owner feels besieged, almost panicked, by the dependency of too many women. And there's an arresting clarity in the picture of Essie Catlett supervising the vegetable gardens of the homeless strikers, hauling her chair out to the weeds and rocking there, issuing instructions.

Or here is Lily, away from home at last, nursing wounded soldiers behind the battle front: "In the stretched silence of the night Lily let herself retreat, for rest from all of them, back into the valley of her mind, almost homesick. She let herself hear the bird voices of her blood sisters. Althea called, 'Lily, I know what you're up to! You can't fool me,' and Mary Rose sang, 'I'm going to tell my mamma on you.' The voices made her smile. The soldiers said that at the front, ten miles away, when the guns stopped, the birds sang."

In one sense, *The Scapegoat* is a straightforward, linear novel. Its four parts cover, in proper order, a single period from 3 o'clock one afternoon to 8 o'clock the following morning. But in another sense, it's more of an octopus shape, with the repercussions from some events branching out to other events, years later, of which we're given glimpses. When I finished the book, I started re-reading it, telling myself that now I could pick up the hints dropped in Part I. When I found myself in Part II, still re-reading, I had to face facts: *The Scapegoat* is hard to say goodbye to. It's a whole slice of a long-ago world, with its leaves still rustling and its voices still murmuring—a quiet masterpiece.

1980

Anne Tyler

All in the Family

Review of *A Mother and Two Daughters*

by Gail Godwin

Gail Godwin already has to her credit a host of memorable women characters. In her five previous books—one short story collection and four novels, including the wonderful *The Odd Woman*—she has created heroines who are intelligent, independent, and ruefully humorous. They're strong, but subject to the usual human weaknesses: insomnia and late-night loneliness. They often make mistakes in their relationships with men, but their lives never totally center on these men. Unlike, say, Edna O'Brien's heroines, these women retain a core of resourcefulness and dignity. Any one of them would make a very good friend.

The women in *A Mother and Two Daughters* are recognizably Godwin women, but in varying degrees and permutations. Nell, the mother, is perhaps the most likable—old-fashioned in many ways, a nurse turned housewife, possessed of a strong sense of duty and moral obligation, but not at all passive or clinging.

Cate, her firstborn, now approaching forty, has much in common with Jane Clifford of *The Odd Woman*. She teaches in a college, lives alone, prides herself on her independence. She's also fiercely, annoyingly self-righteous, and cannot observe a single foible without sermonizing upon it endlessly. As her mother remarks, she's given to "sacrificing people to ideals."

Cate's younger sister, Lydia, is outwardly the more successful of the daughters. She's married well, has two young sons, and lives a life so efficiently organized that it's almost funny. But as the novel opens, she is entering a state of change. She and her husband have separated, and she's planning for a career of her own.

The event that brings the women together is the death of Leonard Strickland, Nell's husband and the father of Cate and Lydia. Significantly, in a novel that devotes much thought to the individual's struggle to survive in a larger society, Leonard's death is brought on at least in part by the social demands of a traditional Christmas party. The dowager queen of Mountain City—a small Southern metropolis not unlike Asheville, North Carolina—asks him first to whip up the eggnog by hand, then to see her maid safely home, which means climbing a steep hill on foot. Shortly afterward, while driving on the expressway, Leonard suffers a fatal heart attack, wrecking his car in the process and slightly injuring Nell.

In reacting to their loss, the three women are convincingly, endearingly true to themselves. Nell is still the caretaker, still smoothing troubled waters even from her hospital bed. Cate is no sooner home than she revives her stubborn feud with the dowager queen. And the practical Lydia, driving toward the funeral with a carload of frozen casseroles, reflects that the L. L. Bean wool shirt she bought her father for Christmas can be given to her husband instead.

Leonard's death is simply a point of entry for the reader. It is not (to my disappointment) one of those drawstring events that gather a plot to a single focus; but it does allow us to see how the three women act with each other before they continue on their separate courses. In the months following the funeral, Nell begins to adapt to widowhood, Cate deals with an unwanted pregnancy, and Lydia, newly single, finds herself a lover, a profession, and an interesting woman friend. We don't see the three together again until summer, after much has changed in their lives—but not, as it turns out, in their relationships with each other.

A publicity sheet that accompanies this book quotes Gail Godwin as saying that she's trying for

> a vision of America, where we've been and where we're going. . . . I see
> *A Mother and Two Daughters* as an attempt to penetrate, often humorously, the way a certain group of characters behave both as their stubborn unique selves, and as part of the interweaving, interacting system we call society.

She has succeeded, I believe. Certainly the three women represent three very different styles of coping with the modern world; and their individual histories reflect enough about their culture to interest an alert sociologist. But the quotation that better sums up the virtues of this novel is the one that occurs to Leonard Strickland just before his death—a passage from Montaigne.

> To storm a breach, conduct an embassy, govern a people, those are brilliant actions. To scold, laugh . . . and deal gently and justly with one's family and oneself . . . that is something rarer, more difficult, and less noticed in the world.

A Mother and Two Daughters has much to say about modern society, but it speaks even more affectingly and more resonantly about the tiny, cataclysmic events that make up domestic life. A grown woman, long since proven competent and successful, still has a feeling of miserable inadequacy when confronting her older sister. A wife supposedly accustomed to widowhood experiences her grief all over again when she discovers the emerging crocuses planted by her husband over twenty years ago. And her grief is unsentimental, unglorifying, and therefore all the more poignant:

> . . . Leonard hadn't been a saint. He had known quite well how to use his gentle unworldliness to evade confrontations; he exempted himself from family squabbles with a maddening sublimity: there he'd be, sitting under his earphones, rapt with opera, or in his study reading a dead Roman lawyer's letters to a friend, while the rest of them tiptoed around, hissing and smoldering at one another. He had driven her crazy many a time while he decided upon a parking place. And . . . she had lost her savor for arguing with him early in the marriage: she would lose track of her best points while waiting for him to finish a sentence.

The little world of Mountain City is as meticulously documented—the rituals of Christmas party and book club meeting; the maid who goes home to the slums every evening laden with hand-me-down clothes and leftover food, "everything in the world but the minimum wage"; the town heiress whose money comes from an ancestral energy tonic that doesn't freeze in winter. There's an observant, amused, but kindly eye at work here, and not a single cheap shot is taken at these people who might so easily have been caricatures in someone else's hands.

And any Northerner contemplating a trip South ought to read about Lydia's conquest of an elderly lady named Miss Mary McGregor Turnbull. Lydia's deference, her willingness to "place" her own last name, her chatty autobiography combined with ladylike reserve—all come straight from an invisible, but nonetheless real, etiquette book for a certain distinct segment of our culture.

Best of all, *A Mother and Two Daughters* demonstrates, once again, Gail Godwin's uncommon generosity as a storyteller. She is openhanded—she's positively spendthrift—with her tales. The most insignificant character travels on a stream of absorbing histories, past love affairs, coincidences, recurring themes. Just look at the story of Nell's semi-seduction before her marriage; or of how old Uncle Osmond lost his nose in World War I; or of Lydia's cold-blooded pursuit of her husband-to-be. Any one of these plots could possibly have been a novel on its own, or at least a short story, but Gail Godwin doesn't measure things out so penuriously. When you read one of her novels, you have a feeling of abundance.

Is *A Mother and Two Daughters* as good as *The Odd Woman?* Is that even a fair question to ask?

The Odd Woman remains one of my all-time favorites, perhaps partly because of the element of surprise—I read it before I knew how much one could expect of Gail Godwin. *A Mother and Two Daughters* lacks that element, of course, and it suffers too from what seems to me an unnecessary summary epilogue—an epilogue that leaps too far ahead, ties things up too suddenly, and takes place, moreover, in 1984. (I don't want to sound pessimistic, but how is she so sure there's going to *be* a 1984?)

There is one improvement, though. In *A Mother and Two Daughters,* the male characters have real depth and texture. Dear Leonard Strickland, and Cate's redneck millionaire suitor, and Lydia's sweetly stuffy husband and her earnest lover—are all solidly believable. For the first time, Gail Godwin's men are equal to her women. And that's saying something.

1982

Anne Tyler

Kentucky Cameos

Review of *Shiloh and Other Stories*

by Bobbie Ann Mason

People who associate *The New Yorker* with fragile, sophisticated, often eventless short stories have been receiving a few surprises lately. One was a story called "Shiloh," in which a trucker temporarily grounded by an accident tried to grow closer to his wife only to learn that she had mentally left him far behind and was preparing to fly. Another was "Nancy Culpepper," about a one-time country girl's return to her senile grandmother's house to search for an antique photograph of her namesake. In "Offerings," a grandmother and a mother tried to put a good face on a visit to the chaotic rural cabin of a young woman with a disintegrating marriage, and in "Third Monday," a woman fell deeply, silently in love with a man who traveled the fleamarket circuit trading pocketknives and hound dogs.

The author of these stories is Bobbie Ann Mason, and to say that she is a "new" writer is to give entirely the wrong impression, for there is nothing unformed or merely promising about her. She is a full-fledged master of the short story, and *Shiloh and Other Stories*, her first collection, is a treasure.

Her characters are backwoods Kentuckians, for the most part, and they're so vividly and lovingly portrayed that we feel we know everything about them. We know their food: the potato and mushroom-soup casseroles, uncooked fruitcake made with graham cracker crumbs and marshmallows, and marshmallow-centered sweet-potato balls rolled in crushed cornflakes. We know their clothing: the women's pantsuits and the men's Worm-and-Germ caps from the feed mill. We know they earn their living selling Tupperware or clerking in Kroger's, the K-Mart, or J.C. Penney, and they pass their free time making latch-hook wall hangings of an Arizona sunset.

They talk of "curtain material, Edda's granddaughter's ovary infection, a place that appeared on Thelma's arm, and the way the climate has changed." They speak of a "datsun dog" and an "old stringling cat." What they say comes through so clearly and directly that their voices ring through our living rooms. "You don't make over me any more," a wife tells her husband sadly. A mother apologizes for a cranky child: "I reckon sooner or later she was bound to show out." Their English is often ungrammatical and filled with gangling, country-style similes, but not a one of these people is described with anything less than complete respect. Characters alone, of course, don't make a story, no matter how quirky or colorful; nor does an eagle eye or a perfect-pitch ear. What matters finally is that the story enlarge our view of human beings, and these do. They are extraordinarily touching, in the most delicate and apparently effortless way. They explore, usually, the sense of bewilderment and anxious hopefulness that people feel when suddenly confronted with change. It is especially poignant that the characters in these stories, having led more sheltered lives than the average reader, are trying to deal with changes most of us already take for granted.

"One day I was listening to Hank Williams and shelling corn for the chickens and the next day I was expected to know what wines went with what," Nancy Culpepper says. The women in "Third Monday" are throwing a traditional baby shower, but the mother-to-be is a proudly unwed thirty-seven-year-old, and since amniocentesis has divined the baby's sex the cake reads WELCOME HOLLY. In "Graveyard Day," a divorcee who's considering remarriage finds herself unable to accept the idea that families should "shift membership, like clubs." A stepfather for her daughter, she thinks, would be "something like a sugar substitute," something like "a substitute host on a talk show."

The trucker husband in "Shiloh," baffled by his wife's body-building exercises and her recipes for "unusual foods" like tacos and lasagna, tries desperately to maintain some link with her.

Norma Jean works at the Rexall drugstore, and she has acquired an amazing amount of information about cosmetics. When she explains to Leroy the three stages of complexion care, involving creams, toners, and moisturizers, he thinks happily of other petroleum products—axle grease, diesel fuel. This is a connection between him and Norma Jean.

In "Rookers"—a jewel of a story that's evidently never been published elsewhere—a lonely father searches for a link with his modern, rather brittle college daughter. Thinking she's taking a philosophy course, he struggles through *The Encyclopedia of Philosophy* until his daughter comes home and tells him it's physics she's studying. In "A New-Wave Format," a middle-aged bus driver who's worried about losing the up-to-the-minute young girl he lives with "suddenly blurts out so much praise for [her] zucchini bread that Sabrina looks at him oddly."

The situations are all the more affecting because the characters try so hard, and with such optimism, to keep up with change instead of fighting against it. They have an earnest faith in progress; they are as quick to absorb new brand names as foreigners trying to learn the language of a strange country they've found themselves in. "Louise," we are told precisely, "threw a Corning Ware Petite Pan at Tom and made his ear bleed." Following an earthquake warning, a family flees to Arizona, "and Dusty took her new set of Teflon II pans with her."

It's heartening to find male characters portrayed sympathetically, with an appreciation for the fact that they can feel as confused and hurt and lonely as the female characters. These truck drivers, bus drivers, and carpenters show an endearing sensitivity and alertness to others.

And "simple" though these people may be, they are fully capable of moments of insight that are remarkably perceptive but never strained. Just watch the wife realizing suddenly why she's spent weeks painting nothing but watermelons after her husband left her; or another wife all at once comprehending what's behind her husband's compulsive calls to the weather recording; or the daughter putting her finger, with perfect accuracy, on the reason for her mother's bringing up a gruesome news story.

There's not an overstatement in the book, in fact. Look at Waldeen, the divorcee, pondering on her ex-husband:

> She is better off without Joe Murdock. If he were still in town, he would do something to make her look foolish, such as paint her name on his car door. He once had WALDEEN painted in large red letters on the door of his LTD. It was like a tattoo. It is probably a good thing he is in Arizona. Still, she cannot really understand why he had to move so far away from home.

Have I mentioned that, for all the sorrow contained in these stories, they are also hilarious? Did I neglect to say you're likely to find yourself in tears on several occasions? But you'll find that out for yourself. Go buy this book. Don't borrow it, don't look for it in the library, but buy it, as a way of casting your vote for real literature.

1982

Barbara Kingsolver

Where Love Is Nurtured and Confined

Review of *Me and My Baby View the Eclipse*

by Lee Smith

Getting a short story off the ground and safely landed again in its few allotted pages is a risk. In a collection of stories, the risk is multiplied, like an airplane flight that includes many stops: There are just that many more chances for failure. It's a rare collection that delivers its passenger smoothly from first page to last without a few hard landings.

Lee Smith's new book of stories, "Me and My Baby View the Eclipse," comes close. There are occasional patches of bumpy air, but like her novels, it is piloted by a clear voice and a secure knowledge of its territory.

That territory is Alabama, the Carolinas, West Virginia: the small Southern towns that deeply nurture and profoundly confine. Neighbors bring over casseroles after an operation or a divorce; women guard their reputations; men who wear Hawaiian shirts are presumed gay. Smith's most appealing and tragic characters are those who have broken out of the mold but still know that as long as they live in the towns that saw them through childhood, they can't really be free.

In "Intensive Care," red-haired Cherry Oxendine, a former high school wild card now facing mid-life and breast cancer, tells her daughter: "When you get too old to be cute, honey, you get to be eccentric." But even so, Harold Stikes loves her intensely. For Cherry, he abandoned his carefully planned house and family and prim wife who characterized their marriage, in a magazine quiz, as "an average love." The town can't feel sorry for Harold now as he watches Cherry die. But Harold believes Cherry's love has briefly, wondrously lifted him up out of the ordinary, like one of those rare folk who've had a close encounter with a UFO.

Most of these stories, in fact, are about love slightly out of control. It disregards beauty-parlor gossip: it leaves a path of kids in its wake: it is as splendid as it is impossible. In "Bob, a Dog," an abandoned wife devotes slavish energy to confining an adopted dog, while the dog shows just as much determination to run free.

In the poignant title story, Sharon, a solid wife and mother, has an affair with a flamboyant younger man. Raymond was ostracized in his youth for wearing high-water pants, but grew up to cultivate fashion sense with a vengeance; now he helps women pick out wedding announcements and drapes. Sharon finally opts to preserve her family, but her moment in the bright, exotic beam of Raymond's attention allows her to view herself as beautiful.

The exceptional story in the collection is its long centerpiece, "Tongues of Fire," a Faulkneresque memoir of a girlhood in a proper, disintegrating Alabama family. While Karen's father has a nervous breakdown, her mother Dee Rose practices her two specialties, which are "Rising to the Occasion" and "Rising Above it All." Dee Rose energetically keeps up appearances, wearing spectator pumps and organizing luncheons, but Karen longs to be chosen by God for some higher, possibly fatal purpose.

Dee Rose has made clear the social ranking of churches: "Methodist at the top, attended by doctors and lawyers . . . Presbyterian slightly down the scale, attended by store owners . . . And then, of course, at the *very bottom* of the church scale were those little churches out in the surrounding county . . . where people were reputed to yell out, fall down in fits, and throw their babies." Karen befriends a coarse country girl, accompanies her to the Marantha Apostolic Church, throws herself on Christ's bosom and is baptized twice in two weeks. It's a comic, heartbreaking exploration of the self-destructive obsessions that sometimes keep children intact when all else fails.

From its wonderful title to its final sentence, this book brims with the poetry of the South, a language whose forte is the understated value judgment. In "Life on the Moon," an exasperated wife sums up her husband: "You can subscribe to the National Geographic for 10 years straight, but there are some people who won't do a thing but look at the naked pictures." And the narrator in "Mom" fondly recalls a trip with her son: "One time [we] both got sick on the pirate ship after eating some kind of weird food cooked by people from a foreign land. The state fair is full of culture, you'd be surprised."

Occasionally the writing lapses: some important factor, such as a child, will be introduced too late in a story: a lover who had "beautiful big brown eyes" on Page 26 has acquired eyes "as blue as the sky" on Page 31.

The book is also rather short (I wonder these days if books are going the mysterious shrinking way of the 50-cent chocolate bar).

Selfishly, I wish the author had taken a little more time with it and given us a few more stories. But those that are here provide a rewarding passage.

1990

Doris Betts

The Fiction of Anne Tyler

I often speculate about how the college courses we teach in writing—which usually means in writing the short story—may be changing the form of the contemporary American novel.

We teach the short story not because it is an easier form to learn—I agree with Faulkner that after poetry, it is the most difficult—but for such practical reasons as classroom time constraints mingled with the impatience of sophomores, and the teacher's need to evaluate finished fictional units.

The result is that a rare student whose creative mind and vision might promise the scope of Tolstoy will instead practice exclusively the skills of an Edgar Allan Poe: brevity, focus, compression, and intensity—much as Anne Tyler did when she was a student of Reynolds Price at Duke University. (At Broughton High School both Price and Tyler had been the writing students of a locally famous teacher in Raleigh, Phyllis Peacock.) At Duke Tyler's favorite author, and Price's, was Eudora Welty, more a short story writer than a novelist, whose effects are most often wrought less from event than from plumbing the depth of her characters and their memories.

What difference, we might ask, can it possibly make if a painter trains his young eye and brush on the miniature or cameo, only later to be commissioned chiefly for murals or chapel ceilings? Which of her early habits would such a painter decide to abandon or modify or—conversely—to practice stubbornly and transmute? By insisting on detail and concentration, by preferring focus and unity over breadth of development and scope, can such an artist modify OUR expectations of what a mural *does* or what a novel *is*?

Anne Tyler's nine novels over seventeen years trace her own accommodation of the methods of the short story, methods geared to change and revelation, until they become adapted to her more novelistic conclusions about a Reality which changes very little, but waits for its runaways to come home and learn at the dinner table how to tolerate even their next-of-kin.[1]

Of course novels and stories are subgroups, not separate species, but the focused structural method and the revelatory intent of the short story mark Tyler's first three novels, which zero in to choose the spot from which the past may be understood and the future implied. Just as Poe's "Tell Tale Heart" has all three verb tenses in its opening sentence and thus makes time radiate, most short stories seek to enter time where they can suggest all three time levels and almost stop their clocks so that yesterday and tomorrow, lying on either side of the moment, can be better understood. Eudora Welty's *Losing Battles*, an example of this structure raised to the size of the novel, may be seen as an older, wiser, cousin to Anne Tyler's first novel, *If Morning Ever Comes* (1964). Both use the same gathering-home; both look through the keyhole of present time at a long past and its meaning.

Short story trainees in our classes prefer summoning characters to those settings where time will cluster most naturally, to home ground, for holidays, reunions, ceremonies, crises, deathbeds—wherever the situation will allow shared memory to solidify. A story writer's second favorite place to arrest time and motion is the circumscribed encounter, sometimes in train stations or airports (Hemingway, Raymond Carver, etc.) where lives intersect for travelers carrying their pasts like undeclared baggage. A story writer attempting a first novel may retain focused time, focused setting, or both. Katherine Anne Porter floated her microcosm out to sea to make her characters hold still for examination in *Ship of Fools*. Styron's first novel, *Lie Down in Darkness*, enters time at a crucial funeral, and recounts the past by flashback.

Early in her career Tyler retains brief times, flashback and restricted setting. Instead of recounting the gradual passage of time before the reader's eye, Tyler enters it at a still spot near some point of change, insight, or decision for her protagonist. Robert Browning's poetry contains even tinier examples often cited in story classes, since Browning, too, can enter a lifetime with a pinprick: showing, for instance, how the only poised chimney sweep we notice is the one about to fall or, in "My Last Duchess," hanging an immobile woman's portrait on the wall, to cause the Duke unwittingly to reveal himself and their entire marriage. Such a revelatory stillspot, or poised moment, is the jugular for which natural story writers have an instinct.

Two of the short stories Anne Tyler wrote for her Duke college class, "Nobody Answers the Door" (*Antioch Review,* Fall 1964) and "I Never Saw Morning" (*Archive,* April 1961), are testing points for her first novel, (1964). Both early stories occur sooner in time than the novel, as if Tyler were walking around the lives of her characters, feeling for a jugular. Like so many short stories, Tyler's first novel has a circular rather than linear structure and concentrates on the *implications* of small events more than the pressure of accumulating cause-effect acts onstage. Its surface ongoing time-level covers just over five present days in the life of Ben Joe Hawkes coming home to Sandhill, N.C., but by memory and association—favorite devices by which stories use moments to suggest entire lives—Tyler draws forward into this five-day period not only Ben Joe's twenty-five years but those of his relatives, including the sister who has also come home and who may now leave.

This novel, like the stories where she tested it first, pierces time instead of tracing Ben Joe chronologically from birth to the present. Even in her first novel, however, Anne Tyler's outlook differs from that of most short story writers who choose the off-balance chimney sweep, a character near the point of change. Tyler has always said she doubts that people *do* change very much,[2] thus her novels more often snap open a shutter on characters who want to change and try, but in the end become what they were fleeing. Because from the beginning her epiphanies have been so calm and slow, if not downright ambiguous, Tyler's development is her reconciliation of a theme of slow-developing realism with modified prose techniques meant for rapid, flashing disclosure. At twenty-three in this first book, Tyler relies on short story method, but has since been steadily tinkering to adjust it to the more ponderous inevitability which magnetizes her rebellious characters home.

Her second novel, *The Tin Can Tree* (1965), still has a dense center to which events cling for resonance and insight. Her plot direction still moves down through layers of meaning, not across time from left to right. This novel is as chronologically compact as the first, six successive days, and again enters time at a selected crisis point—Janie Rose's funeral and the disappearance of her brother. But Tyler has now begun tinkering with the unity of story, and her first attempt to increase the size of one of fiction's elements is the most obvious: she increases her cast of characters. She crowds members of *three* separate but interdependent families into a single house, still keeping unity of surface time and place, but entangling more, and more complex, relationships. Again the novel's structure drills down into grief and guilt to the bedrock of past causes, but diversity of character saves the action from seeming static. Though this second novel seems neither longer nor larger in size than the first, it *does* feel heavier. This compressed weight, which will become a Tyler trademark, predicts one way her novels develop, from a round marble to a round ball bearing, from china to steel.

Like Eudora Welty, Tyler chose early to make character bear her heaviest load of meaning. Outlining any Tyler plot will illustrate Welty's definition of plot as the "why" of story, the steady asking of "why?" and having the question replied to "at different depths."[3] Tyler's strategy keeps but deepens and weights the basic strategy of Katherine Anne Porter's story, "The Grave," where a forgotten incident thrusts itself across twenty years' time to become clarified while the narrator is walking a street in another country. And Tyler has also learned to walk Welty's "Worn Path," not pursuing any buildup of suspenseful events, but because the real journey is the deep descent into the life of Phoenix Jackson. Or perhaps Tyler absorbed her time structure from Faulkner's story, "A Rose for Emily," where the entire present action occurs on one day of Emily Grierson's funeral but below that day, like a mine shaft, drop sixty years of past events, all forced upward to claim their true meaning in the grisly discovery waiting up the stairs in a dusty bed. These good story writers (as well as talented novelists tinkering with their methods) suspend time long enough to drive readers down the layers asking "why?" with such aroused curiosity that they forget the more primitive question of "what happened next?"

By her third novel, *A Slipping Down Life* (1970), not only Tyler's structure but recurring themes seem clear. Her microcosm is the family, containing its two extremes, the stay-at-home and the runaway. Dare I call them types of the Classic and Romantic? In Tyler's family cacophonies one lonely individual voice sounds stronger among other lonely voices, recalling Frank O'Connor's famous study of the short story, *The Lonely Voice,* which identifies the mood of the form. Other persistent Tyler motifs are: leaving and returning; the desire for dream-parents and dream-lives but the confrontation with real ones; conflict between individual freedom and duty to others; the pull between private and social life. Often Tyler's novels end with reconciliation (some call it resignation) to a reality which may include drudgery, in homes where possessions threaten to own their occupants. (Some resolutions are made with a passivity which my liberated women students find very close to masochism. Last month we read Tyler's *Earthly Possessions* just after Fowles's *French Lieutenant's Woman;* the coeds want and fully expect to become Sarah Woodruff, and never Charlotte Emery.)

By Tyler's third novel, *A Slipping Down Life,* she decides to tinker with her surface time span. Suddenly it flowers from a few days into a full year in the life of Evie Decker, a fat teenager who carves with nail scissors the name of a rock singer on her forehead. Evie is one of many Tyler characters with a longing to be set apart from the rest, at least by a mark, at best by full bodily escape. But Evie is also more *vivid* than earlier characters. According to Stella Nesanovich, Tyler has described the characters in her first two novels as "bland" ("Individual" 7), so in this gloomier novel she not only spreads time but outlines its occupants with darker lines, like Rouault. This time she shrinks again the size of her family unit as if abandoning the experiment with mere numbers in favor of experimenting with intense individual portraits, almost to the point of caricature. Critics have called this her most Gothic novel. Here again are the Tyler themes: escape, kidnapping, non-communication, the final return home—although here Evie will enter an empty house to examine the stopped-time smiling photograph of her mother whom no one now living remembers. (Tyler's use of photographs, especially in *Earthly Possessions,* will be more fully treated later, since a short story is to a photograph what a novel is to a motion picture.) But Tyler's biggest adaptation of story form to novel intent in *A Slipping Down Life* is the more novelistic time span in which she uses more sharply etched character.

With her fourth book, *The Clock Winder* (1972), Tyler covers an entire decade, 1960–70, and for the first time begins tinkering with point of view. Most modern short stories achieve unity and impact through tight viewpoints, and Tyler's early novels have been persistently focused through one character, *The Tin Can Tree* through two. In *The Clock Winder,* Tyler enters many more characters, though still treating each like a protagonist in a separate short story, with assigned chapters in each one's point of view. These divisions make the novel's structure match its controlling metaphor since each character, even when synchronized with the others, will tick separately in the novel, just as many clocks tick in separate rooms in the Emerson household. Again Tyler's favorite themes recur: families, individuals escaping families, with focus on the title character Elizabeth Abbot, who can wind all the clocks properly to keep the same time, who in future novels will be the almost inadvertent, half unwilling, nurturer of others. Elizabeth, incidentally, believes in reincarnation, surely Tyler's ultimate expression of the motif of departure and return!

In this fourth novel, Tyler not only tinkers with viewpoint and extends her scale, but also expands her unified story writer's setting. Elizabeth, a native of North Carolina, comes to live with the Emersons in Baltimore, so for the first time Tyler has *not* located past and present in the same place. Although shifting points of view can easily become separate stories, her increasingly novelistic overview is also larger, more interlaced. She even tries here a section of letters, and provides more action and triggering action before the reader's eye instead of retrospectively.

She keeps but modifies further her viewpoint expansion in *Celestial Navigation* (1974), perhaps her most revealing novel about her own literary progress. This time-coverage extends to thirteen years, most of them spent in a dark, three-story boarding house (still vertical space, not horizontal) on a narrow street in Baltimore, where the boarders who come and go resemble an extended family. The return of two sisters for their mother's funeral again opens the novel but, significantly, despite reliance on memory, this novel moves forward along events which occur after this entry point of crisis. Unlike Tyler's now familiar survivor-women, Jeremy Pauling seems a new kind of character, Tyler's first portrait of the artist, whose development from collage to sculpture seems to parallel Tyler's literary progress from story to more and more complex novel. Jeremy begins his career with pasteups inside fixed borders, using items which, selected and clustered, suggest a whole which reveals even more than its parts. He progresses to more intricate collages, then thickens their layers to bas relief, and at last molds sculptures, a steady progress in dimension, a steady move toward using human character. The process takes Jeremy a decade; Anne Tyler in ten years and five novels has also enlarged her story skills through a process of added dimension.

When asked, Tyler called Jeremy Pauling "wholly imaginary" ("Individual" 123), a character barely suggested by an ex-mental patient she knew for only one day—more than sufficient time for a story writer's trained laser vision. Besides, when most writers call a character "wholly imaginary," we often mean secretly that we went down deeper for him than we knew or cared to tell, that we formed him by feel alone of our unconscious dust in the dark. As a girl, Tyler has said, she wanted to be an artist, not a writer ("Still Just Writing" 13).

Artist Jeremy Pauling also provides one answer (perhaps the answer creative women have historically given) to the artist's eternal question about choosing between the life and the work. Despite complaints, even allowing for his eventual withdrawal from the interruptions of family living, Pauling's art is first brought alive and nourished by the intrusion of children, clutter, love. In his life first, then his art, he makes a parallel shift from the use of objects in his collages to inclusion of human beings.

Six years before *Celestial Navigation* appeared, Tyler's writing teacher Reynolds Price also published a novel animated by Yeats's question, called *Love and Work* (1968). I hope a critic will someday compare the two, for *Celestial Navigation* seems almost a response to Price's, a yes-but response; and both novels contain similar content. Price's protagonist does choose work over life; though in the end Jeremy rejects life for art as well, the final images of his moored boat moving only in circles, of his old age spent in a locked and darkened house, seem to say that a high cost has been exacted for the "great, towering, beautiful sculptures" he makes late in his isolated life.

Anne Tyler's essay "Still Just Writing" details her own conflict between life and work. Like so many writers who are also wives and mothers, she chose both; she stayed home with art practiced the hard way against the contrary pull of domesticity; but she has said her children have deepened her and her work. "Who else in the world do you *have* to love, no matter what?"(9)

A stronger resemblance between Tyler and Jeremy, then, may be the way he sees life in a series of brief flashes which arrest motion in midair, faster even than photographs, the other metaphor Tyler uses in almost every novel. Story critics have compared the photograph with Hemingway's "Hills Like White Elephants," Irwin Shaw's "Girls in Their Summer Dresses," even William Carlos Williams's "The Use of Force," calling these stories the polaroid shots of literature. Click. The black and white essence, caught. Click. Stopped movement. Sufficient. Yet mysterious.

Jeremy's clicking eyesight is specified early in *Celestial Navigation*. "That was the way his vision functioned: only in detail. Piece by piece. He [Jeremy] had tried looking at the whole of things but it never worked out"(45). Even as an artistic child, Jeremy could not draw an entire room, but would produce a closeup of wallpaper pattern showing one electric wall socket with "its screws neatly bisected by microscopic slits." Although Mary Tell (one of Tyler's simultaneous rebels and nurturers) will bear Jeremy's four children, they will always *see* different things. She has left one husband and will eventually leave Jeremy, but although Jeremy (who early reminds us of Bartleby) rarely leaves his house, he deduces the entire world from evidential detail observed through his third floor window.

This vantage point of seeing, this use of detailed parts arranged inside a frame, sounds like Tyler's developing literary method. She remains a writer who selects her time entry points but heads toward magnitude, whose life is both private and domestic but who prefers not to teach writing courses much as Jeremy finds art students an ordeal. Nor will you hear Anne Tyler speaking at the South Atlantic Modern Language Association; she has said, "I will write my books and raise the children. Anything else just fritters me away. . . . I hate leaving home" ("Still Just Writing" 15).

And as Jeremy's art work thickens with glued-in layers of ordinary objects like Dixie cups and shoestrings, so have Tyler's novels. Family and its clutter remain her metaphor for life. She does not examine political, social, class, or economic movements, but like Jeremy keeps increasing texture, depth, dimension, of the small, earthly possessions which come to hand. Olivia calls one of Jeremy's structures "a cross section of a busy household." Anne Tyler's later novels, Jeremy's later art and the symbolic photographs can all be described by another character in *Celestial Navigation,* Mrs. Vinton. "Moments that you just witnessed are suspended forever while you yourself recede from them with every breath you take. The moments grow smaller and yet clearer. You see some sorrow in them you have never before suspected"(145).

Following her portrait of the developing artist and his developing art, Tyler's last four novels consolidate her gains, the short story form now so imbedded inside the larger novel that its overlapped, glued-down edges blend and hardly show. Novel number six, *Searching for Caleb* (1976), like Jeremy's final towering sculptures, is Tyler's largest family and longest time coverage—five generations of Pecks who look alike but aren't. Their 1912 runaway, Caleb, was always drawn away from the others by any stray music he might hear. Once more Tyler unravels time backwards, since Caleb disappeared sixty-one years before the novel opens; but this great volume of time has become historical, affecting generations, with older causes, longer meanings, below the surface action. In *Searching for Caleb,* Tyler has also grown more comfortable with enlarged scope, relaxed enough to be more humorous. Though the actual finding of Caleb and his second disappearance will occur over the span of one summer, this time Tyler also tinkers with the breadth of her persistent themes. Her runaway/stay-at-home conflict has sometimes warred within one character, then between two, or between one family member struggling with the rest; but among the Pecks of fashionable Roland Park, whole groups of kin of all ages have these contrasting natures. Having multiplied the conflict, she also synthesizes it by joining one representative of each type, Justine and Daniel, in partnership to find Caleb. More than usual, in this novel Tyler seems to choose sides with the vagabond family group, allotting this time to the runaways those qualities she typically affirms—steadfast endurance and the will to keep on loving. In the end Justine is moving on, but stripping her house not of love—only the family furniture.

The distance is not great from that scene to Tyler's seventh novel, *Earthly Possessions,* in which Charlotte Emery also wants to strip herself of all encumbrances, objects, possessions, perhaps even people, in order to take alone the long refugee march of her life away from the romantic homeland of childhood, toward the revised, improved, romantic true country of dreams.

Tyler's frequent use of photography becomes in this novel a central metaphor which functions much like Jeremy's art. I was reminded of Jeremy's quick flashes by a recent exhibition at UNC-Chapel Hill of thirty-five of the black-and-white photographs Eudora Welty made during her 1930s work with the Mississippi WPA. Reynolds Price has called Welty's the "keenest eyesight in American letters." Tyler's eyesight is also keen and her shutter snaps open and shut in many novels, even the first, when Ben Joe finds his captured younger self photographed riding a long-ago wrecked tricycle. In *The Tin Can Tree* a main character is a professional photographer, Joan Pike photographs the family and thus makes visual her absence from it, and a dead child is outlived by her printed image, the mortal features beginning to fade among surrounding splotches of Queen Anne's lace which have since withered. The photographs, like Jeremy's art, "suspend moments forever, while we recede from them with every breath" (*CN* 145), and see their hitherto unsuspected sorrow.

In *Earthly Possessions* photographs are most consistently used to freeze time and to pin people inside its case like collected butterflies. Photographer Charlotte Emery, who drifts into using the studio she inherits from her father, discovers that using props (a sword, a flaring lace shawl) can coalesce personalities on film and develop the ghostly true image up through the routine identity. Photographs can also be used to do what Faulkner said the writer does, to "say no to death," though sometimes Tyler's seem to say yes to it. Early in *Celestial Navigation* a photo holds somehow at home the father who "went out for a breath of air 34 years ago and never came back." And just as Jeremy's collages turn ordinary objects into symbols, just as mortality and transience are challenged and admitted by the photograph, Anne Tyler's literary entries into time bring back and save those arrested moments which imply the whole. In *Caleb* one photo of Caleb playing the cello in a stable loft is said by the pose alone to reveal not Caleb, but the personality of the photographer.

In her later novels, having married story's methods to novel's goals, Tyler can flash into place a single face before it shows the grim genetic trait, can glimpse through her camera lens, though inverted, the start of loving desire just as it metamorphosizes into the propagation of the tribe. The mood of the short story, like that of the lyric poem, is youthful, trusting illumination or luck; but Tyler has now learned to tell us at length that the more things change, the more they stay the same: caught forever, lost forever, all at once, like photographs.

Photographs may be too neat a metaphor as *Earthly Possessions* seems too neat a book. It is her most criticized, perhaps because her tinkering here has become too conscious, not gently relaxed as *Caleb* was. Her tinkering with viewpoint has become first person, too thin a wire on which to hang so much. Her tinkering with structure this time seems arbitrary and mechanical, an alternating sequence of past and present chapters, dividing past from present far more neatly than seems Tyler's habit. Perhaps she wanted the reader to feel he was turning in rhythm from this year's photograph album to focus on an older one. An undergraduate called this novel "overworked," too patterned, with too many then-and-now kidnappings to be plausible, too many pre-and-post insights, too many neat black-and-white parallels developed.

Many readers prefer her eighth novel, *Morgan's Passing* (1980), which began, Tyler writes in "Still Just Writing," with a bearded character who wandered into her mind and who, if "organized," might cause a novel to "grow up around him"(3). By accident Morgan also enters in 1967 the lives of two puppeteers and becomes their impromptu obstetrician. This novel moves progressively twelve years to 1979, though it circles to end at another puppet show. Popular because of the vitality and appeal of the scene-stealer Morgan Gower, for that reason it recalls Kay Boyle's famous discussion of short story technique and her description of what she called the "wallpaper story." In such a story one character, often eccentric and memorable, enters lives, makes a certain pattern, and exits; by his very nature he will probably move on and repeat the same pattern in the next life in the next town. A story example she cites is Carson McCullers's "A Tree, A Rock, a Cloud." The tramp, the wise old man, the good witch, the childlike spokesman for innocence, the philosophic clown, are typical wallpaper characters. Though Morgan seems to come home to love Emily and will not continue to produce long patterns of twined leaves and rosy ovals in other lives, he *could;* he could easily *keep* passing, could easily go, like Caleb, off to Wyoming without notice just a few more pages beyond the novel's end.

Far more satisfying is Anne Tyler's most recent novel, *Dinner at the Homesick Restaurant* (1982)—still set in Baltimore, still centered on one family, the Tulls, still opening at the crisis point when the mother, Pearl, is dying at eighty-five. As usual, the narration moves back thirty-five years to reveal Pearl deserted by her traveling-salesman husband and dandy, a figure Tyler sometimes makes a paradigm of male mobility. Here Mary Tell, Charlotte Emery, and Elizabeth Abbott, among others, live in their kinsman Ezra Tull—for sometimes Tyler's separate families from all nine novels seem like one large family, like a clan even larger than the Pecks. They even sound alike: Tell and Tull, Peck and Decker, Peck and Pike, Emery and Emerson. Unlike Jeremy, Ezra Tull does not expect art from life; he only wants to create a restaurant with a family atmosphere, a homesick restaurant—the name expresses Tyler's usual paradox: sick FOR home, sick OF home. In spite of all Ezra can do, the Tull family meals end in squabbles and quarrels. Yet the family is curiously bound together in spite of desertion, child abuse, and the betrayal of one brother by another. Tyler's homes are not merely broken but often crazed like a glass vessel but the vessels still hold; blood is still thicker than water. That the family should all be nourished at the same dinner table, despite estrangement, despite those members who fling down their napkins mid-way and go, seems Tyler's perfect symbol.

If Ezra is Pearl Tull's stay-at-home boy as Jeremy was Mrs. Pauling's, and if he is outwardly also the novel's loser, Cody and Jenny are this family's runaways. Cody even takes with him in a kind of latent kidnapping for jealous revenge the woman, Ruth, whom Ezra meant to marry. Again there is homecoming for Pearl's death, the revealed contrast of their different memories of what she, the mother, and they, the children, were really like. Even their father Beck Tull, who like Jeremy's father ran away years before, will come home now to eat the funeral meats at Ezra's homesick restaurant.

This runaway father seems to summarize for Tyler what she considers semi-heroic. Beck Tull admires but cannot be like those who can endure "the grayness of things, the half-right and half-wrongness of things," the stay-at-homes who cope. But since Beck Tull will leave again as soon as possible, and because Tyler must evidently keep working through her long stay-and-go conflict over and over, book after book, we might measure her stay-at-home allegiance and her vision as only 60-40, that is, 60 percent a classic vision.

In Murray Krieger's study, *The Classic Vision,* he concentrates on those authors who know what extremity is and means, but reject it and "turn away toward the wholly compromised human condition,"[4] without illusion, sentimentality, or false expectations. He says they are the Leech Gatherers, the Michaels. They are Dostoevsky's remarkable peasant women of faith who have no idea that they are remarkable. And they are Anne Tyler's self-sacrificers, although some 40 percent of her heart is always running away from this compromise and fleeing for dear life with the non-conformists.

If Tyler were depicting them in short stories, her dutiful characters intensely rendered closeup might appear simple-minded, perhaps saccharine, whereas a novel like *Stoner* by John Williams, or one like *Dinner at the Homesick Restaurant* can give dimension to the sad but "good" person.

Anne Tyler has been learning dimension at a rate of one novel every two years, from age twenty-three to age forty. By tinkering she has learned also how to outwit the weaknesses most writers risk when they first switch from short story to longer novel form. One risk is that their themes will be too small to stand up under coverage of 80,000 words or more without being watered down; early in Tyler's career she already had a classic vision, at least 60 percent, which demanded size. Another risk is that a cast of eccentric, overblown characters will be transposed in full hyperbole to the longer work, and seem narcissistic there, and too theatrical. Some of Tyler's characters are, but she imbeds these deep in the collage of the others and she gives her longest attention to ordinariness. A talent for story writing and for short bursts of intensity can produce nervous though vivid novels peopled by static navel-gazers. Like Jeremy Pauling, Tyler has avoided that risk by her steady thickening of realistic representational work, and by her willingness to avoid sensationalism, the way Jeremy carved his friend's head in "wood, because that is slow and takes patience." Some story writers who take up novels cannot break the habit of producing each chapter like a mini-story, one bead on a string of beads. Last month, by accident, I met Anne Tyler's mother, Phyllis, who told me every titled chapter in *Homesick Restaurant* had been designed so it could be published as a separate story. I had not noticed.

Though Tyler's range does not aspire to *War and Peace,* though her work with time and family does not become Faulkner's historical South, though there are subjects she passes over with minimal treatment—sex and philosophy; and though some complain that she never experiments much with her very competent style, her persistent tinkering with story methods has produced a distinctive, dense, Tyler-type novel, dependent on character, made resonant by memory. About 60 percent of the time, she continues to do variations on the unfashionable and rather Southern theme that those who can live generously in close quarters at home are facing the world as it is, not as it should be. The other 40 percent of the time, Anne Tyler runs off with her vagabonds and rebels in their capes and costumes.

Her ratio is just about right. Any writer who has been more than 60 percent tamed, even when entering her forties, is probably not vivid enough nor honest enough to make us pause in our own preference for running away, to hear her home truths.

1. Even more than these endnotes might show, my observations on Anne Tyler's novels are indebted to earlier work by two women scholars, and have been affected by and enriched by both. The first was a paper read in 1981 (before *Homesick Restaurant*) by Susan Hull Gilbert (Meredith College) entitled "Returning Home in Anne Tyler's Novels: or Ending at the Beginning." The second source is the only dissertation on Tyler's work, "The Individual in the Family: a Critical Introduction to the Novels of Anne Tyler" (1979) which was written by Stella Nesanovich at Louisiana State University; she is now teaching at McNeese State University. In addition to the novels, Nesanovich makes use of other sources, correspondence, and stories, in tracing her theme through Tyler's seventh novel, *Earthly Possessions* (1977). Her recommendation in her conclusion that the influence of Welty might be a fruitful subject first suggested this brief essay on short story structure itself. Both she and Gilbert comment in even more detail on Tyler's use of photography.

2. See Nesanovich dissertation, 74, citing Tyler's 1972 interview with *National Observer*.

3. See Eudora Welty, "Looking at Short Stories," in *The Eye of the Story* (Random House, 1970), 90.

4. See Murray Krieger, *The Classic Vision* (Baltimore: John Hopkins Univ. Press, 1971), 44.

1983

Doris Betts

Review of *Celebration*
by Mary Lee Settle

At the heart of Mary Lee Settle's ninth novel is a Jesuit named Pius, 6'9", originally a prince in his native Dinka tribe, a nigger in the city surrounding Georgetown University where he studied, a nignog in the book's setting in London, but "priest everywhere. He clung to that, as he clung to that old rugged cross till its burden at last he could lay down. That had been the first song he had learned in Washington, D.C., the first time he had been invited anywhere." Besides Pius, there is an intangible "black monk" who lives in the mind of Teresa Cerrutti—a figure composed of psychic fragments from her own Jungian animus, Chekhov's story, a remembered childhood friend, a foreshadowing of the real Pius, and what we might call her own soul-voice or conscience.

Such a reverberation from natural to supernatural is typical of *Celebration,* in which real events in 1969 ripple until they merge first into biography, then history, at last mythology. Settle, best known for her five-volume Beulah Quintet covering Virginia from the 1600's to now, won the National Book Award for her eighth novel, *Blood Tie,* which showed her expanding fascination with cross-cultural history as it shades into anthropology and religion. There she wrote of expatriates in Turkey; here they are living in England and Western culture but leaving complex, international lives behind them like comets' tails— the part that vaporizes but also gives the only light.

The novel opens by following one of those flights directly. Teresa

Cerrutti and her husband Michael, anthropologists, are on a dig in Kurdistan, where sacred objects are buried in layers of collapsed civilizations, and where the locals have learned to "salt" the territory with counterfeits. Michael descends into a tabooed well he believes is a shrine and dies from its real taboo—a tangle of poisonous snakes at the bottom. On the plot-surface, these mistranslations of reality continue. Russian and American agents in Turkey play chess while trying to reduce an ancient world to cold-war terms. When the widowed Teresa has healed her grief and moved to London, she is spied upon by a C.I.A. agent who interprets her international circle of friends as a Communist cell.

But apparent reality, to Settle, is almost comic relief. The real story is one which Jung, E. M. Forster, Sir James George Frazer and Mircea Eliade have continued to read below the surface of written history and which the priest Pius identifies at a joyous party celebrating America's first moon-landing, spinning a globe as he talks: ". . . like this globe, this room contains a world, a globe you can't see. It was in this room that we stepped on the moon and saw ourselves blue in space, a little pendant orb, and here tonight we celebrate a wedding of each other, a wedding of the soulscapes that in this room make up that world. I knew a man once who called it the country behind his eyes. You . . . have in your soulscape the mountain where Noah landed."

In the novel's plot-surface of apparent reality, Teresa falls in love with Ewen, Scottish geologist afflicted by malaria he got in Africa; meets again her childhood friend Noel, homosexual, mourning a lost, Hong Kong love, and serves as the reader's surrogate to hear their life stories that are, of course, archetypal soulscape journeys of love's persistence and life's value. Even for Pius, who is specifically in love with the Christian God rather than promiscuous among the crowd of deities said to inhabit mankind's unconscious, personal history reaches back to Ethiopia; his understanding of human pride touches Hammurabi. If his rosary were stamped with the date of manufacture, it might say B.C. as well as A.D.

At a time when the novel as a form seems often the size of one solipsistic psyche—sometimes the narrator's, sometimes the novelists's—Mary Lee Settle has steadily moved the boundaries of her region out to encompass the human spirit. Early critics said she had made Virginia her Faulknerian Yoknapatawpha, traced it and the nation's history through recurring characters. Instead of giving us full details of suburban car pools and women's rooms, Settle has extended her early process to the scale of what Eliade calls in his subtitles "archaic realities." Like E. M. Forster's, her crisp prose always telegraphs her empathy for people displaced or misunderstood. She takes her readers into a worldwide Marabar Cave of her own, but unlike Mrs. Moore, she does not agree that "everything exists, nothing has value." *Celebration,* which ends with two ceremonies, a funeral and a wedding, leaves no uncertainty about Settle's recognition of death and her celebration of life. Even the book's cover shows the mythical snake and Michael's death-snake juxtaposed against the mythical flower-mandala of fruition and life. In the end, Teresa has accepted Pius's conviction that "you lived within other people, in what he called their soulscapes . . . she felt full of light and constructed by the love she had been given, and held within her."

"Only connect," E. M. Forster advised. Mary Lee Settle has followed his advice in novel after novel until her connections have grown very large and generous, while still respecting mystery.

1986

Doris Betts

Tyler's Marriage of Opposites

A friend at Chapel Hill and a fellow Tyler fan, Professor George Lensing, once remarked that as he moved along library shelves choosing books, he would often open an unfamiliar novel and examine its first and last sentences as clues to whether or not he would enjoy reading the whole.

(Naturally a thrust of acid pierced me during instant recall of my own unsatisfactory opening closing sentences.)

However, once I had become about the millionth reader to notice that Jane Austen's novels open by discussing money and progress toward concluding with marriage and security, I decided to examine Anne Tyler's early novels and test how her fictions start and stop. If home is said to be the place where you can scratch anything that itches, home is central to many Tyler openings—and so is somebody's itch to get away from it.

"When Ben Joe Hawkes left home . . ." are the opening words of *If Morning Ever Comes* (1964), for instance, but the reader soon learns that Ben Joe is actually enroute home *again* to Sandhill, North Carolina, because his sister has left *her* home and husband and recently fled back to *their* parental home. *The Tin Can Tree* (1965) begins with the statement, "After the funeral, James came straight home . . . ." That funeral is only one of Tyler's many opening funerals initiating her plots, this one to bury Janie Rose Pike, aged six, killed in a tractor accident. One of my two favorite Tyler novels, *Celestial Navigation*

276

(1974), opens with Amanda's only section of narration, in which she introduces her brother Jeremy Pauling, a 38-year-old bachelor who has never left home at all, and is now telephoning to summon her back home because of their mother's death. A mother is also dying on the first page of my second favorite Tyler novel, *Dinner at the Homesick Restaurant* (1982); and during the first scene of *The Accidental Tourist* (1985, Tyler's first novel to be made into a movie) because of another random, meaningless child's death—the murder of their son Ethan in a fast-food restaurant—the marriage of Macon and Sarah Leary is dying. The widowed Mrs. Emerson needs a "clock winder" (CW) after a death, her husband's. And in *Breathing Lessons* (1989), Maggie and Ira Moran will spend almost half the novel attending a funeral that echoes, even attempts to duplicate, the dead man's wedding.

This rather amusing funeral first appeared as a separate story in a holiday issue of *The New Yorker*, July 4, 1988, entitled "Rerun." In her eleventh novel, this funeral, Max Gill's sendoff to his *eternal* home, has the same cause-effect function of generating the story as do funerals for Pearl Tull or Mrs. Pauling, or even in Tyler's third novel, *A Slipping Down Life* (1970), precipitating change. Here the funeral comes near the end as Evie returns home from arranging last rites for her father, only to discover her husband Casey in bed with her best friend. As usual, death is not Tyler's final word—the novel concludes after Evie has left Casey to await alone the *birth* of their baby.

In Anne Tyler's reality, there is always life after death, literally, in the plots; the marriage of opposites produces it. In *Breathing Lessons* the two who respond to death with lively sex and are found in bed together after Gill's funeral are a couple twenty-eight years married, Ira and Maggie Moran.

Perhaps Tyler's steady and positive counteracting of death by love or new life, her italicized hope which some attribute to her Quaker background, are partial reasons five of Tyler's novels have been Book-of-the-Month Club selections, and *Breathing Lessons,* although a smaller work than my two favorites, received the 1989 Pulitzer Prize. Many Tyler novels begin where other contemporary writers would write "The End." Death only appears to conclude events, then it becomes her precipitating event for change, plot, and subplot. I can imagine *For Whom the Bell Tolls* would come out of Tyler's typewriter following Maria on her headlong horseback ride behind Pilar into a different life; or that Tyler's Chapter One might show Nick Carraway departing from final rites for Gatsby enroute to new adventures in the midwest. Although her plots do include other crises—quarreling, suicide, death, even sex, though rather understated sex—in Tyler's fiction climactic events become early cause; her characters work through them toward later denouement or conclusion. She remains more interested in how her people survive and persist *beyond* crisis during their long, steady, three-meal-a-day aftermaths.

Though her affirmations have won her a wide audience, her insistence on chronicling what the *Baltimore Sun* called "the mundane"[1] has had two interesting effects on her literary career. Her popularity makes some literary critics wary that her vision may be too rose-colored. Yet, despite her popularity, she has never become lively copy for *People Magazine* because her own life has included one long marriage and motherhood, nor does she get interviewed about the pleasures of domesticity for housewives' magazines. The reclusive Ms. Tyler would never let Barbara Walters inside her front door. Though she did attend the premiere showing of *The Accidental Tourist* where she was seated in a theater section roped off from others, she has since her first novel appeared in 1964 secluded herself to write, and maintained equal unconcern about being popular, fashionable, or avant garde.

Make your own list of newsworthy literary categories that, like Procrustean beds, will not contain her comfortably. Does Tyler write the self-consuming metafiction of Coover, Barth, Barthelme? Would you classify Anne Tyler as a post modernist? How about mixing genres—does she blend history with fiction like Doctorow, journalism with fiction like Capote and Mailer? Does she write Writing with a capital-W like Updike; is she a Raymond Carver minimalist? A conscious practitioner of artifice like John Fowles? Is she locked into her despairing existentialist self? Have you heard Anne Tyler deconstructed often? Would she agree with Walker Percy that it is "better to be a drowning man than alive and well in East Orange?" Since she grew up in North Carolina, does she fit the profile for the self-conscious "Southern" writer? Which Tyler novel can be categorized as surreal, topical, political? Does she belong to the '80's "brat pack" in whose brightly-lighted, big-city prose we always hear the fast click-click of computer keyboards? Is she a Maryland version of those women writers producing mall and K-Mart fiction? Why isn't Anne Tyler as flashy as beatniks, yippies, yuppies? Would Geraldo Rivera cross the street to ask her about pornography?

Can we even call Anne Tyler by that capital-F word, *Feminist?* One conclusion I draw from *Breathing Lessons* is that Tyler understands the differences between the male and female consciousness more intimately than Gloria Steinem; but because Tyler's women often collaborate with the chauvinist enemy, and by staying married try to merge those opposites into one flesh, her heroines are seldom angry enough to star in the average Women's Studies syllabus. Passion or rage do not deter Anne Tyler long. On their wedding night, when Maggie Moran comes out wearing her sheer white nightgown and Ira sucks in his breath in awe and admiration, Maggie "thought that would go on forever." Tyler writes about all the rest of married life that goes on instead.

Since 1964, unencumbered by literary trends and categories, Anne Tyler has kept moving along her own main line, employing a vision that may seem rosy to contemporaries because it is more classic than romantic. Her eleven novels reverse today's more typical alienated linear progression by moving her plots from grave to cradle, from death to birth or rebirth, with themes which only sink briefly, then rise from the depths onto ordinary weekday plateaus where she presents, as she has said, "how people last." Her characters oppose, juxtapose, and resolve; and they perform this complex dance of life inside the family, although during her publishing career demographics have indicated a decline in or at least reshaping of the nuclear American family. While some would say the family has almost died out during the last quarter century, Tyler's families break, mend, and persist; she seems in tune with the Moroccan proverb: "None but a mule denies his family." However modified, this family unit remains on center stage where her characters play out, as she told Mary Ellen Brooks, "how people manage to endure together—how they grate against each other, adjust, intrude and protect themselves from intrusions, give up, and start all over again in the morning."[2] You can't get much closer to true

Women's Studies than that nor, indeed, to the mood of the final page of *Breathing Lessons*. When Cecil B. deMille was asked why he had so many films based on the Bible, he shrugged: "Why let 2000 years of publicity go to waste?" Tyler is unwilling to waste the ancient human microcosm arranged around the hearth, and especially the family unit of the last several centuries.

Had Friedrich Hegel been a wife and mother forced to do his thinking between the crib and washing machine, Hegelian philosophy might have sung the music-of-the-spheres to Anne Tyler's tune: Thesis/Antithesis/Synthesis—all of them banging together in a domestic blend down the hall, or being stirred into wistful synthesis at the dinner table, or sometimes resplit by slamming screen doors. Novelists typically arrange their selected polar opposite characters and contrasting themes into struggles between protagonists and antagonists, but Tyler's protagonists also take—or long to take—that third reconciling step in the direction of synthesis. She almost seems as homesick as Ezra Tull to feast on a happy ending.

Yet Tyler usually resists the temptation to attach with Velcro a hackwriter's happy ending to her final page. She tries to make her characters earn solutions, step by step, or be dragged into happiness as Macon Leary is, by a dog and a dog trainer. Having learned in her own kitchen the art of dividing a cake so everybody thinks he got the biggest slice, sometimes Tyler does try—like Maggie Moran—to work more magic for her surrounding characters than they can digest and she may, in *Breathing Lessons,* dramatize her own artist-conflicts through Maggie. But usually, if Jane Austen's novels begin with money and end with marriage, Anne Tyler's stop short of absolutely happy endings to close with small convergences: people make temporary rest stops on life's journey; they take catnaps in the marriage bed or drop anchor at sandbars somewhere in the relentless flow of time. Even when Tyler's last sentence seems to make a temporary truce with fate, readers suspect that if they could read onward beyond her back cover, her still-fated people would soon be setting off again.

The contrasts Tyler sets up within families are part of the general pattern of contrasts in fiction. The fantasy world of Don Quixote needs the foil of Sancho Panza's common sense. In literature, comic effect results whenever flat content is rendered in lofty form. Readers choose sides between Faulkner's Snopes and Sartoris families; readers like heroes and villains even when stereotypes are softened by subtlety, relish the counterpoint between real and fantastic in *The Lord of the Rings,* believe themselves in on the joke when the real England is exaggerated so they view with double vision the strange, yet familiar travels of Lemuel Gulliver. Thanks to Kafka, readers even know how it feels to be treated like a giant insect. Most fiction first sets up a contrast, then amplifies to active conflict by turning up the volume. Tyler moves from death into noisy, hectic life.

But contrasts are not essential to literature alone. An ability to see right through contrast with double vision, perhaps all the way to unity, seems vital to every creative activity. Frozen dilemma produces no forward movement. The process of thesis/antithesis/synthesis, run by verbally at 100 m.p.h., is metaphor—called by Aristotle the one gift that cannot be taught. To think in metaphor is a talent: to superimpose unlike objects and achieve something new so that when Juliet calls Romeo a "beautiful tyrant" we know in the tension between two words what is meant. Kepler's particular talent saw the link between the motions of the tides and the motions of the moon. Creative talent made Pythagoras discover musical harmony while watching blacksmiths hammer iron bars of different lengths while each sounded at a different pitch. With metaphor, one scientist expressed the connection between energy and matter—E equals MC^2—and the gospels depict one long metaphor, "God is love."

But Anne Tyler's metaphorical work, to posit opposites and reconcile some, occurs where more than charity begins, at home, where she has lived as daughter, wife, and mother of two daughters. In her essay, "Still Just Writing,"[3] she specifies antithetical partitions in her own mind that separate the domestic and professional halves of her life. Once, she says, she made the mistake of trying with a tape recorder to capture those wonderful story ideas that came during the buzz of the vacuum cleaner; but the experiment failed because she had violated essential divisions in her life. She decided, then, that her method would be to keep hold of two strings: when she went into her study to write fiction, she needed to drop in the hall the string of her domestic life and pick up the writer's string waiting for her across the threshold. Many working American women will sigh and nod to this household schizophrenia they also live forty-eight hours per day, in a setting where blood certainly *is* thicker than water, even when spilled or sucked. (Evidently Tyler also carries two separate strings for her private and public lives, and rarely picks up the public one.)

Reading about Tyler's strings of identity made me remember 1964, the year she was publishing her first novel, written during her first six months of marriage when, she says (perhaps nostalgically?), she didn't have much else to do. By 1964 our children were aged four, ten, and eleven, and I had far too much to do; so I was famished to find some Handy Dandy Shortcut to writing, any system that would help me spew out twenty pages of prose in about twenty minutes stolen daily time. Published in 1964, besides Tyler's first novel, was Arthur Koestler's *The Act of Creation,* which examines far more cogently than I can the nature of the creative process, suggesting that it occurs—whether for Sophocles or Charlie Chaplin—whenever two unrelated causal chains collide and perhaps merge or reveal something new. Rothenburg has called this simultaneous recognition of opposites "Janusian thinking," after the Roman god Janus, whose two faces point in opposite directions. Our month January is named for his doubleness, facing both New Year and Old, and the two-faced Janus appears on the Dell paperback edition of Koestler's book about oppositions and collisions and syntheses. In a pun, for instance, Koestler says two strings of word-thought get tangled into an acoustic knot. In novels, conflict causes plot, just as in the Chinese language the word "crisis" is composed of two characters—one represents danger, and one represents opportunities. The foundation of quantum physics is also laid on an apparent contradiction between particle and wave images.

So encouraged was I in 1964 by Koestler's analysis that I set out to fuse it with my desperate need to speed the writing process. I would disturb equilibrium by focusing on contrast and thus leap overhead into the "Eureka" of new stories! Toward that end I drew up a long list of apparent polarities. Meditating on youth/age, body/soul, night/day, sweet/sour, life/death would by dynamic tension alone fling high my yin/yang ingredients for cooking up fiction.

The 1964 short stories resulting from this attempt to make my left brain consciously teach "breathing lessons" to my right brain were, as you would expect, terrible.

Though Anne Tyler surely never wasted time compiling such a list nor cooking up fiction after deliberate manichaeanism, criticism of her work usually takes note of its repeated pull between contraries and toward balance. Stella Nesanovich's 1979 LSU dissertation, "The Individual in the Family," could in spots have been "the individual *versus* the family." An earlier article of mine divided Tyler's characters in her first nine novels between stay-at-homes and runaways. "Without contraries," said William Blake, who married Heaven and Hell, "there's no progression."

Even Tyler's titles produce doubling or marry opposites. In *Earthly Possessions,* for instance, one hears the first obvious meaning and then a reversal echo, "What on *earth* possessed you!" The restaurant in her ninth title reminds a reader of how it feels to be simultaneously sick *for* home, and sick *of* home. That cliche, "armchair traveler," gets flipped to the logo on Macon Leary's guidebooks, "traveling armchairs." In fact, the title is nearly an oxymoron—how can a tourist be accidental? Tyler has played with this particular contrast before by featuring the non-tour at the end of *Earthly Possessions* where Charlotte and Saul (like Macon Leary, like Ralph Waldo Emerson) have traveled extensively at home. In fact, Tyler's pilgrimages frequently turn into the one the Queen described to Alice, "It takes all the running you can do to keep in the same place." Her running/staying characters have personalities that also contrast or clash, like Cody with Ezra in one novel or, on a larger scale, Morgan Gower as Jeremy Pauling turned wrong-side out. Typical Tyler clashes and mixtures resonate across all eleven novels, in which readers will recognize similar names, situations, cardgames, prodigal fathers, funerals, kidnaps and near-kidnaps—the same elements stirred and restirred. The portrait painter Sir Joshua Reynolds was famous for the subtle tones he achieved in flesh and fabric, and when asked, "What do you mix your colors with?" replied quickly, "brains." As Tyler's novels accumulate, her mixtures also grow more subtle, her sketches of individual families widen into murals of the human family.

The title of her Pulitzer prize-winning novel blends an action that is reflexive, autonomic, natural—"breathing"—with a process deliberate, cerebral, learned—"lessons."

Keeping in mind Ben Jonson's claim that "all concord's born of contraries," look more closely at how Tyler marries opposites in

Breathing Lessons, so printed by Knopf that when the reader flips through the book its pages will alternate subliminally, with the word "breathing" printed atop each lefthand page, "lessons" atop the right.

First, examine the dustjacket on the hardcover edition, a painting Anne Tyler approved, by New York artist Tom Woodruff. Its interlocking circles certainly suggest the eternal rings of double wedding bands and bonds, but these particular circles have been formed by midair birds in flight, perhaps shortlived sparrows like those which in Jesus' time were sold for a farthing and thus symbolized brief, anonymous life, though He said the Heavenly Father noticed each one. In *her* created world, Anne Tyler also seems to notice every sparrow-gray character, those who fly and those who fall.

Below these birds-of-a-feather flying on the cover runs a small road with double ruts that "rise to converge" on the horizon. This overall scene with golden light emanating on all sides was suggested to the painter by that moment in the novel when Maggie and Ira Moran scare up birds as they drive along the road. Whatever has sent them into air, these wild birds have superimposed themselves into a pair of almost harmonious circles—I say "almost" because in Tyler's world one or two birds are always loose from the flock.

This cover illustration, like a ghost picture on the reader's retina, overlays Chapter 1 in which Maggie Moran hears on her car radio a call-in broadcast on the topic of ideal marriage. After twenty-eight years Maggie, 48, and her husband, Ira, 50, have not an ideal but a *real* marriage, warts and all; but what their son Jesse has is a broken one. Though Maggie knows what the Swiss say, that "marriage is a covered dish," she so often hears what she wants to hear that on this Saturday morning she is convinced that one radio caller's voice belongs to Jesse's divorced wife Fiona, announcing on the air that having once married for true love she will now do the opposite and remarry for security. Shocked, Maggie immediately hits the accelerator instead of the brake and while locked in this opposition is herself hit by a Pepsi-Cola truck.

With that opening moment of start/stop/collision, while the air is full of broadcast news of an old and new marriage, in the context of an upcoming funeral to be conducted like a renewal of wedding vows, Tyler begins this journey which will cluster her contrasts in a single day.

Her plot seems simple, since Tyler's plots are usually means to her ends of revealing character and theme. This time her main characters have grown older, the marriage and conflict are longer lived. Maggie Moran is 48, as Tyler was in October of 1989—not that life begins at middle-age, but that's where it does begin to show. If in middle age you try on a bathing suit in front of a floor length mirror, you realize that "skin tight" isn't that accurate a description. It's certainly the right age for a Janus view, remembering the past, looking with some anxiety toward the future.

Part I, told from Maggie's middle-aged point of view, contains three chapters. The first provides context for the Moran family: Maggie and Ira, Jesse and Fiona, and their daughter Leroy. Chapter 2, the self-contained portion excerpted by *The New Yorker,* moves the Moran couple ninety miles north of Baltimore to the funeral of Max Gill (Gill is not, ah, breathing anymore) in Deer Lick, Pa. These last rites have been planned by his widow Serena Gill as a reenactment of their nuptial rites, complete with pop love songs to be resung by aging friends from the original wedding party who, like Maggie, have not just *kept* their youthful figures but doubled them.

Chapter 3 describes the wake at Serena Gill's home, during which silent home movies will be shown depicting the corpse as bridegroom a quarter century ago. During this event, which brings alive neither Gill nor the Sixties, Ira and Maggie slip upstairs and counteract death by enjoying spontaneous sex in the dead man's bedroom.

Part II, almost a separate story, is only fifty pages long, the only section narrated by Ira, and again almost a sandwich filling between thicker slices of "what Maggie knows." Headed home from Gill's funeral, Maggie, annoyed by a bad driver, yells at him that his wheel is loose. She is stricken when the driver, Daniel Otis, believes her lie and also turns out to be both old and black, a double assault on her conscience since good-hearted Maggie works with the aged in a rest home. Mr. Otis becomes one more stray person Maggie keeps inviting into their lives; Ira sees this incident and their involvement with the Otis family as a hyperbolic expansion on her earlier instant intimacy with a waitress in a roadside cafe.

In Part III, four chapters through Maggie's point of view, her Good Samaritanism becomes even more fullblown, though not every injured neighbor proves grateful. The long marriage of Ira and Maggie is contrasted with the brief marriage of Jesse and Fiona seven years earlier; both of these form a contrast with the "ideal marriage" broadcast into the Platonic ether in Chapter 1. If the first marriage evolved into a wedlock in which two different people have learned to live as partners, the second turned into a deadlock from which Jesse and Fiona escaped. Maggie, who once believed marriage would be "an alteration in people's lives, two opposites drawn together with a dramatic crashing sound" (*BL* 246) now understands that every individual problem of the bride and groom will persist afterward, become entwined, perhaps even synthesize.

In Part III, Ira and Maggie, still headed home from the funeral, take the detour Maggie demands to invite Fiona and Leroy home to Baltimore overnight. Once Maggie has them under her roof she begins her old efforts to turn white lies into bandages, trying unsuccessfully to bring Jesse back home as well. She, not they, will tie their marriage bond again. A meddler, a unifier, an improver, Friedrich Hegel in an apron, Maggie sees the world "out of focus, the colors not within the lines" (*BL* 312), and still believes that if she could only make a correcting adjustment then "everything would settle perfectly into place" (*BL* 312).

During the domestic conflicts that result, Maggie relives her early days as mother-in-law. By then she had already acted out Samuel Butler's remark, "Life is like playing a violin solo in public and learning the instrument as one goes on," and she wanted Jesse and Fiona to master her particular epithalamion. Literally the "breathing lessons" learned were those Maggie helped Fiona practice when she was pregnant with Leroy. Now at 48, Maggie is certain that everybody's childhood lessons in piano playing, typing, equations, driving—none of these provided training in the skills needed for "living day in and day out with a husband and raising up a new human being" (*BL* 182). Maggie makes readers recall that moment post partum, when nurses shooed them into a car and placed a strange and fragile baby in their laps. "If I'm a parent," everyone thinks at that time, "they must have lowered the requirements."

In his own way, Jesse did try to master those requirements seven years earlier. As an expectant father, he devoured baby books (Jeremy Pauling also read up on fatherhood), believing, like many American males, that "reading up, getting equipped" would put him in control. But despite book lessons, Jesse has become one more failed amateur at marriage and fatherhood. Ira thinks him a failure as a son as well. For all her clumsy, sometimes misguided meddling, Maggie could not "teach" him and Fiona then, nor on this day seven years later, the lessons that "real life" has slowly imparted to her in the School of Hard Knocks. Nor has she herself learned every other would-be teacher's lesson. She rejected the one taught by Ira's embittered father Sam, for example. She has remained deaf to the sad instruction of seniors in the rest home where she works, whose lives are worn beyond repair. She has not lowered her sights to the level from which commonsense Ira views the world.

Ira's diagnosis is that since Maggie believes the people she loves are better than they are, she changes reality to suit her view of them—a charge also implied against Anne Tyler as author by Edward Hoagland in his *New York Times* review of *Breathing Lessons*. Tyler is "not unblinking," he writes; she skips over racial friction even though it regularly occurs in the very Baltimore neighborhoods she writes about. In all eleven Tyler novels, he says, "Her people are eerily virtuous, Quakerishly tolerant of all strangers, all races. And she touches upon sex so lightly, compared with her graphic realism on other matters, that her total portrait of motivation is tilted out of balance."[4]

Some might argue that Hoagland's view of sex as prime mover is influenced by his gender, but Tyler draws complaints from militant feminist readers as well. Her focus on family may shortchange unmarried, divorced, childless or single-parent career women as heroines and as a reading audience. Other feminists frown over that scene in *Breathing Lessons* where Maggie rushes to the clinic to persuade Fiona not to go through with her planned abortion. Though Tyler's description of pro-lifers who are demonstrating angrily at curbside hardly seems sympathetic, some pro-choice readers want to be sure which of Maggie's anti-abortion arguments belong to Maggie and which belong to Tyler. One might as well insist that *Sense and Sensibility* take a stand on Napoleon, that *Emma* be more forceful about the War of 1812, or that *Persuasion* concern itself with the 1817 riots in Derbyshire over low wages.

Reading audiences do change, however, and if Jane Austen's novels develop toward final marriages, it may be less persuasive to reconcile plots that same way in 1989—ending as *Earthly Possessions* and *Breathing Lessons* do in the marital bed. In the latter ending, Ira is still awake and at a complex stage of his solitaire game, symbolizing his approach to life; Maggie has just kissed him before getting a good night's sleep so she'll be ready to travel on tomorrow, symbolizing hers.

What about the other endings to Tyler's novels? Are they unblinking, feminist? Do they constitute a synthesis arrived at after the clashing of opposites? What kind of synthesis?

At the end of *The Tin Can Tree*, P. J. climbs into the car and falls asleep with her head on Peter's lap. In *Earthly Possessions,* Saul and Charlotte in the old sleigh bed decide not to take a trip because their lives are the trip. "Go to sleep," says Charlotte, and he does—a small reversal of who has the insomnia from *Breathing Lessons*. A much older Miss Vinton has the last word of *Celestial Navigation,* looking at herself and Jeremy Pauling as they must appear to the eyes of a lighthearted whistling boy, who sees them as not at all star-crossed, just an elderly couple at the end of the dusty and unremarkable journey of their lives. *Dinner at the Homesick Restaurant* ends as Cody leads Beck back toward the family meal, the funeral meats. In *The Accidental Tourist* Macon is leaping from his Paris taxicab because Muriel is waiting by the curb, just as Morgan Gower (*Morgan's Passing*) starts humming while he walks toward another curb where Emily holds Josh on one hip. No rebellious Nora goes slamming out of her doll's house in these conclusions; no woman is swimming out to where horizon meets sea or going mad from seeing creatures swarm inside her yellow wallpaper.

Yet Tyler's reconciliations must not be made to seem as easy as Blondie's with Dagwood; she knows these risks. In *Morgan's Passing*, the puppet show does not end with the beast changing into a prince because "we use a more authentic version" (83). And usually Tyler presents opposing views, as through Sarah Leary, whose reaction to her son's murder is to decide that life is meaningless, and human beings evil. It would not suit the tone and purpose of *Breathing Lessons* to conduct marital conflict at the level of Medea vs. Jason, yet Tyler does catalogue those maddening habits of men and women which drive husbands and wives crazy. She even dares make almost stereotyped assumptions about gender roles in America: Ira is too quiet and self-contained; disorganized Maggie confides in absolute strangers. Don't most T.V. sitcoms also pair the impetuous meddling female with a patient, less excitable male? When Maggie storms out of the car and threatens to leave him forever, Ira does drive away and stay away just long enough to fill one episode. In his taciturn Gary Cooper way he says in the final moments of *Breathing Lessons*, "Maggie, honey" (*BL* 314) or "There, now, sweetheart" (*BL* 326). After twenty-eight years of rehearsal, the Moran disagreements have taken on the skills, stratagems, and compromises superficially sketched on the Cosby Show, but a novelist can enter her characters' minds, not just their apartments, and characters can read one another's thoughts. Maggie, for example, understands Ira's mood by the tune he whistles. (Tyler's father did this kind of whistling.)

Like other Tyler characters, the Morans are amazed at how their lives have turned out. Even Ira's marriage proposal seems an accidental by-product of a quarrel with his father, while Maggie's bridal candidacy resulted from a mistake she made about which soldier was dead. She considers Jesse's and Fiona's divorce almost accidental as well, the result of missed communications. The Morans live out their amazement at unpredictable life in ways associated with standard male/female attitudes: Maggie still busily trying to tinker with and repair life, Ira meditating more abstractly on the wastes of mortality and time. During his brief narration, Ira achieves the theme of "Our Town," through one of his periodic insights into how much he loves his awkward, lopsided, transitory family, whether he tells them out loud or not. His other half, Maggie, already knows she loves hers, tells them, and also wants to darn their lives, like socks. Unlike feminist writers who have mocked gender roles, or who have made marriage a battlefield between the sexes, Tyler carries sexual stereotypes to deeper, more complex levels to attempt in fiction what Josef Albers aspires to in his painting, "to make black and white behave together instead of shooting at each other only."

What I have called Tyler's use of thesis/antithesis/synthesis becomes for Mary F. Robertson in *Contemporary American Women Writers* a pattern of strangers disrupting a family's ordered life, then altering it into something new.[5] One possible dissenter to us both is John Up-dike, obviously a Tyler admirer, who nonetheless complains of one weakness: "a tendency to leave the reader just where she found him."[6] Updike believes the ends of Tyler's novels have *not* actually moved far from their beginning pages into new syntheses. Charlotte, after all, is back home with Saul; Jeremy ends up at home with a substitute wife/mother; Beck has come home to the dinner table even if he insists he'll leave again before the wine is poured; and, in *Breathing Lessons*, Maggie is gong to sleep on her side of the bed much as she must have gone to sleep the Friday night before the novel opened on Saturday morning.

In Tyler's fiction, the marriage of opposites does not produce radi-cally different offspring. The real adventure is not to light out for the territory with Huck Finn but to function as the Hallmark card ad-vises, even with all the risks of sentimentality that affirmation entails, to "Bloom where you are planted." Some find her developing work to be more positive than realism warrants. It is said that Tyler only chooses to review those books she expects to like, and in fiction, too, she seldom lingers long on characters who are actively mean spirited.

But in his *Times* review, though Hoagland finds her "Quakerish," he does not call Tyler's themes sentimental but links her with Henry James. Both, he says, produce a "literature of resignation—of wisely settling for less than life had seemed to offer . . . a theme more Euro-pean than New World by tradition." Such a theme, Hoagland thinks, is now coming into its own with the "graying of America into middle age since World War II."[7]

No one is more aware than Tyler of the risks either of boring compromise on the one hand or—worse for us women writers—sentimentality on the other, in such resignation. One slip of her pen and certain Tyler characters might begin warbling, "Brighten the cor-ner where you are," or quoting Edgar Guest, "it takes a heap o'liv-ing/to make a house a home" or—as Maggie sometimes does in *Breathing Lessons*—exhibiting too predictable a mixture of tend-erhearted with madcap-cute, like Lucille Ball. I agree with critic Joseph Voelker that sometimes Tyler casts on Maggie Moran an eye almost as cool as Graham Greene in *The Heart of the Matter* casts upon Scobie, though the issues are much smaller.[8] And I prefer *Celes-*

tial Navigation and *Dinner at the Homesick Restaurant* precisely
because the issues are larger, the opposites more distinct, the ambiguities in their resolution more persistent. But many of Tyler's most
devoted readers would disagree, would even claim that Maggie's outlook on life duplicates her creator's.

Nor do I want to be counted with those critics who object to Tyler's
fiction *because* her work aims steadily at reconciliation. William Gass
once remarked that the Pulitzer prize traditionally went to mediocre
talent, an opinion that underscores his own preference for stylistic
experiment. Those who prefer experimental work have a tempera-
mental distaste for Tyler's content, her emphasis on life-as-journey, her
mature willingness to accept and absorb conflict, her characters' decisions not to seek finality so much as the will to enter tomorrow still
doing what one song advises breezily in two novels, "Keep on Truck-
in'." Some contemporary critics will break out in allergic hives at any
literary content containing the slightest histamine of didacticism, affirmation of life, positive thinking.

But Tyler's positivism has more of the tough realism that underlies
Madeleine L'Engle's essay about her very old and very ill mother,
about the importance of loving her still, loving her enough "to accept
her as she is, now, for as long as this dwindling may take."9

Quiet acceptance need not minimize the hardships of life, death and
despair. In much of her work Tyler has permitted death and despair to
intrude, but not to win.

Leslie Fiedler's famous essay about shouting "No, in thunder!"10
against life's chaos and its daily grind, despair at its brevity and fury
over the pious banality of society's advice to cope, seems to assume
that to *see* the abyss is automatically to scream at it; to assume that
those others who may see it, look down, then turn away silently and
get on with the necessities of living are bound to be less sensitive, more
superficial, even blind. Women often consider his a romantic, luxury
view—available to those who've always had the option of
knighthood, war, shipping out on whalers or to the French Foreign
Legion, but partially foreclosed, say, for Emily Dickinson, who could
only climb the stairs. For those left home to nurse the old folks
through their long vomits of fatal cancer, shouting "no" would get no
bedpans emptied. Tyler's feminism is of this less dramatic sort—she

admires the people, often women, who have an abyss running right through their own backyards and still hang out the laundry.

Anne Tyler depicts the non-shouters, those people who "go on meaning well," ordinary people who seem "funny and strange to me, and touching in unexpected ways. I can't shake off," she says "a sort of mist of irony that hangs over whatever I see."[11]

So *The Accidental Tourist* opens in the rain as *A Farewell to Arms* closes in the rain. And if a denouement is usually the point in fiction that *un*ravels the tangles in story plot, consider for contrast the spontaneous *duet* of Ira and Maggie which is joined in the supermarket, their voices after much disagreement still plaited, braided. At the end of *Breathing Lessons* Ira stops Maggie's latest scheme to bring Leroy to live with them and brighten her own future days as well as his by enrolling in the superior Baltimore schools. Ira stops her by saying, "'Maggie, look at me.' She faced him, hands on her hips. 'No,' he said" (326).

Contrast Ira Moran's not very thunderous "No" with what happens in the end of that ultimate pop novel, *Gone With the Wind*, a novel Leslie Fiedler calls part of our national myth, as "southern" as our movies are sometimes "western." Many male writers would end that novel with a "no," at least in moderate thunder, by stopping where Rhett Butler says, "Frankly, my dear, I don't give a damn," and departs. In fact, thousands of readers (who have not been polled by gender) remember both book and film as ending exactly on that note.

But Margaret Mitchell (who called herself "a dynamo going to waste") ended her only novel in the same tone Tyler's chief characters in her also popular novels stubbornly employ. "Tomorrow will be better," thinks Scarlet O'Hara at the end of *Gone With the Wind*, just as Maggie Moran—stopped by circumstances, stopped by her husband's firm "No"—may seem to drift into sleep acquiescent although the previous 325 pages have made clear that for Maggie, too, tomorrow will always be a new day. Even in dreams she will be scheming up ways to use tomorrow, to improve the ordinary people living there and remold them nearer to the heart's desire. It is as if, with Tyler's women, indeed with many heroines at the end of novels by women, the closing mood is: "And that's semi-final!"

In her long consideration about opposites and how they marry, after eleven novels about love, home, family, and survival, *Breathing Lessons* is surely semi-final, and Anne Tyler is already dreaming up Novel Number 12.

1. Carl Schoettler, "New Anne Tyler Magnifies the Mundane" [rev. of *Breathing Lessons*], *The [Baltimore] Evening Sun*, 1 September 1988, sec. D, p. 1.

2. "Anne Tyler," *Dictionary of Literary Biography*, vol. 6: *American Novelists since World War II, Second Series*, ed. James E. Kibler, Jr. (Detroit: Gale Research, 1980), p. 337.

3. In *The Writer on Her Work*, ed. Janet Sternburg (New York: Norton, 1980), p. 9.

4. "About Maggie, Who Tried Too Hard," *The New York Times Book Review*, 11 September 1988, p. 44.

5. "Anne Tyler: Medusa Points and Contact Points," in *Contemporary American Women Writers: Narrative Strategies*, ed. Catherine Rainwater and William J. Scheick (Lexington: University Press of Kentucky, 1985), pp. 119–142.

6. "Loosened Roots" [rev. of *Earthly Possessions*], *The New Yorker*, 53 (6 June 1977), 130.

7. "About Maggie, Who Tried Too Hard," p. 44.

8. A remark made by Joseph C. Voelker in an open forum at the Anne Tyler Symposium, Baltimore, April, 1989.

9. *The Summer of the Great Grandmother* (San Francisco: Harper & Row, 1974, 1979), p. 149.

10. "The Power of Blackness: Faustian Man and the Cult of Violence," in *Love and Death in the American Novel*, rev. ed. (New York: Dell, 1960, 1966), p. 505.

11. "Still Just Writing," in *The Writer on Her Work*, p. 12.

1990

Communities

The perception of community in the South elicits dual images. On the one hand, there is the landscape of imposing monolithic solidarity, of common purpose and sentiment from Mississippi to North Carolina. On the other hand, there is the snapshot of many small towns with courthouses and Baptist churches at their center surrounded by vast rural areas that are splattered with numerous small farms and dotted with a few large plantations. Increasingly, both of these images have faced revision. Beneath the cloak of presumed solidarity emerges at least two Souths, one black and one white, and many others. Even small-town southern life has had to confront urban and suburban mores.

Just as community has been transformed, the literary impulse that has emerged from it and defined it also has sought redefinition. The experiences of many, a pluralism of lifestyles and ideas, give voice to writers of different traditions and experiences. Women writers have flourished in such an environment. In their work they have engaged these issues and at the same time discovered new forms of community. Despite the many differences of style and subject matter, they demonstrate a continuity with the past. While the traditional subjects may be in some ways disappearing, there does remain "a stubborn sense of place." As Margaret Walker suggests, "It is impossible to read our most distinguished writers without being conscious at once of the land as well as the people . . . . There is not a southern state that has not figured prominently in literature" (p. 29). The importance of place—of shared idiom, locale, and experience, however separated by physical space—lingers with contemporary writers even as the very conception of the South undergoes revision and expansion. Thus, when writers gathered at Furman University to discuss the subjects of community, place, friendship, and connection, they continued in many ways the conversation begun by others on a panel at Wesleyan College twenty-five years earlier.

Josephine Humphreys

A Disappearing Subject
Called the South

To tell the truth, the South is once again in ruin.

Our first ruin—slaves let loose and mansions burnt—ought to have been a fortunate fall, the kind of collapse that clears an old bad life for new good things. But we are here again, witness to a second devastation, and not only witness, but party. We have done it to ourselves.

I am talking about visible ruin—the real physical destruction of our places. Let us call it, for purposes of irony, "development." Development is the dirty family secret of the South, and, like most dirty secrets, it is known to everyone.

A writer friend from Florida tells me that one can't really write about Southern development anymore. The topic is stale. Too many writers have milked the condo-golf resort scene; too many books have pointed out that the South continues to become more like the North every day. Maybe so, I say; but stale news may still be true and urgent. Recently I drove through the urban labyrinth of Charlotte, North Carolina, with a Yankee writer, and after studying the scenery for an hour, which is how long it takes to get from one side of Charlotte to another, he finally said, "Nothing prevents this from being New Jersey."

Nothing prevents it. That is why, no matter how overworked the topic, we must continue to write about development. We must prevent it. Writers in particular have a duty to prevent it, because for us what's at stake is lifeblood.

There's a peculiar relationship between fiction and place, one that is rehashed daily in literary seminars; it remains peculiar and fascinating. Fiction must *take place*. Without what Shakespeare called "a local habitation," there can be no good narrative, only "airy nothing," a poor brain's fiddling. But whenever story can locate itself in reality, it will draw on reality's mystery and power, becoming that oddity of literary endeavor, true fiction. This geographical imperative exists because fiction has as its natural subject the real world and real man in it, and all the complications brought on by one clear fact: *We are here.* The writing of fiction must always involve both the *we* and the *here*.

The writing imagination is fueled by real places. A writer living in Disney World, like the last of the dusky seaside sparrows, would be so removed from his real original home that fiction (true fiction as opposed to its opposite, pure romance) would become impossible. In the past, the South had a vast supply of real places. But the first gradual and now swift metamorphosis of our geography has changed our literature.

We have, of course, already lost our original home, the Eden of the great forests, swamps, rivers, islands, mountains. What's left now are tiny pockets, museums of artificially sustained wildness run by the Park Service. Southern writers have felt the loss. In William Faulkner's Yoknapatawpha County it looms, a constant awareness of paradise surrendered to sawmills and plantations and towns. Here is the so-called "sense of loss" that is said to characterize Southern fiction. It is not that we lost a war. It is that we lost our place. We must forget the Southern wilderness; it is as finally gone as a lost love, and nothing but pain to recall.

But towns! Towns are another matter. Towns are what I grieve for now. The natural setting of Southern fiction is not wilderness, nor farm nor city. It is town. For the most part, that is where our fictional vision has been focused; that is the place that has seemed most fitting for the kinds of stories we have wanted to tell—narratives of the human community. While one life may form the spine of a novel, one life alone is not enough in a Southern novel. Our subject is the concert of human lives.

We've never really had a strong tradition of literary individualism. No Southern Thoreau has emerged to celebrate the individual Southern consciousness. Maybe Jefferson's voice was one early solo trumpet, but Jefferson's overriding concern was still with society, how men must live together. In fiction, there has been no Southern *Moby Dick,* no novel so thoroughly stripped down to the single mind and its mad, glorious quest. Our best match for Melville is Poe, not a novelist at all.

Supposing Mark Twain to be the first great Southern novelist (and incidentally the greatest American novelist), I see our early need to re-create the South and show it to the rest of America as well as to ourselves. To wish to do so is not necessarily apology. We are a self-conscious region, suffused with the kind of inwardly turned interest that accompanies a sense of separateness. We've never really felt American. We've always tried to show why.

The easiest and truest answer is the long-lived disaster of slavery; I would say it is the only answer necessary, except that I always feel there is something more, some schism of mind and soul that pre-dated slavery, that maybe even enabled it. All my life in the white South, I have heard apologists diminish the importance of slavery: it was not a direct cause of the Civil War; it was a system that actually benefited the slaves; it was an economic necessity and therefore excusable. But the human mind, while it can superficially deceive itself, has a deep knowledge of moral truth. True crime against nature—like slavery or development—cannot be committed unknowingly. An entire society may, for a time, look the other way, but at heart it will know the truth. Its writers will tell that truth, sooner or later. They will maneuver for a good view of society, and they will tell what they see. Their best vantage point will be a town.

A purely rural setting is hard ground for the novelist; more often than not, he'll widen the rural scope by taking his people to town now and then, or by hauling in travelers. But a purely urban setting is hard, too, because community itself is not to be seen in most cities; the proportions of the place have gotten out of hand and are no longer of human scale. Town alone is that community in which community itself is discernible.

Reynolds Price has said that fiction is best set in a town of fewer than ten thousand souls, "a town from whose center open country [can] be reached by a fifteen-minute walk." He goes on to give the reason: fiction's deep need for a vision of the permanent beauty of the world. The city, he says, can mostly support only "bad poems and novels full of neon light on wet asphalt, unshaven chins, scalding coffee at four a.m."

There's something else, too. Something happens there, at that spot imagined by Price, the place where you can see the end of town. At that margin, the mystery of human community and the mystery of non-human beauty touch. A street dead-ends in a cornfield. The last garden fence keeps out thicket and vine, and a railroad track curves off into woodsy nowhere. Even sounds stop, fly into thin air. Stand there awhile, where you can see both town and no-town, and you will know something about life on Earth. You will know enough for a novel.

Where I live, in the South Carolina Low-country, towns are hard to see. Some, like Mount Pleasant, have been swallowed whole by neighboring cities. Some, like Summerville, have spread themselves outward to link up with a neighboring spreading town, and the original boundaries of both have been lost. The perfect town of McClellanville is being colonized, its edges blurred by a slow accretion of new houses. For the fullest sense of community, shouldn't a person be able to see the limits of his settlement? If he can't see the end of his town, won't he have a diminished notion of home, and no notion of an unknown territory beyond home?

In parts of the South, we are actually building fake towns. Places called "Seaside" and "Charleston Place" in Florida are merely developments costumed as towns. A real town is the work of a kind of collective dream, the sum of a thousand individual urges belonging to real people: the urge to love, to form families, to educate and worship and fight and eat and invent. The new fake towns signal our desperate need for town, but they do not fill it. They are "quaint" in the original sense of the word: wrought with skill, clever. I see a parallel tendency in our fiction, the increasing output of "Southern" works set in a "south" that can't be found in reality or even in history, an exaggerated and quaint fake place.

There are, of course, still Southern towns. I have seen them—set out to see them, in fact, on a journey that took me looping from South

Carolina through northern Georgia, Alabama, Mississippi, and Louisiana to Texas (where I figured I could make out the limits of the South itself) and then back along the coastal route into Florida, and home. They still exist, places like Talladega, Alabama, and Jefferson, Texas, two of the loveliest.

But I had the feeling all along that these towns too were endangered. I had the feeling that one day the Southern town may exist only as a town-museum, its houses precious objets d'art, its "way of life" annually re-enacted in period costume. Some are already approaching that museumized condition. Talladega's houses are marked with plaques and listed with the National Register of Historic Places. Jefferson has come under the sway not of the National Register but of a thriving bed-and-breakfast enterprise, which also labels its houses. These towns and others like them have discovered that tourists will come, and will pay, to see what a real town looks like.

But once a town is museumized, it loses the very authenticity that tourists enjoy and writers crave. Its useful force as a real place dissipates. I don't predict what will happen to our fiction when writers can no longer put themselves in touch with that force. But I suspect that we will depend more and more on the "South" as setting, where there may be antebellum houses and Spanish moss and horse-drawn carriages, but where there is no community.

Our better writers may then turn to the secret towns, those that are still real because no one wants to develop them, or even lay eyes on them: the poor towns like Tchula, or Indian towns like Pearl River, in Mississippi; towns hidden within cities, like Prichard, Alabama, inside Mobile; and the nightmare migrant towns of Belle Glade and Immokalee in Florida. Nothing picturesque or festive or quaint or even comfortable here. These are real places, with more force and more story and more community than any of our developed places. *We are here,* in Pearl River, in Tchula, in Belle Glade. We are still here, and from here may again reconstruct ourselves.

1988

Mary Hood, Lee Smith, and Leigh Allison Wilson

A Stubborn Sense of Place

During the summer of 1986, *Harper's Magazine* asked nine Southern fiction writers to comment on the place of the writer in the new American South. What follows are Hood's, Smith's, and Wilson's remarks.

Leigh Allison Wilson: We're all of us in my family East Tennesseans, have been ever since our one-legged forefather, James Patrick McGuire, came hobbling out from Fermanagh County, Ireland, to settle in Jefferson County, Tennessee, searching for riches in 1792. He didn't find them, and neither has anybody else in my family. His failure must have killed the spirit of adventure in the rest of us, because for 200 years nobody has moved around much. A few people have been to Los Angeles and New York, and there was a second cousin once removed who got stationed in Japan during the aftermath of World War II, but he shot himself there, confirming everybody's suspicion that what was good for America in strange places wasn't all that good for people in our family. If they can help it, my family mostly stays put.

This is not to say that they think of themselves as regionalists, or even Southerners. They are Jefferson Countyists, perhaps, or Wilson-Blackburn-McGuireists. What they usually are, no doubt about it, is selfish, self-righteous, and self-referential, just like everybody else is half the time. There's no getting around incredible foolishness and incredible pride, even in your own home. Most especially in your own home. When you know every twisted tree and misshappen rock and paint-chipped sign on the way to Cas Walker grocery store, you can't help but think you know just about everything worth knowing in life. I don't think this is particularly Southern, though I do think it might be peculiarly American. Most likely it's simply human.

I went off to college in New England, an anomaly in my family, and during the first few weeks there a great change came over me. At home I'd been demonically opinionated and, I thought, intellectual as all get-out; I could squeeze the humanity out of any Southern social problem and turn it into a grand abstraction, a generalization as smooth and polished and bloodless as a pebble. After holding forth at college for a while, though, things came to a crisis. One day I had a vision of my family, all of them—aunts, uncles, grandparents, cousins, the whole bunch—and I had a vision, too, of the places I'd know, the details of home that, one after the other, were the summation of my life until then. And in that vision I saw other people, complete strangers, coming to take their places beside my family, people from Hamblen County and Knox County. Then more people came, crowding in from Georgia and Mississippi and Florida, all of their faces different, all of their lives a complete mystery to me. Next all I saw was a map of the South, the states in different colors but turning dark with teeming pinpricks that stood for people. And at the very end of that vision, there was just a globe of the world with no people on it anywhere. Nothing I cared about existed any longer, and neither did I. That's when I turned against those kinds of generalizations.

Since leaving Tennessee to go to college, I have made homes in Virginia, Massachusetts, Iowa, California, and New York. In all of these states there are details that have formed me, people I have loved, places whose images burn in my mind like recurring dreams. I don't think this is because I am from the South. I think it's because we all of us on earth appreciate the familiar and titillating and mysterious details of our homes, wherever they are, whoever lives there. That the South has been blessed with many great writers is, it seems to me, simply a fact, not some sort of grandiloquent and puzzling truth. The truth of things lies in much smaller details, a twisted tree here, a skyscraper there, a greening cornfield or an embarrassed smile somewhere else. My family are all East Tennesseans, have been for two centuries. They mostly stay put. They are selfish, self-righteous, and self-referential when you give them the chance. They all of them know so very much about the things and people around them, and so very little, and that's just like everybody else.

Mary Hood: Because my father is a native New Yorker and my mother is from Georgia, I have never felt comfortable with the we/they dichotomy. Even if I could, I would prefer not to choose: I am both. Though I was born in Georgia and have spent all my life here except for travels, as a child I never thought (nor do I now) of "up North" and "down South" as being anything but geographical distinctions. In me the twain met. I am like Laurie Lee's fabulous two-headed sheep, which could "sing harmoniously in a double voice and cross-question itself for hours."

I cannot think of a single more important influence on my writing, and certainly upon my life, than my parentage. It has given me a duty toward both no-nonsense brevity and encompassing concatenations: the Northern preference for sifting out *why* in twenty-five words or less and settling it once and for all, the Southern for interminably savoring *how,* cherishing the chaff of irrelevancy around the essential kernel. It must have been a Northerner who invented the questionnaire. A Southerner would have been more likely to think up—but not bother to apply for a patent on—the essay response. (A Southern always issues an essay response unless suffering fools.)

Suppose a man is walking across a field. To the question "Who is that?" a Southerner would reply by saying something like "Wasn't his granddaddy the one whose dog and him got struck by lightning on the steel bridge? Mama's third cousin—dead before my time—found his railroad watch in that eight-pound catfish's stomach the next summer just above the dam. I think it was eight pounds. Big as Eunice's arm. The way he married for that new blue Cadillac automobile, reckon how come he's walking like he has on Sunday shoes, if that's who it is, and for sure it is." A Northerner would reply to the same question (only if directly asked, though, never volunteering), "That's Joe Smith." To which the Southerner might think (but be much too polite to say aloud), "They didn't ask his name, they asked who he *is!*"

When I began to write fiction, I made a conscious decision to try to sound like the Southern talkers I had heard tell such wonderful things, but every word I wrote had to pass the sternest censorship from that Northern conscience in me—the one that stands ready, tapping its foot, jingling the car keys, rustling the map, wanting me to *get on with it,* asking with every turn and delay of plot, "So?" I didn't set out to try to sound like Southern *books.* (I hadn't read all that many.) Rather, I imitated the actual talkers in my own daily life: kinfolk, neighbors, strangers on street corners, passengers in the bus seat behind me; I strove for an accurate transcription. I thought of myself as American, blooming where planted—which happens to be with a Southern exposure. But I believe that if I had been anywhere else when I set buds for such bloom, I would have adapted to that climate as well and flowered in season. Because the people I was writing about were Southern, I wrote "Southern."

I had not researched the genealogy of the noble house of Southern Literature, whose heritage seemed grander than any to which I, with my library card and secondhand paperbacks, could lay claim of kinship. It was, then, a great surprise to discover that I had already and automatically inherited it, was in fact a Southern Writer, without even trying! I found it out in New England, and the one who broke the news to me was a Long Island novelist who, upon hearing my accent and discovering that I was from Georgia, by assumption conferred on me fraternity into that worthy tradition to which I had not yet become reconciled—Southern letters.

"How far are you from where Flannery O'Connor lived and worked?" she asked me.

"About thirty years," I replied. But I'm catching up.

Lee Smith: Well to answer your question, yes things are changing down here.

Things are not what they used to be.

Take Miss Everdeen Foscue's house on the corner for instance, you know the one with all the gingerbread on it and the widow's walk they put up there for her Aunt Elizabeth who lived with them because she never got over the fact that her husband Clarence Lee failed to come back from New Orleans where he went apparently on business? and she used to just stand up there on that widow's walk and look down at all the little Bible School children drinking red Kool-Aid at ten o'clock in the morning on the playground of the First Presbyterian Church next door and cry her eyes out. I guess she knew by then she'd never have a child or a man either one . . .

Well that house has got a health food store on the first floor now and the Turkey Jackson Insurance Agency (that's State Farm) on the second floor, and Louise Rideout's combination Beautyrama and Tanning Salon up on the third floor where she's got these big box things that look like coffins and you get in them nude and get a tan. You would not catch me dead in one of them, just on principle, not to mention the ultraviolet.

You can't tell who's nice anymore, either, not like you used to could back in the days when you just naturally knew everybody in town and what their daddy did. Now people that you have almost never heard of are running everything. I mean the guy from high school who used to wear the soft brown flattop, you know the one I mean. You just can't remember his name. Or his last name anyway—you *think* his first name was Dave. Dave! What a dumb no-account lackluster name, nothing like Fontaine B. Barrett IV or Hogface Haines. In high school he wore highwater pants that showed his white socks and short-sleeved plaid shirts or shirts that had a little all-over pattern? and a pen-and-pencil set in a clear plastic case in his breast pocket? Now he's grown up and bought him some *Miami Vice* clothes and got a portfolio. He's running this town, and nobody even *thinks* to ask who his daddy was.

About the only thing down here that is still the same in fact, if you ask me, is the way Southerners will *talk*. On and on and on. I mean, whether you want them to or not. I mean, if you just ask them a simple question such as "Where is the post office?" they will start in about one time their cousin was going to the post office and she got bit by a mad dog, or how the postmaster has not got enough help in there and it is clear to all that he has been shorting the public and bought a bassboat. In fact I had an uncle who used to say, if you asked him *anything*, "Well, I'll tell you a story about that." I don't know if you know what I mean or not. It's like everything is a story, I mean even things that somebody from Ohio, say, would not even bother to *mention*, much less think it was a story.

Sometimes I think I can see these tendencies in myself, and I tell you, it gives me pause. In fact I think I might already have caught the deadly Southern Door Disease, which attacks white women of a certain age and makes them unable to leave a room without holding the door open for a minimum of fifteen minutes meanwhile talking talking always talking . . .

1986

Bobbie Ann Mason and Elizabeth Spencer

Remarks on Contemporary Writing

In the winter of 1987 *Michigan Quarterly Review* posed this question to a number of distinguished American fiction writers:

> Granted that contemporary American fiction is a variety of things, what kind of recent writing interests you especially, and, in your opinion, is most deserving of more attention and more readers?

What follows are Mason's and Spencer's responses.

Bobbie Ann Mason: Although I admire many individual writers of various styles and subjects (and I'm usually partial to stylists), I'm especially interested right now in the new American fiction about the lives of so-called "ordinary people," people whose lives weren't written about much before, but whose dreams and difficulties are nevertheless complicated and rich. I hear these new voices coming in from all over—small towns, farms, prairies, factories, reservations, night shifts, car radios, backyards, prisons, shopping malls, condos, big city apartments and offices, riverboats. It cuts across class lines. It's "people like us" instead of romantic heroes.

American fiction since "Huckleberry Finn" has been about the alienated hero (usually male) who rejects society because of its corruption and goes off to follow his own rules. But nowadays there are so many of us, and so many feel left out and are in no position to reject society and light out for the territories, that the focus has shifted away from the romantic hero to the ordinary person's struggle to get by in a mass society. Now the emphasis is on characters who make up the mass culture and away from the privileged few who can remove themselves from it. The new arena for fiction is the mainstream. Instead of the hero going outside society, we have people carrying on their daily lives within it, in spite of it, and we have marginal folks trying to get in, to get some basic advantages they've been denied. In the past we weren't willing to take sales clerks, for instance, seriously in fiction—especially black female sales clerks. But now we are. And that's important, I think.

Elizabeth Spencer: American writing at this time seems spread out over the whole country. No one area or ethnic approach seems to dominate. There are pockets of first class writing on the West Coast, in the South (as usual), suburban to New York (to be expected), and around Houston, Texas, to mention a few areas I know of. The poet Yeats's dire prediction, "the center cannot hold," has come true for us in just the ways he meant it: there is no one controlling myth, tradition, or set of critical values. Yet we have fine talent—readable, serious, informed, entertaining, and working hard.

We are all—in terms of supermarkets, shopping centers, schools, "housing," wars, assassinations, and national politics—living a similar life, bound historically to that crazy roller-coaster ride we call our own time. Fewer American writers are trying to bring us news from abroad: more, from a position in the here and now among us, are searching outward (Richard Ford in *The Sportswriter*), looking back (E. L. Doctorow in *World's Fair*), looking forward (Walker Percy in *The Thanatos Syndrome*). Yet the American experience outside the country can still be explored with great imaginative force, as witness Norman Rush's *Whites,* a collection of stories which limns the cultural encounters, often perilous, often comic, of the U.S. civil servant in Africa. As witness also Cecile Pineda's *Face,* creating out of a few facts the courage of an accident victim in Brazil.

Overworked though it may have been in the past, the Southern scene can still be brought to vivid new life, fresh as a flower from an old root: here note Padgett Powell's moving *Edisto,* Nancy Lemann's *Lives of the Saints.*

1987

Furman University

The Woman as Writer and Reader:
A Panel Discussion

Furman University, 24–26 March 1988. Panelists: Ellen Gilchrist, Gloria Naylor, Josephine Humphreys, and Louise Shivers. Moderators: Willard Pate and Ann Sharp. Questioner: Barbara Hardy.

Pate: We would like first to have all four of you entertain the question "Do you think of yourself as a woman writer?" Then we will ask for supplemental questions from the audience.

Shivers: Well, I don't know how to answer that question but maybe as we talk, more will come to me. I really do try to write stories. I *am* a woman and I'm, at this point in my life, very happy about being a woman. So that's the way it's going to come out, but I really don't think about it that much.

Gilchrist: I wrote an answer down but I wouldn't have had to because Louise just said what I'm thinking. That doesn't mean that it isn't a good title for a panel discussion, but I decided that if I do this I *have* to tell you exactly what I think whether I am popular with you or not. Because like all well-raised children, I was raised to try to get people to like me. But I don't think of myself as a woman when I write because I think of myself—I wrote this down—"As part of the physical universe which includes the reaches of the stars and the sub-atomic particles." I think it's a terrible mistake for a writer to start limiting their conception of themselves. But Louise just said exactly the same thing much more simply and probably more beautifully.

Naylor: This is a question that has only been asked of writers in the last 20 years or maybe even 15 years. I cannot imagine anyone having said to Richard Wright, "What is it like to be a black, male writer?" or to John Irving, "Tell me, how is it to be male and a writer?" Because we assume naturally that anything that is indeed male, writes. So, therefore, in texts you will have the writer, *he* uses the pen and uses metaphor. That's a problem that does not exist with the people on this panel. It exists with the way we perceive things in this society. If we make the assumption that there is a norm, and if that norm is indeed male or if that norm is indeed white, upper middle-class male, then anything that's not in that norm has to explain their existence and explain what they are doing.

The whole process of writing, folks—before the word processor— took a piece of paper and a pencil, and it took a desire to have something to say. From Homer on, every writer has articulated through their own particular experience. Shakespeare's Egyptians, his Venetians, his Caribbeans all spoke like Elizabethan English people. Because that was what Shakespeare was. But now, lo and behold, Alice Walker will come along and she will articulate through her experience and will be asked to explain, "Why did you write from that perspective?" You know it is like saying, "Why do you breathe, Gloria?" "Why do you breath, Josephine?" And I don't take exception to it; I am not insulted by it. But I am a bit put out by the closed-mindedness of our society that has not accepted the reality that women have been here writing about their experiences at the same time men have been writing. And that is what we have to change.

Humphreys: I never considered this question at all while I was writing my first book. But suddenly after publishing and talking to people and having people react to my work, I realized it *is* a question. At first it annoyed me every time it came up. I didn't want to talk about being a woman writer, and I didn't like the distinction made between a woman's book and a man's book. However, in an insidious kind of way all of that thinking has made me think the opposite. There are some things in my own personal life right now—a lot of emotional turmoil that I think is related to being a woman, and in particular with children—that affects my writing a lot. So I hesitate to say that I'm not affected by the female experience and that it doesn't affect my writing.

In a way, though, writing affects my femininity more than femininity affects my writing. It's sort of an opposite thing for me. Writing has
changed my life in so many ways, and that's one of them. It seems to
be constantly modifying my perceptions of myself and of what I am
doing.

Questioner: I'm curious to know how you are able to write, as well
as cope with the many demands in women's lives—children, family,
husbands, dogs.

Humphreys: This is part of my whole problem now. When I began
writing I handled the problem by becoming schizophrenic and dividing my life completely down the middle. Doing children half my time
and writing the other half. Well, children *and* family, but everything
else disappeared out of my life, including friends. And that is the
worst loss. Everything else too—all my contact with community. At
the time I was clearly glad to be rid of it. But this is 10 years down that
road now, and I find that the lack of friends and the lack of contact
with the human community is killing. It really is very, very difficult to
maintain over that long period of time. And though I give some
thought and effort to restoring myself in that respect, I have a feeling
that I will cut back even further, so that I'm eventually going to cut
back on the things that are crucial and important to me and that I
love. So it's frightening to me that there seems to be, to me anyway,
almost a danger in writing.

Naylor: I understand what Josephine is saying. That's one of the
reasons I teach. Because it forces me to leave my home and to reach
out to people and listen to what they are saying and communicate.
Because as a writer you are rewarded for staying inside, for becoming
a recluse. That's one of the ironies of the whole process. The more you
hold yourself off from the world, the better you're able to re-create the
world that you've sort of shut off. Unlike the women on my left and
right, I don't have to worry about the nuclear family. There was a
husband once, but I got rid of him, and so there are no small children
who are dependent upon me. So there's even a greater danger that
there'll be no one demanding my time outside of me. And you don't
want that. You want to be a whole human being if you possibly can,
but it becomes a fight.

Gilchrist: I'll tell you what I was thinking about when Gloria was
saying that. My first book of fiction was supposed to be published the

same month that my first grandchild was being born in New Orleans. I've always thought what a lucky and fortunate and star-created situation that was for me because it saved me. I remember I called Eudora Welty sometime in August, and she said something about I know you're excited about your book, and I said I am. And then I said, "Eudora, the baby's going to be born exactly the same time, and I don't know which one to be more excited about." And she said, "Oh, Ellen, they're not in competition." Oh, wasn't that wonderful? And they aren't; and I thought about it a million times. But they are. Since I am an obsessive person, I have to do what Josephine used to do—I have to go from obsession to obsession, but I've been doing it for 53 years, and I'm real comfortable with that.

Shivers: Even though my children were late teenagers by the time I started writing, I still have almost the same problem I think Jo was talking about. We have a very close family and even though they're now grown people with husbands and wives and I have a grandchild, they're constant, every day problems. I mean, they still *are* your children. I was so intense about finally getting the chance to be a writer and not wanting to miss the chance to tell these stories that I finally found out I could tell, and at the same time wanting to keep the family. That's all—I don't do anything else. I'm either writing or with the family, and there are some relationships and friendships that hurt to give up, but you do have to give up some things if you are a writer. That's for sure, and I've been there. It's worth it.

Gilchrist: I've learned a wonderful thing from having that happen to me, though. I've learned what it is when a man becomes obsessive about his work. I know now he doesn't dislike me, he's not tired of me; he's excited about something he's doing, he's moving toward a goal that he has created for himself, real or imaginary. And not only a man. I say *men* because I have sons, and my sons are at the age where they're beginning to really fulfill their mature lives, and I see them get an idea in their head and start going toward it, and nobody else is going to exist for them for weeks or months. And it's wonderful to know that that's okay. They're going to come out the other end and say, "Where are my friends? Where are my children? Where's my mother?"

Questioner: Mrs. Shivers, it seems to me that both Roxy and Georgianna, whom you shared with us in your reading this morning, seem to be very aware of their roles in society as far as being mothers and taking care of their houses. You mentioned that you married very early and that you didn't start writing until you were about 40, and I wondered if their experiences and your experience are parallel, if you're trying to send a message about a woman's place in society through Roxy and Georgianna, and the difference now from then.

Shivers: I probably am. Neither one of them really had much choice. Georgianna certainly, in the late eighteen hundreds, didn't have any choice. There were no libraries and bookmobiles. There she was in this little town and she was raised to—you know, you're a wife and a mother and you cook meals and take care of the men and there you are. That's your life. And then Roxy came on in 1930 and did the same thing. Well, I was raised the same way. I'm sure most of y'all were raised that way. The woman steps back. You give the man the biggest piece of meat and you wait until he eats. Yes, I am still working out something in myself about that. And I see it in my daughters, though they've already gone far from it. I think I started giving them a message pretty strong, "Get out there and go." But I still have some problems with myself, and, of course, I'm writing through those problems.

Gilchrist: Nobody ever told me that women were supposed to take a backseat to anybody. I just didn't ever perceive it as being between men and women. You went out there and fought with your brothers for whatever you wanted—this is the kind of stuff I say that makes me unpopular. I saw being the only girl in the family as a position where I was the only one who could run to my mother and grab hold and hide behind her and say, "He hit me! He hit me!" I always started it!

Questioner: This question is directed to Mrs. Shivers. I heard you say at another workshop that the tender trap for most Southern girls was being daddy's little girl or something to that effect. That it was a trap that was very difficult to get out of.

Shivers: It was for me. I did have this wonderful father, and he was just very tender and sweet. And then I had all these brothers. It helped me stay a victim a lot longer. Because they were protective, I was safe. I was really safe. I had Daddy and the boys. And that's not all bad. My Daddy was a sweet thing, and I do think of him as *sweet*.

I didn't start writing until after my father died. And that's part of
the thing that made me go on to do it, I'm sure. One of the things that
feels so good about all this is I know how proud he would be that I
finally did it. But I also know now that he would have been proud if I
had gone ahead and done it a long time before I did.

You know, I like men and I never had any big awe about men. I was
surrounded by them all the time, not only the ones at home but all the
boys who worked at the funeral home, so it wasn't any great mysterious thing. But somewhere in there I had just gotten that message
from the time I was born: "Keep quiet and be sweet and they'll *love*
you better." I have a part in the new novel I just finished where I say,
"Maybe that kind of compassion and all this Southern, loving way is
just another way to say fear." Maybe it was just another word for fear.
So I'm still trying to figure all this out.

Gilchrist: It's another word for Oedipus complex, if you *say all that.*

Now that is amazing. All that a female child can do from the time
she sits up and walks and talks is repeat that relationship that she had
with her daddy. And all that a male child can do is repeat the one he
had with his mama. And it's not bad. It's just how the human mind
works, but you can never finish sounding the mysteries of the Oedipus
complex.

Humphreys: I had no brothers at all and no boys my own age to
talk to and went to a girls' school. So my father was the only male in
my life. And though I couldn't wait until he died to publish, he wishes
that I had.

The messages to me when I was growing up were you need not
compete with men, and women can do anything that men can do.
And you *must* get all A's in school and you *must* be the best that you
possibly can, but *never* let anyone know how smart you are. Especially don't let men know. And *never* . . . let's see, the things that
you could do that might ruin your life included number one, getting
pregnant, number two, going on the stage, number three, publishing
something. And those were explicit rules.

Pate: This is very Southern.

Naylor: Yeh, very Southern. Although my folks are from Mississippi and I was conceived in Mississippi and they moved to New York a

month before I was born, I grew up in somewhat of a Southern home. But not quite as Southern as what I am hearing.

I am the oldest of three girls. My dad wanted sons and my mother told us that he told her when I first came, "Okay, okay, I'll give you that one, but I want sons." And then the middle sister came and the baby sister. My mother said, "Then I closed up shop." So he reconciled himself to the fact that he was going to be raising females. And that was good for us because we were taught by a father that you can do anything you want to do. He was so afraid that we would have to become dependent upon men that we learned how to change tires. I learned how to unchoke my car, that sort of thing. And also just to go out and do what I had to do in the world. *But,* somehow you knew that after you did all that, you did get married. Become very independent so in case he leaves you, you can take care of yourself. There was supposed to be a *he* who would be there. That's the kind of home it was.

But as far as my writing is concerned, I never had any worry about my parents' having to be senile or dead before I could say the things I've said. They've been quite proud of the fact that I do write. I think a lot of that comes from their background. They didn't have the privilege of going on to college or even being allowed to use the public libraries where they were.

Questioner: If you had advice to give to a person who wants to write, what would you tell them?

Humphreys: If you are 20, I would tell you to read as much as you possibly can. That would be the first thing to do. If you are 30, I would tell you to work as hard at writing as you possibly can. And I think those are two things that all writers should do, all beginning writers and all practicing writers also. Hard work is the secret to me and it is the way that you get to page 300, which is always the crucial thing. You just have to keep at it.

Shivers: I would say learn to respect yourself, and respect that desire to do it. Read and write, and just write about things that you are passionate about. And *do* it. It really comes down to being that simple. The day came when I said to myself, if I am going to do it I've got to do it and not keep talking about it.

Naylor: I have found that if you have to tell a person to read, they're normally not a writer by inclination, because all writers begin as voracious readers and then somehow just spring off from that. You also want to articulate your own story. So the reading is just natural, more than even desire—an almost unquenchable passion for you. You just absorb language.

To reiterate, it's hard work. And you have to understand the loneliness of it. We have this Hollywood conception about what it means to write, but it takes tremendous hours and not just hours where you are sitting around, but hours of intense concentration and self-examination. That's work. But if you have a story you feel is worth telling, you don't mind that sacrifice of friends, of community, of time and even having it be all wrong sometimes. And then you have to have the courage to start over and to keep believing that somehow that story is in you.

Pate: This would be something that would be true for a man or a woman.

Naylor: Exactly. That's the whole thing about this panel. Ninety-nine and forty-four one-hundredths of the process is indeed not only genderless and raceless, it's even humanless at times. It's about dredging up things that are down there in the human spirit, in the gut. Yes it's words, it's language, which is the province of everyone. It just becomes problematic when you begin to filter it through thousands of other perceptions or assumptions.

Questioner: When you want to write about something that involves people you know, is it a problem? Do you say, "I am going to do it; I don't care who's offended?" How much of that kind of editing do you do as you write?

Naylor: It's really censorship you are talking about.

Questioner: Yes, censorship. Self-censorship.

Naylor: What will happen is that I will often see the character start to evolve and take on a life of his or her own. I might catch glimpses of people in my family, perhaps, or of friends in that character, and I just simply let it go. Because if you step in and say, "Oh, God, this is my mother. This is a story she told me when she was 20. She'll kill me. She'll cut me out of her will. She'll cancel her insurance policy." If you do, if you pull yourself in and you say let me chop this off, then the writing becomes flat. And I think psychologically something happens because you know that you cheated. After that it's like playing dominoes, everything will fall flat.

It takes a lot of courage and I think understanding from the people around us. You can only write from what you know. And things you've imagined and things you wish to meet. And they'll have to understand that it's not them. Perhaps it may be just little bits of them. And if it is them, I think it's a compliment. You know what we have told you about how hard it is to write—you spend that much time talking about your mother. She should be glad.

Humphreys: Also, the thing you are writing about tends to change as you write and to become less a true event or a true person and more your own creation or own mixture of the two. In the end it's something new.

Questioner: I have heard different writers refer to a character they had created taking on a life of its own, speaking to them. If you've had such experiences, could you share them with us?

Humphreys: I used to hear people say that, and I thought it was baloney. That's before I was writing. And now I get that same feeling. I think what happens is that when I am writing, part of my rational brain shuts down. That's almost necessary in writing and is what we call inspiration. It is not really that at all, but it is something coming from part of the brain that we are not always in control of or in good touch with. And so it seems as if the book is writing itself or your character is taking over. Obviously that doesn't happen; it's obviously the creation of your imagination, but you may not know exactly how it's working.

Gilchrist: It's like, "Who is driving this car? Who's skiing down this hill?" You are not really thinking about it. It may not be as difficult to write a book as we would like to think. Once you get past all the inhibitions and fears and problems and questions—you just write. It feels like memory, which means you thought it up very fast and you are just remembering the parts.

Questioner: As an aspiring writer, I wonder when do you make the differentiation between talent or lack of talent? Is there a certain number of rejection slips that tell you that?

Naylor: That should be the least of your concerns. That, or even reviews. If you are literate, you have a talent for putting words on paper. Though it becomes a bit more than that—things we have been telling you about—dedication, willingness to hang in there, the passion for language itself. If anything, that is what separates the girls from the women.

Sharp: Today, we'd like to talk about the place of the woman writer in the literary tradition. In recent years, there has been a growing concern about past failures to include women writers in standard collections like the *Norton Anthology*. And there has been an effort to have more women included.

Would you tell us what women writers you read when you were growing up?

Gilchrist: I'll start with Pearl Buck who I think won the Nobel. And Edna St. Vincent Millay, wonderful, wonderful sonnets which I think will someday be revived. She's represented in anthologies, but not well represented.

I think that at least half the books I read must have been by women. I was a voracious reader and I naturally moved towards books by women. Because I had so little experience with the world to bring to the things I was reading, at least a woman's sensibility would be speaking to me. My brother was in the other room, and, you know, we had the sexist country at our house. He was over there reading the Hardy Boys and I was reading Nancy Drew. We thought that was okay.

Humphreys: I actually read a lot of boys' books when I was young. I read the Hardy boys and not Nancy Drew. I just didn't have Nancy Drew. I think that was the only reason. But I also read every single Louisa May Alcott book, and those books were extremely important to me. It's about a family of girls, which is what I lived in. And the oldest girl, who was a writer, was named Jo.

Shivers: I think it's terribly unfair that you actually got to be named Jo.

Humphreys: I used to do the things that she did. She would take apples up into the garret and write. I didn't like apples but I took them up there, in an attic where no one had been for hundreds of years. It was 93 degrees up there and I wrote. It was an amazing influence on my life to do that. I think if a child reads something with a character with his name, it's really powerful. It would be nice if we could find one for everyone else.

Hardy: You were lucky because that's one of these androgynous names.

Humphreys: Oh, yes. I realized that also from an early age. I was sort of a tomboy. I thought my parents wanted a boy rather than a girl. I didn't have any brothers, but it took me a while to realize that it was okay to be a girl. I read Pearl Buck at a later age and Edna St. Vincent Millay as well. But I didn't really notice which books were written by women and which were by men.

Gilchrist: It never occurred to me. The only reason I wanted to know the names of authors was so I could get the rest of their books. I had no curiosity whatsoever about the author.

Hardy: I also read a lot of boys' books and boys' magazines, but I also read an awful lot of tripe, or trash. I had a wonderful aunt who was the least academic of her family, and she once said when I picked up one of her women's magazines, "Well, I'll say this for Barbara, she'll read anything." She was very pleased.

Shivers: Other than Louisa May Alcott—at least I almost got Louisa—my favorite book was *The Secret Garden.* I still love it so much.

And also around the house there was a copy of *Pride and Prejudice,* which my mother had left over from her days at Meredith College. I read it over and over and over. I loved it; Darcy was so wonderful. But I always read whatever, too. Just whatever was there. In fact, my first learning about sex was from my brother's Boy Scout manual.

One other thing that was a big, big influence on me. I remember exactly the moment when a teacher came in and read "Patterns" by Amy Lowell.

Hardy: I read a lot of books that, like the books by Louisa May Alcott, were about America. All the *Anne of Green Gables* and so on. I didn't realize for a long time that they were about America.

Humphreys: I thought they were British.

Gilchrist: I could never read *Anne of Green Gables* or any woman who would allow herself to be a victim in literature, or really even the Alcott books. They would begin to bore me. I fought for a living. I fought with my brothers for excitement and fun. It was my greatest pleasure in life. And I could not understand anyone being in a position where they couldn't fight. So I didn't understand why they didn't. Or else I would be empathizing so much. To this day in a film if someone is going to be struck or hit I'll leave the theatre. I have never been able to see the middle part of *Fannie and Alexander* when that child was beaten. I literally can't face it.

Questioner: It seems that not much writing by women is included in the established canon. Just a little sprinkling here and there. Would you like to voice an opinion about why?

Hardy: Publishers are doing a lot about it. There are good presses, and women's presses have been introducing a lot of new stuff. Feminist critics have been attacking the exclusiveness of the great tradition, and I would have thought things were moving.

Humphreys: I think in the last 10 years or so there has been a renewed interest in some of the nineteenth century and early twentieth century women writers. But it is still sort of grudging. I mean it's for women. These women writers are being dug up for women to read. It's not like they're being restored.

The reason I think that women writers are not part of the grand tradition and graduate school work is that graduate school teachers don't like to give much value to domestic fiction, to stories of the family. Immediately there is a reaction against that subject matter. And they won't come out and say so; they use the term "limited palette."

Questioner: Don't you feel that women will read what are considered to be male books on male topics while men will not read about domestic issues? I will read *Sports Illustrated* or *The Right Stuff* or some football book my husband has, but he would never turn around and read my book.

Gilchrist: You've just got this bigger palette.

Hardy: It's also because women's liberation has outstripped men's liberation.

Questioner: I hate to be the devil's advocate here, but my husband just read *Hot Flashes* and loved it.

Gilchrist: Well married!

We have got to stop a minute here, because it is one thing to talk about fiction, but I am more interested in the poets of the past. I have always felt like women poets—women poets in America—are well represented in anthologies. They dominate to some extent. My God, Emily Dickinson dominates the century practically.

Hardy: There's something very interesting about this. It is possible to write a history of English poetry, of the whole of the canon up to the end of the nineteenth century mentioning only one woman poet, Emily Bronte. I am speaking now not about American poetry, though you haven't got many in the nineteenth century you need to mention. But you could not write a history of English fiction and leave out women. And I think women's experience has allowed women to write novels, but it has been very much more difficult for women, whose emotional range has been very, very restricted, to write poetry. I do think there is a big genre difference here. You've got Emily Dickinson in the nineteenth century and we've got our Emily.

Gilchrist: In the late fifties all of a sudden we've got Sylvia Plath and Anne Sexton. We've got this burgeoning of incredibly powerful women poets in the United States; and all the women in the United States including myself that aspired to write began to write poetry in the shadow of Sexton, primarily Sexton, and then all of the ones after.

Humphreys: I think Virginia Woolf said that fiction had attracted in the past more women than any other art. And she said the reason is that it is the easiest. But I like to think that what she meant was that it's the most accessible. Women have been able to do it in secret without anyone knowing—you know, hiding their work and working at it in spurts. I did that myself, so I know you can hide it. And I think that's one reason that we may have gravitated towards it. I don't know exactly why poetry also couldn't be clandestine.

Questioner: Given what you've just been discussing, would each of you comment on the way writing has affected your everyday lives?

Humphreys: My everyday life has been totally transformed by writing because I have come to think and see in a totally different way. My normal life before I started writing, which was happy and healthy, is now neither one of those things. I am constantly questioning things. I have gone from being very conservative in most things to what I consider extremely radical. Because writing questions things. You fall into that frame of mind. And my everyday life, more or less, has disintegrated. I can go to the grocery store now, and I can cook food.

So there are a few things I can still manage to function in, but I'm on the edge of it. I'm always looking through things and looking through experiences and people to try to figure out what the answer is. And I don't think that's a normal everyday life. I think in the long run it can be very disturbing. And the more I write the more I become like that. It's a kind of circular process.

Shivers: I will have to say it's affected me in entirely the opposite way. I was never healthy and happy because I was always trying to find that missing thing. I never was able to fit in. I never found people to talk to, so that kept me unhealthy and unhappy. This may be us finding it at different ages or many other reasons too.

Hardy: One very obvious thing—the reason I think a lot of women have not written is that women leading a conventional, domestic life tend not to have solitude. And you have to have solitude.

Questioner: Mrs. Humphreys, would you say you are losing your identity through this?

Humphreys: No. The opposite. I am gaining my identity, but I'm losing the capacity to find an identity that doesn't include writing. Writing—it's like a fungus—it has taken hold and taken control.

Hardy: One of the most outstanding little examples of writing in everyday life is Jane Austen, who didn't have a study. She used to have a blotter and as soon as visitors came—she couldn't get away from the visitors so she would slide her manuscript under the blotter. The amazing thing is that she wrote anything at all. She had to do it in this crowded world over which she had absolutely no control. She couldn't say, "Oh, I'll go upstairs now. I'll go and write."

Gilchrist: You can't ever tell when all of a sudden you're going to need long periods of solitude. And I don't mean all afternoon or all weekend. It may take three or four months. You may need to get in the car and go somewhere for three or four months. It's very difficult—you can't explain this to young children. Though maybe if the children grew up with it like Jo's have grown up with Jo writing, maybe they think it's well she's out of their hair.

My children love to think that I am on a piece of work because they know I won't call them up at 8 o'clock in the morning and give them some advice.

Questioner: Nineteenth century novels tend to end in marriage. It seems like recent novels begin in divorce. What's happening to the American family in novels?

Hardy: Some nineteenth century novels, because they didn't have the possibility of ending in divorce, ended in death. I think family life has always been rightly suspected. It's always been looked at as suspiciously comic or tragic—nineteenth and twentieth century.

Shivers: I think we are all trying to deal with that, in the books we are doing.

I had to kill a couple of men off in my first book. In the second one you have a divorce, but you also have a marriage. We are trying to figure all that out.

Questioner: Yesterday Ms. Shivers said she wrote for herself. I took that to mean that it was her standard that was important, not the standard of the *New York Times.* But how important to you is publication? And who is that dear reader in your mind when you write?

Shivers: That goes back to what I just said in answer to the other question. I am trying to figure it all out. I am trying to figure myself out. And so, therefore, I am writing for myself.

I think the thing about publishing is that that's the way to do two very important things. By being published and being acknowledged you get a little money and a little respect. Somebody knows that you are doing something. Before you are published, people just don't take you seriously. The other thing that publishing does is that it's given me friends. I have had a chance to meet other people who are writing and I didn't have that chance before. Until you publish you don't usually have that chance.

Questioner: Who do you think your audience is? Would each of you please answer that?

Humphreys: I have two audiences in mind. One is a very vague, general bunch of people that I can't identify but who are probably a lot like me. In that sense I am writing for myself. But I also frequently have in mind real people whom I want to win. The first one happened to be someone who was no longer alive, which made it an odd undertaking. I have specific people in mind. I want them to like it.

Questioner: I was struck by what Louise Shivers said about the importance of making friends through her publications—that is, friends who are also writers. I would be curious to hear what the members of the panel might say about what role other writers, currently writing writers, play in their lives as writers. What do you get from them?

Shivers: Knowing that when you are sitting in that room by yourself, and it's just as painful as it has ever been, you are not by yourself.

Next week we will be back wherever we all are. I will be back home; I'll know that Gloria is back. But I'll hear that hurricane that she read about, and I'll think . . . "Well, she's lonesome too." I remember one day, about a year and a half ago—maybe I shouldn't tell this—but Jo and I were really feeling in the pits about the books that we were writing. I either called her or she called me and we just talked to each other. She said, "God, this young adult novel I'm writing!" And I said, "Well, I'm writing this stupid romance novel." It helped just to know she was there. We didn't have to see each other or talk that much. It just helps to have somebody to say it to—to know that you've got other people out there who care.

Hardy: For people starting out who may not have met writers, it's very important to know that literature isn't written by gods and goddesses and doesn't come out in printed form. It is written by people with arms and legs, and written with pens and on typewriters. I think it is very important to get the ordinariness.

Humphreys: It's also nice to realize that essentially literature is not competitive—though that's easy to forget in the system we have today. I like to know that there are other writers with whom I am not racing and that we like each other's work. That we are in some ways working toward the same end.

Sharp: I thought what Ms. Hardy said underscored the impetus for having this symposium. It's important that we hear the voices of writers. It's also important to see that they really have arms and legs and hair and everything, and to identify with the person behind the printed page. I think it has been a great experience. I want to thank them. They have been incredibly giving of themselves.

1989